Introduction to International Relations

Introduction to International Relations

Theory and Practice

JOYCE P. KAUFMAN

ROWMAN & LITTLEFIELD PUBLISHERS, INC.
Lanham • Boulder • New York • Toronto • Plymouth, UK

Published by Rowman & Littlefield Publishers, Inc.
A wholly owned subsidiary of The Rowman & Littlefield Publishing Group, Inc.
4501 Forbes Boulevard, Suite 200, Lanham, Maryland 20706
www.rowman.com

10 Thornbury Road, Plymouth PL6 7PP, United Kingdom

British Library Cataloguing in Publication Information Available

Library of Congress Cataloging-in-Publication Data

Kaufman, Joyce P.
    Introduction to international relations : theory and practice / Joyce P. Kaufman.
        pages   cm
    Includes bibliographical references and index.
    ISBN 978-1-4422-2118-5 (cloth : alk. paper)
    ISBN 978-1-4422-2119-2 (pbk. : alk. paper)
    ISBN 978-1-4422-2120-8 (electronic)
    1. International relations—Philosophy.   I. Title.
JZ1305.K378 2013
327—dc23   2013003201

∞ ™ The paper used in this publication meets the
minimum requirements of American National Standard for Information
Sciences—Permanence of Paper for Printed Library Materials, ANSI/NISO Z39.48-1992.

Printed in the United States of America

Contents

Preface

Understanding international relations (IR) is an important part of an undergraduate student's education, whether as a staple of a political science program, an introductory course in an international relations/international studies track, a class on globalization, or simply as a guide to better understand the world in which he or she lives. Yet, increasingly, international relations texts are chock full of details about theories and ideas that are abstract and seen as removed from reality rather than helping the student apply the theories to the "real world."

This concise text takes as its starting point a discussion of the theoretical frameworks that are the foundation of current international relations. The book draws on and explicates the traditional international relations theories, but also makes a place for understanding the areas that lie outside of or cannot be explained by those approaches. Although levels of analysis will be the primary unifying force, one of the strengths of the book lies in addressing the flaws of this approach in understanding the contemporary international system. Integrated throughout the text are applications of the theories so that students can see how learning the theories will actually help them better understand the "real world." That, in turn, will also help them make decisions about issues pertaining to current international events.

The book is organized around the various "levels of analysis" or the primary actors who play a role in international relations, since, despite its flaws, it still provides a fairly easy unifying framework. The goal of this book is to be a short and concise guide to international relations that will allow a faculty member to use it as one of a number of books in a class. Each chapter also includes suggested readings, such as additional articles on each topic, so that each faculty member can augment this concise text with the readings that he or she feels is appropriate. The notes and web sources will also provide a guide for faculty and students to more detailed study of each of the topics raised in the book. Clearly, it will be up to the faculty member to determine the approach that he or she wants to take in the course and identify readings accordingly.

As I noted in an earlier U.S. foreign policy text, virtually everyone who teaches undergraduates thinks that she or he could write the ideal text. I am not sure that this is it. However, the approach grows from years of teaching undergraduates. I owe special thanks to two undergraduate students: Deyla Curtis (Whittier College, '12), who was in both my U.S. foreign policy and my International Relations classes and who read and responded to early drafts of this book, and Anthony Akkawi (Whittier College, '14), who was also in a number of my classes and who took the time to read every page of the latest version and offer his comments, feedback, and suggestions. Since this book is written for undergraduates, having their input was very helpful. I owe a special debt of gratitude to every student in any of my IR classes since I came to Whittier College in 1985; they know who they are and are too numerous to name. It was from them that I really learned how to teach the material, and I hope that the lessons they taught me are reflected in this text.

My thanks to my dear friend and colleague Irene Carlyle, who, as in the past, was willing to take her time to read a draft to see if I could convey the ideas to an interested lay-person. I deeply value her insights on the book, as well as on many other things. I want to thank the two reviewers who read and commented on various drafts of the manuscript; special thanks to Eric Leonard, not only for taking the time to offer written comments but for his willingness to talk through some of his ideas with me. I hope that I did justice to his important feedback.

My own training in International Relations clearly has had an impact on my approach to the subject, feminist perspectives aside. My introduction to the field started when I was an undergraduate at NYU and Robert Burrowes taught my first political science class. He then become my undergraduate advisor and when it was time to go to graduate school—and by then there was no doubt as to IR as my major field of study—he urged me to consider the University of Maryland specifically so that I could work with Jonathan Wilkenfeld. I took his advice, went to Maryland, and worked for—and continue to work with—Jon Wilkenfeld. While both Professors Wilkenfeld and Burrowes roll their eyes at my turn toward research in feminist IR, both remain dear friends and supportive colleagues. I owe each of them a huge debt for helping direct and mentor me. Each of them can take credit for the parts of my work that they would like to—and disavow the parts that they do not agree with.

My deepest thanks also to my editor at Rowman & Littlefield, Susan McEachern. By coincidence, my husband, Robert Marks, and I have worked with Susan on our various book projects for many years and she has become far more than an editor, but a good friend. This project would not have moved forward without her. Also at Rowman & Littlefield, thanks to production editor Alden Perkins, copyeditor Catherine Bielitz, and associate editor Carrie Broadwell-Tkach. All responded to questions and comments promptly, which made the various stages moving to publication much easier. The excellent feedback and input of all involved notwithstanding, any errors or omissions are my responsibility.

Finally, no preface would be complete without thanking the person who really started me on the path to understanding the importance and role of short, concise texts and of writing in my "teaching voice." My husband and colleague Robert Marks has been a role model in many ways, as well as everything else he is to me. Those roles are too numerous to elaborate on here—but he knows what they are. And, of course, there's Stanton. As I promised Susan, I hope that one day Stanton and Sydni will join the ranks of Rowman & Littlefield authors.

Introduction: International Relations in a Globalized World

On September 11, 2001, why did nineteen men affiliated with the terrorist group al-Qaeda hijack four planes and attack the twin towers of the World Trade Center in New York and the Pentagon outside Washington, D.C., and attempt to crash the fourth one perhaps into the White House or the Capitol? Who were these men, and what were their motives? What did they hope to gain from this attack, and did they achieve their ends?

Almost ten years later, in May 2011, U.S. Navy special forces (SEALs) attacked a compound in Abbottabad, Pakistan, killing Osama bin Laden. Abbottabad is home to a large Pakistani military base and a military academy of the Pakistani army. Pakistan, a supposed ally of the United States in the fight against al-Qaeda, was not informed of the raid in advance. Furthermore, following the raid, serious questions emerged about what the Pakistani military did—or did not—know about who lived in that compound. If Pakistan was aware of bin Laden's whereabouts in the country, shouldn't they have notified the United States, an ally? How could bin Laden, a wanted criminal, have lived within a mile of Pakistani military forces for so long undetected? Should the United States have notified its alleged ally prior to the raid? And did President Obama make the correct decision in authorizing the raid and then bin Laden's burial at sea immediately after? Who else was involved in these decisions?

Here is another set of questions to ponder that might strike a little closer to home. How does Wal-Mart, one of the largest corporations in the world, influence policy not only in the United States but in the countries in which it has factories? What is the trade-off between allowing you, the consumer, to purchase goods at a relatively low price if that possibly comes at the cost of exploiting the laborers who produce those goods? Or looking at this another way, is the labor really exploited when working for Wal-Mart in a factory in Bangladesh is the difference between a worker being able to put food on the table or starving? How can a company, which exists outside the bounds of government, have so much power?

These are all examples of questions that we ponder and study in the field of international relations.

WHY INTERNATIONAL RELATIONS IS IMPORTANT

International relations (IR) as a field of study deals with decisions that are made within a country that have implications for relationships outside the borders of that country. But it also asks a number of other important questions: Who makes those decisions? Why? How are they made? Who is affected by them? And what are the likely responses to those decisions? But what makes the study of international relations especially complex is the range of actors who could be involved with answering any and all aspects of those questions.

One of the really important questions to ask is: What does IR have to do with me personally? These seem like really big questions that are removed from most of us. But the reality is that they are not. Every time a country decides to go to war, it has implications for what happens not only to the people in that country but in other countries as well. For example, when President George W. Bush authorized the invasion of Afghanistan in October 2001 in retaliation for the September 11 attacks, he committed U.S. forces to fight. That meant ensuring that there were enough U.S. military forces available to fight that war. But it also meant supplying the military for that invasion, which resulted in more money being required for the Defense Department. Tax money spent for the military cannot be spent for other things, such as education; this is known as "guns versus butter." So directly or indirectly, that decision affected you.

Other countries are also affected by terrorist attacks and therefore have a vested interest in confronting al-Qaeda. So it became necessary to round up allies to work with the United States in Afghanistan so that the United States did not have to bear that burden alone. That is the role of *alliances*, specifically bringing in other countries to work together in pursuit of common goals. So other countries, and the people within them, were affected by the decision made by President Bush. And clearly, so were the people of Afghanistan.

Let's look at another case. The economic instability in Europe in 2011 and 2012 and the decision of the euro zone to bail out Greece and Spain might seem irrelevant to you. But in a world in which countries are interdependent, economic instability in Europe can affect the U.S. economic system. Entities in the United States own European debt just as China owns U.S. debt. The possibility that there could be a default on that debt in Europe could panic the people in the United States who own the debt, which in turn could lead to more economic uncertainty in this country. Similarly, there are some in the United States who are concerned about how much U.S. debt China owns. Does that mean that China "owns" parts of the United States? These questions are all a function of an interdependent globalized world that, in some ways, brings countries closer together. But it also illustrates the dangers of that close relationship, where uncertainty in one country or region (in the case of the euro zone) can have a marked impact on another.

The bottom line is that these are very difficult issues that generate complex questions, and if we are ever going to attempt to answer them, we need to find a way to simplify the reality so that we can focus on one aspect of the problem at a time. For example, in the case of September 11, if we want to know more about the hijackers, we can focus on the men who acted together as part of a terrorist group that sought to inflict damage on the United States. Or put into IR terms, we are looking at the impact that a nonstate actor (al-Qaeda) had on a major international actor (the United States) in order to influence U.S. policy in some way.

Or we can look at it another way that also would provide some explanation for the actions of 9/11. In this case we can start by identifying the nineteen men as individual actors who were part of a larger group and agreed to engage in a suicide mission. If we were to take that approach, our focus would be on the men as the actors and on what motivated them to act as they did. This would be a smaller or more microlevel response.

Or we can approach it in yet another way: We can ask why Osama bin Laden, as the leader of al-Qaeda, wanted to inflict damage on the United States, which he saw as the ideological enemy of all that he believed in. In that case, our focus would be on an individual leader who made decisions that had an impact on many other people. This is an even smaller or more micro level—that of a single individual.

No one of these approaches is a right or wrong way to begin to understand the complexity of the 9/11 attacks. But if we take them apart, we can focus on different aspects of the attacks that allow us to begin to answer some of these questions. When we put them together, we can get a more complete picture of the various actors involved (bin Laden, al-Qaeda, the nineteen hijackers), what the motives of each of them were, the decisions that each made, and the outcome of their decisions.

Conversely, we can look at the same event from the perspective of the United States, the country that was attacked. We can focus on the options available to then president George W. Bush as the primary decision maker, and what he ultimately decided to do (the micro or *individual* level). We can concentrate on the Congress and the support that the Congress gave to President Bush when he asked for authorization to use military force (*government* level). We can focus on the role of the American public as it (as a whole) tried to understand what happened and why (level of *American society*). And we can look at the United States acting as if it were a single entity, which weighed options and then responded. That response committed the United States to a course of action. The focus on the United States as a whole is the largest and most macrolevel response, that of a country (or *nation-state*, in IR terms). Again, as in the above case, each of these approaches allows us to focus on some aspect of the U.S. response to the attack; taken together, they give us a more complete picture of who made the decisions, how they were made, and what they meant for the United States.

By breaking the attack into these smaller pieces, it is possible to answer questions about the event that might seem way too large to answer as a whole. In other words, we are breaking a complex event into its component pieces while holding the other parts aside, so we can arrive at some answers that will help us understand the event as a whole.

Similarly, we can look at different aspects of the events to determine the primary actor or actors who made the decisions. This can range from an individual (e.g., bin Laden or Bush) to the government (Congress and/or the executive branch in the United States), the public as a whole, or even the nation. This levels-of-analysis approach, then, allows us to pick the pieces apart in order to analyze one at a time.

And we can do this with virtually all of the examples given above, or almost any other example you can think of. For example, in the case of the attack on the bin Laden compound, we can focus on an individual—President Obama as the primary decision maker, and his national security team—to try to understand the processes that led to the decisions not only to attack but also to leave Pakistan uninformed. This will help us understand the inputs or factors that led to the decision that ultimately was made. We can focus on the nation-state level and the interaction between the United States and Pakistan, as a way to understand more about this alliance and its weaknesses. And we can focus on the perceptions of the American public as they reacted to the news of bin Laden's death.

Or in the Wal-Mart case noted above, we can study and try to understand the impact of this corporation from the point of view of the American consumer (individual or culture/society), the workers who produce the goods (individual), or the corporation itself and its relationship to the nations in which it is based (nation-state). Or we can look at the role that Wal-Mart plays in influencing or affecting the economies of the various countries in which it has a role (global or international level). Focusing on each of these levels of actors/analysis gives a different picture of the question; when taken together, they allow us to understand the whole.

We will describe the levels of analysis in more detail later. But this short overview should help you understand how we approach some of these big questions in IR—and how we can answer them!

Why Study IR?

Traditionally, international relations is the most macro level of all the subfields of political science, as the international system and the actors that make up that system are the basic units of analysis. Rather than looking at the specific political processes within nation-states (such as the study of American government) or across different political systems (which is comparative politics), IR looks at the ways in which decisions made within a country affect that country's relationships with other countries or nation-states. The focus remains on the interaction between countries or among countries and other actors in the international system, including nonstate actors such as multinational corporations (MNCs), international organizations (IOs), and nongovernmental organizations (NGOs). It also looks at the impact of these macrolevel decisions on the various actors who exist within the nation-state and how they, in turn, affect these major decisions. Hence, IR looks at who makes the decisions (from the role of the government to the individual decision maker) and how those decisions then affect the people, society, culture, or even individuals within the nation-state or other nation-states. In short, IR looks at "big picture" questions.

We live in a world today in which nation-states are not only interrelated and interdependent, but in which nonstate actors have also emerged as major players, as noted in the example above. Clearly, terrorist groups such as al-Qaeda have affected the behavior of states, not only as a response to actions that al-Qaeda actually has perpetrated, but in anticipation of what the group *might* do. If you have gotten on a plane recently and at the airport had to take your shoes off for security and put your resealable plastic bag with shampoo and toothpaste in it through the X-ray machine, you have seen the increased security designed to prevent a terrorist action. In other words, policy is made not just based on what did happen but on what *might* happen.

The presence of nonstate actors has tossed on their head many of the questions that have guided traditional IR. Nowhere is this seen more dramatically than in the case of al-Qaeda, a terrorist group that crosses a number of state borders, is clearly tied to an ideology and culture, has taken actions against a number of nation-states, and has in turn evoked a response from those nation-states. Yet whom are these countries fighting? Is it possible to "declare war," traditionally the purview of the nation-state, on a nonstate actor? If so, doesn't that require violating the sanctity of a nation-state in order to attack a group that exists within its borders?

In addition to terrorist groups, other nonstate actors play a critical role in affecting or influencing the decisions made by various actors in the international system. Multinational corporations (MNCs) have become major players in the international system, and because they straddle the boundaries of many countries, they have some influence on them as well as on the international system as a whole. Again, going back to the example used above, where and how does the levels-of-analysis approach account for the role of an MNC, such as Wal-Mart? Understanding this, and the impact that a major MNC like Wal-Mart has on the policies of various countries with which it does or has business, will help us see more clearly the impact of globalization.

A series of Pulitzer Prize–winning articles published in the *Los Angeles Times* in November 2003 clearly describes the impact that MNCs such as Wal-Mart can have on a nation-state, society, culture, and even individuals as consumers—but also on the people who produce the goods that Wal-Mart sells.[1] Rather than taking a position or making a judgment, articles such as these point out the power that an MNC can have and the dangers that come with corporations that seem to exist outside the boundaries of traditional and established international law. The main point is that in a world in which economic power equals political power, corporations like Wal-Mart, Exxon Mobil, Shell Oil, and Bank of America all have power. Yet in many ways, they exist outside the reach of any single nation-state, and it can be difficult to hold them accountable. Questions and issues surrounding the role of MNCs, which are an integral part of international relations today, will be discussed in more detail in chapter 5.

International organizations are also important actors. In addition to the United Nations, regional organizations such as the European Union (EU) take on power internationally that is far greater than the power that any single member country would wield. But the integration and desire to create a single foreign, defense, and/or monetary policy for the group that comes with organizations such as the EU also brings with it a challenge to the very notion of sovereignty that is central to the essence of any nation-state. The recent crisis in the euro zone also illustrates clearly the dangers that instability in one country could easily spread to others, especially when a single policy affects all of them.

Understanding how to reconcile the apparently contradictory conflicts of integration and sovereignty is another aspect of international relations. But it is even more important to understand the role that international organizations in general play in a globalized world. We will discuss all these concepts in more detail later in this book.

Many of these examples point out one of the flaws of the traditional levels-of-analysis approach to international relations. Specifically, the field of international relations is premised on the idea that the nation-state is the primary actor, meaning that it is state-centered or *state-centric*. But the contemporary international system has seen the emergence of a host of nonstate actors, all of which play a role in what happens in international relations. Yet they exist outside the traditional levels of analysis that guide most international relations theory. Therefore, one of the dilemmas facing those of us who study IR is how to account for those nonstate actors; more specifically, what framework can we use that incorporates them as major players in the international system? Doing so will allow us to answer an expanded range of questions about what is going on in the world today.

Just as there has been a growth of nonstate actors that have called into question some of the basic approaches to IR, the newer theoretical frameworks seek to account for the role of these actors and the changing nature of the international system. For example, *constructivists* argue for the need to take variables such as identity and other socially constructed realities into account in order to better explain the decisions made in the contemporary international system. *Feminist IR theorists* also discount the centrality of the traditional patriarchal/hierarchal assumptions about decision making in order to focus on the role of women and other actors who not only play a role in the decisions that are made (albeit often an indirect one), but without whose presence the decisions would not be implemented successfully. Could a country go to war to protect the "mother country" without the symbolism of women? In thinking about broad IR decisions, feminist writers in the field also tell us about the need to study those within the country who are most affected by the decisions that are made. Women and children are the ones most removed from foreign policy decision making, and yet they are often directly affected by the results of those decisions.

These are all prominent and real questions that have been prompted by recent events, and yet, technically, international relations has no set framework for responding to these questions. Or when it does, the framework often is limited and inadequate. This does not in any way suggest that the traditional approaches can or should be rejected. Rather, starting with and trying to understand the present and the complexity of the world as it currently exists will give you some relevant and current examples to grapple with as you try to define a framework appropriate for dealing with these questions.

While the levels-of-analysis framework provides the guiding structure for this short volume, grappling with the need for the emergence of a new theoretical framework or even a paradigm shift that addresses the role of nonstate actors and a globalized world in which nation-states and nonstate actors interact regularly is not a trivial exercise. Just as IR scholar and realist theorist Hans Morgenthau[2] proposed in 1948 to recast our understanding of international relations so that it is focused on power, so too, we now need to rethink the larger international system and broaden our understanding of how to address nonstate actors and the role that they play in a globalized world.

Doing so will illustrate the importance of having a theoretical framework that is appropriate for the realities of the twenty-first century.

IR as a Field of Study

The main point made thus far is that by simplifying an otherwise complex situation, we can start finding answers to our often complex questions. That is why the study of international relations is such an important part of understanding our world today. It provides a theoretical framework that allows us to break the component pieces apart, identify the relevant actors, understand their approaches, and draw conclusions that help us answer these questions. And it also helps us understand what assumptions we need to make about the behavior of individuals/groups/nations in order to answer those questions.

As you will see, there are advantages to the theoretical approaches outlined in the field of IR, but also disadvantages. The field itself emerged after World War I, when sovereign nation-states eclipsed monarchies and empires as the primary actors.[3] Thus, the field tends to be very state-centric, assuming that the traditional nation-state is—and will be—the primary actor. But as the examples of al-Qaeda and Wal-Mart show, nonstate actors have emerged as major players in the international system in the twentieth and certainly the twenty-first century. To some extent, the emergence of nonstate actors has changed the field. The traditional model has little room for other than nation-states, the societies that make up those states, and the people and governments who lead them. Does that mean that we need to throw out the old models? Absolutely not! They can still help guide our approaches both to asking questions and answering them. But now we need to do so with an awareness of the limitations of those same theoretical approaches and models.

Understanding international relations is an important part of an undergraduate student's education, whether as a staple of a political science program, an introductory course in an international relations/international studies track, a class on globalization, or simply to better understand the world in which he or she lives. While international relations theory still relies heavily on the basic theoretical paradigms (realism, liberalism, and constructivism, for example, to be explored in more detail in the next chapter), there has been a proliferation of other theoretical approaches. These all have some merit, although they might appear to be bit esoteric to someone who is trying to understand basic questions, such as why there is so much war and conflict, or why there is a global economic crisis. In fact, one of the hardest parts of studying international relations is drawing the distinction between learning the way things are supposed to operate in theory and using that theory to understand how they actually do operate. For example, why do countries behave as they do? Why do some societies rise up against a leader, as was the case in Tunisia, Libya, and Egypt early in 2011, and why are others quiet, even in the face of tyranny? Why did a leader make the decision that he or she did, and who helped the leader make that decision? Thus, the real dilemma for the student trying to understand international relations comes in trying to apply all that theory to real-world questions.

In order to be able to do this—that is, to apply the theory to an understanding of real-world issues or problems—it is necessary to have not only a basic grounding in the theory but also an approach that will help guide us through the complexity of the real world. That is what this book will help define.

The Levels-of-Analysis Framework

Levels of analysis will become the overarching framework as we begin to understand international relations. Levels of analysis "presumes that decisions are made at different and distinct levels, that is, from a fairly micro-level, such as the role of an individual decision maker (who is usually male), to society and culture, and then becoming more macro-level, moving to the nation and finally the international system."[4] Another underlying assumption is that each level exists fairly independently, with little interaction between or across levels.[5] However, the reality belies that assumption. Events that take place at one given level of analysis have the potential to impact other levels. For example, a president or prime minister can move a nation to war, which in turn has an impact on the society and the individuals within it. And while the levels of analysis can provide an important guiding framework, the limitations of the approach must also be noted; we have alluded to them already and will discuss them in more detail in the next chapter.

Briefly, though, because of its emphasis on the nation-state, the framework does not really have a place for nonstate actors or even supranational organizations such as the United Nations. Rather, it assumes that all actors within the international system are nation-states, with a defined leader/decision maker who heads a government, and that decisions are tied to the values and goals of the culture and the society. Collectively, all of these make up the nation-state. As seen above, the Wal-Mart and al-Qaeda examples point out quickly the flaws in this approach. Even with its limitations, though, levels of analysis provides a clean, unifying model for approaching international relations and is a useful tool—as long as we remain clear about its weaknesses.

The levels-of-analysis framework allows us to ask who or what we will be focusing on as we try to get answers to some of our questions. In many ways, the approach is somewhat circular. The questions we ask will determine the appropriate level of analysis that will be our focal point. But it does allow us to focus on one level at a time while holding the others constant, thereby allowing us to simplify the approach we are taking.

Broad Theoretical Perspectives

From a theoretical perspective, *realism* (both classical and neostructural/ structural) is the bread and butter of basic IR theory. It puts the state firmly at the center of our analysis, and it then puts states' actions into terms of power and balance of power. This is fairly easy to understand intuitively, and there are numerous examples of applications of the theory. Furthermore, this approach is grounded in history. But again, it is very state-centered, which raises questions when we try to apply it to the world today.

Since the end of the Cold War especially, a plethora of new theoretical approaches have either emerged or gained prominence in order to explain what is and what has been taking place in the international system. *Liberalism* and *constructivism* are two such approaches, both of which focus on different levels of analysis in order to better describe and explain the behavior of the international system. Where constructivist theorists focus on social structures both within and outside the states and the impact that these have on states' behaviors, liberal theorists make other assumptions about what drives a state's behavior that are more normative (or what "should be") in approach. Note that in this case, *liberal* does not refer to ideological perspective (versus *conservative*) but to a particular theoretical approach.

Growing from the desire to integrate women—their roles in the international system and the impact on women of political decisions made at various levels—another approach was born; feminist international relations theory not only provides a critique of the existing theoretical approaches but also offers an alternative that looks at international relations through gender-sensitive lenses.[6] As you will see, feminist theory is featured prominently throughout this book. I am not trying to proselytize; rather, my own research has highlighted the importance of looking at IR, and some of the basic questions in the field, with gender-sensitive lenses in order to get at more complete answers to the questions. In fact, feminist IR theorists argue that unless you look at all the actors who are involved with or are affected by a decision, it is impossible to get the complete picture. This is a very different way to approach the study of international relations. While I try not to privilege one theoretical approach over another, I do believe that the feminist perspective is valuable for posing different questions and positing answers regarding international relations and therefore deserves to be included in our study of IR theories.

It is important to note that, although the theories included here are often depicted as competing with one another to offer the "best" explanation of why countries behave as they do, an alternative model would be to look at them as offering complementary explanations depending on the questions asked and the level of focus. Thus, it is not necessary to assume one must take a particular theory as the single guiding framework. Rather, it is possible and sometimes beneficial to move between and among theories, depending on the question or focus of the inquiry.

As we continue our discussion of IR theories, it is also important to remember that in this field, a theory cannot be tested as it is in the sciences. We cannot hold one part of the world constant while we test another, as we would do in a laboratory. Rather, in the field of IR our laboratory is the world, and we do our best to approximate the variables so that we can describe, explain, and predict. Some political scientists even in IR use mathematical models as a way to improve our explanatory power. But the main point is that the world we deal with is complex and full of uncertainties, and our job is to try to describe and explain events that occurred and why. Theory can help us do that.

An example can best illustrate what is meant by all of this. The first Persian Gulf War in 1991 was an example of a coalition of the willing, which involved a group of countries coming together to use military force against Saddam Hussein. Iraq had invaded Kuwait, an ally of the United States, and the first President Bush (George H. W. Bush) worked with the United Nations and a group of countries to apply political pressure, and later the use of military force, to get Iraq to withdraw from Kuwait. From a *realist* perspective, this is an example of a group of countries uniting to use their collective power (military and political) to counter the actions of a single state, Iraq. From that perspective, power triumphed and helps us explain the event.

But this same case can be examined from other theoretical perspectives. For example, *liberal* theorists might argue that this is a case of countries working together to achieve a common goal. They worked first within the framework of the United Nations to try to bring about a peaceful settlement of the issue through negotiation. When that failed, countries cooperated to achieve a particular end, which was to get Iraq to withdraw from Kuwait. From that theoretical point of view, the important thing to consider is the idea of cooperation, rather than conflict or power as we saw in the realist approach. Here the emphasis is on how countries could and did work together to achieve a common goal, rather than the assertion of military power.

The *constructivists* would focus more on the individual leaders, as well as the social and cultural constructs of the states and societies involved. So a constructivist might ask what Saddam Hussein wanted to accomplish given his role, the countries with which he interacted, and the political structure of Iraq—and then, given all that, try to understand the responses of the coalition partners. Or from the other side, a constructivist might ask how President Bush's perceptions helped him determine what responses to take in this case. The constructivists do not ignore the central role of the state but rather put the state and the leaders into the broader social and political constructs that led to the particular processes and decisions that we are studying.

Each of these theoretical examples also relies on a different set of assumptions and focuses on a different level of analysis. When viewed separately, they will allow us to explain some portion of the event in great detail; taken together, they can give us a more complete picture of the entire event.

Clearly, it is important that students of IR understand the role of theory and how theory and the basic paradigms that exist in the field guide our understanding of international relations. Similarly, it is important to understand circumstances under which the existing theories don't explain events adequately, let alone predict what might happen in the future. The role of the major theories will be woven throughout each of the chapters in this book and will provide an important unifying theme throughout the narrative. Each of the major theories offers some explanation as to why countries behave as they do. In addition, all rely heavily on the notion of levels of analysis to help frame the approach.

This concise text takes as its starting point a discussion of the theoretical frameworks that are the foundation of current international relations. The book draws on and explicates the traditional international relations theories, but it also makes a place for understanding the areas that lie outside of or cannot be explained by those approaches. Although levels of analysis will be the primary unifying force, one of the strengths of the book is addressing the weakness of this approach in understanding the contemporary international system—that is, a globalized world. Integrated throughout the text are applications of the theories, so that students like you can understand that learning the theories will actually help you better understand the "real world." That in turn will help you make informed decisions about issues pertaining to current international events.

INTERNATIONAL RELATIONS IN A GLOBALIZED WORLD

In this chapter, we begin with a very broad overview of what studying international relations means in a world that is globalized. In contrast to the world of nation-states, upon which most of IR was premised, globalization offers challenges that come with understanding a world in which those states and even nonstate actors are interconnected. But before we can begin to address globalization, we need to define the fundamental actor in the international system: the nation-state. (This idea will be developed in even more detail in chapter 3, where the focus is on the nation-state level of analysis.)

The Concept of the Nation-State

This concept is two-pronged: the *nation,* which is a group of people with similar background, culture, ethnicity, and language, who share common values; and the *state,* which is an entity with a defined border under the rule of a government that is accepted by the people. The concept of the nation-state originated in Europe and can be traced to the Treaty of Westphalia (or Peace of Westphalia), which ended the Thirty Years' War in 1648.[7] Along with the emergence of the nation-state, the Treaty of Westphalia also specified a governmental order *within* each of the new states, as well as the relationship among them. Paramount among the concepts that emerged is that of *sovereignty,* which means that within a given territory, the government is the single legitimate authority and no external power has the right to intervene in actions that take place within national borders. Within the past few decades, since the Cold War ended, some governments seem to have abrogated their right to protect their own peoples—for example, either committing or permitting acts of genocide and ethnic cleansing to take place. These actions have called into question the concept of sovereignty, as other countries' governments have debated whether it is appropriate to intervene to protect basic human rights even if it means violating a state's sovereignty. We are going to explore these concepts in more detail in a later chapter, but until then, it is important to get the fundamentals.

Forces of Integration, Disintegration, and Self-Determination

Until the end of the Cold War, which fostered the era of globalization,[8] most of international relations was based on and/or tied to relationships between and among nation-states and the assumption that each state is a sovereign entity. However, that changed after 1991, when the prevailing patterns of international relations shifted. No longer were relations between and among countries tied to the United States and the Soviet Union—"West" versus "East." In fact, without the dynamics of the two superpowers, relations between and among countries became far more fluid. Rather than a world of discrete nation-states competing with one another for power, which was the old order, the globalized world that we see today is characterized by the integration of nation-states into larger regional blocs, such as the European Union (EU), that are developing common policies not only on economic issues but increasingly on issues of foreign policy and security. While this does not suggest that the era of sovereign nation-states is over, it does suggest that countries believe that they can benefit from cooperating rather than competing with one another. In terms of IR theory, this might suggest acknowledging the primacy of liberal thought at the expense of realism.

Similarly, while some countries have been working together to pursue common policies, others have been dividing into component pieces, as the various "nations" within the states seek self-determination—the desire to be recognized as a nation and to be able to govern themselves. Thus, we see the peaceful breakup of Czechoslovakia into two component pieces (the Czech Republic and Slovakia) and the bloodier disintegration of Yugoslavia into six republics, each of which has become an independent country. In contrast, the Palestinians are a stateless people, who seek to create their own state with defined borders and a government that is sovereign. The Kurds, a distinct ethnic group who possess their own language, traditions, and lifestyle and account for substantial communities in Iraq, Turkey, and Iran, seek to create a country of "Kurdistan" that will guarantee them their sovereignty free from the strictures of another state. More recently, we have seen the country of Sudan divided into two parts, Sudan and South Sudan, following a referendum after a peace treaty ended a decades-long civil war. The implosion of the Soviet Union in 1991 led to the creation of fifteen countries, all of which had been "constituent republics" of the larger group. (See map 1.1.) While the initial breakup was relatively peaceful, conflicts remain, leading to bloody wars and terrorist attacks regarding the status of Chechnya and subsequently the status of other areas of the Caucasus. Thus, as recent history has shown, it is not that easy to create a new nation-state. In other words, being a nation does not necessarily mean that there is justification for a state or that the outside world will recognize that state.

Many would argue that none of these changes—forces of integration and disintegration, desire for self-determination, and so on—would have been possible were it not for the end of the Cold War. In fact, the Cold War, which dominated international relations from the end of World War II until the unification of Germany (1990) and the breakup of the Soviet Union (1991), can be seen as critical to providing a stabilizing framework for nations' interactions. The ongoing threat of nuclear war and the fears that came with it helped keep countries in check. Many governments were afraid to appear too aggressive out of concern that if they did so, either the United States or the Soviet Union would intervene, which would inevitably provoke a military response by the other country. In order to avoid any direct military confrontation, the United States and the Soviet Union interacted through what became known as proxy wars, where battles were fought indirectly through their allies. This meant that the United States would sometimes take the side of repressive regimes, rather than allowing a communist government (which would appear to be loyal to the Soviet Union) to take control of a country. For example, when the left-leaning Sandinista government took control of Nicaragua in 1984, deposing the U.S.-backed Somoza family, hostility toward the United States caused the new government to turn to the Soviet Union and Cuba for support. This set the stage for a U.S.-backed counterrevolution, with the United States arming the opposition forces, or the Contras. Thus, although the United States and the Soviet Union did not directly confront one another, they were involved through their respective allies.

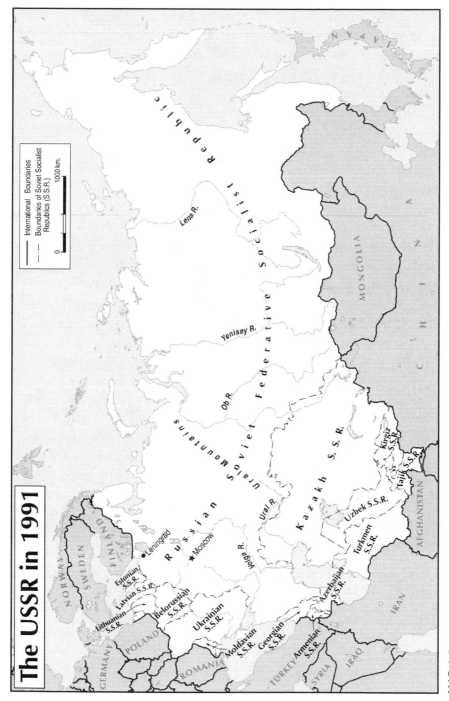

The USSR in 1991

International Boundaries
Boundaries of Soviet Socialist
Republics (S.S.R.)

0   1000 km.

Russian Soviet Federative Socialist Republic

Ural Mountains

Lena R.

Yenisey R.

Ob R.

MONGOLIA

CHINA

Kazakh S.S.R.

Kirgiz S.S.R.

Taj. S.S.R.

Uzbek S.S.R.

Turkmen S.S.R.

AFGHANISTAN

IRAN

IRAQ

SYRIA

TURKEY

Armenian S.S.R.

Azerbaijian S.S.R.

Georgian S.S.R.

Moldavian S.S.R.

ROMANIA

POLAND

GERMANY

Ukrainian S.S.R.

Belorussian S.S.R.

Lithuanian S.S.R.

Latvian S.S.R.

Estonian S.S.R.

NORWAY

SWEDEN

FINLAND

Leningrad

★ Moscow

Volga R.

Ural R.

MAP 1.1
The USSR in 1991

During the Cold War, it was also important that the respective allies remain firmly within the Eastern or Western bloc. For example, when the government of Czechoslovakia, one of the Eastern bloc countries, got out of hand in 1968, the Soviet Union came in and forcibly suppressed the nascent rebellion. The Soviet Union did not want any dissension or rebellion that could upset the delicate balance of power that existed. What happened in 1968 stands in contrast to what happened in 1993, following the end of the Soviet Union, when Czechoslovakia peacefully split.

This introductory overview is designed to stress a few main points as we begin the study of IR: that the nation-state has always been seen as the fundamental actor in international relations; that the concept of nation-state has a number of component parts, many of which can now be questioned; that the nature of the international system is and has been changing, and no doubt will continue to; and that the old world of "balance of power," whether as it existed traditionally or as seen through the Cold War, has now ended and has been replaced by a globalized world in which nonstate actors (actors other than the traditional nation-states) are playing an increasingly major role.

What does all this mean for understanding international relations? In order to understand the changes to the international system, it will be important to understand the fundamental building blocks: the nation-state, the concept of sovereignty, and the notion of power, to name but a few. But it also means that we really need to step back and look at the world today, and at what it means to be living in a world that is globalized. The very nature of globalization, with the interconnections among countries that help define the concept, has changed the nature and understanding of international relations.

GLOBALIZATION

We are beginning our study of international relations by asking a number of very macrolevel questions, which means that we are looking at the questions that affect the international system as a whole. In order to do this, we need to know what assumptions we are making and to define some basic terms and concepts. In this section, we will focus on issues of political stability and economic equality, what they mean, and why they are important when we consider the international system.

We are going to start with the international system as it exists today. To look at the international system in the twenty-first century is to look at a world that is interdependent—that is, what happens in one state directly affects what happens in others. Why is this the case and when and why did this happen?

What Is Globalization?

We are going to begin by asking a very basic and important question: What do we mean by *globalization*? This is a term that we hear all the time, and it is one that can generate a great many negative feelings. For example, recent meetings of the Group of Seven (now Eight) industrialized countries, and meetings of the World Trade Organization (WTO) have been disrupted by protestors. These protestors wanted to point out what they saw as inequities in the global economic system and especially the role of those major economic powers that are seen as the ones who make the rules. But can protests really change what has become a global reality? Can anyone stop or reverse the process of globalization? A more realistic set of questions might be: What do we mean by the current international economic system? How did it get here? And can it change?

Globalization as Historical Phenomenon

In order to answer these questions, we need to look at the concept of globalization not as a current phenomenon but as a historical one. For example, Thomas Friedman, columnist for the *New York Times*, describes three periods of globalization. In his estimation, the first lasted from 1492 (the voyage of Columbus) until around 1800. According to him, this phase of globalization "shrank the world from a size large to a size medium. . . . [It] was about countries and muscles." In his estimation,

> the key agent of change, the dynamic force driving the process of global integration, was how much brawn—how much muscle, how much horsepower, wind power, or, later, steam power—your country had and how creatively you could deploy it. In this era, countries and governments (often inspired by religion or imperialism or a combination of both) led the way in breaking down walls and knitting the world together, driving global integration.

Again, according to Friedman, the primary questions asked during this phase were "Where does my country fit into global competition and opportunities? How can I go global and collaborate with others through my country?"[9]

Friedman looks at the second era of globalization as lasting from around 1800 to 2000, interrupted by major events such as the two World Wars and the Great Depression, during which the world shrank still further. In this era of globalization, "the key agent of change, the dynamic force driving global integration, was multinational companies. These multinationals went global for markets and labor, spearheaded first by the expansion of the Dutch and English joint-stock companies and the Industrial Revolution."[10] Friedman also notes that it was during this period that we really see the birth of a global economy. What he is also telling us is that the international system changed in nature to include countries and companies working in collaboration. With this, we start seeing the impact of nonstate actors. All this was made possible by changes in technology that helped encourage more rapid movement of goods and information, as well as increasing the means of production.

He then identifies what he calls the third era of globalization, which he sees as beginning in 2000, and he says it

> is shrinking the world from a size small to a size tiny and flattening the playing field at the same time. . . . And while the dynamic force in Globalization 1.0 was countries globalizing and the dynamic force in Globalization 2.0 was companies globalizing, the dynamic force in Globalization 3.0—the force that gives it its unique character—is the newfound power for *individuals* to collaborate and compete globally. (emphasis added)[11]

Hence, Friedman tells us that the world/international system in general and the economic system in particular is changing, that it is getting smaller, that individuals and multinational corporations now make more of a difference, and that all this has happened relatively recently.

Historian Robert Marks, in his book *Origins of the Modern World*, similarly identifies a number of cycles of globalization that exist in historical context. However, he looks at the first globalization as part of a system of trade among the then nations, or more accurately, empires, going back to the 1200s. He notes the three primary trade routes that linked the major subsystems that existed at that time: East Asia, which linked China and parts of Southeast Asia to India; the Middle East–Mongolian subsystem, which linked Eurasia from the eastern Mediterranean to Central Asia and India; and the European subsystem, which linked Europe to the Middle East and the Indian Ocean. According to Marks, these subsystems "overlapped, with North and

West Africa connected with the European and Middle East subsystems, and East Africa with the Indian Ocean subsystem."[12] Again, what is important about this is that it suggests that there was a very well-developed trade system that linked most of Africa, Europe, and Asia as far back as the thirteenth century. And according to Marks, one of the important things to note when looking at and trying to understand the development of the international system from the perspective of globalization is that, like political scientists, "until quite recently, historians have practiced their craft taking current nation-states as their unit of analysis, rather than adopting a more global approach."[13] Thus, he argues, the international system actually pre-dates modern nation-states, and we need to look at and understand components of the international system and globalization from this very broad historical perspective.

He also takes this approach out of the realm of the realist thinkers, and he claims that the thirteenth-century world system "functioned without a central controlling or dominating force. To those who conceive of the modern world system as growing under the domination of a single state or group of states, the idea that a system could work without a controlling center is somewhat novel." He looks at a world that is *polycentric*—that is, "it contained several regional systems, each with its own densely populated and wealthy 'core,' surrounded by a periphery that provided agricultural and industrial raw materials to the core, and most of which were loosely connected to one another through trade networks." (See map 1.2.) And in his estimation, the world retained this polycentric character until around 1800, with the expansion of European colonization.[14]

If we look at the current international system, Marks traces its origins to the late nineteenth and early twentieth century, with the solidification of the modern concept of the nation-state system. He claims that the advent of *nationalism*, or the desire for national peoples to have a state, was congruent with the growth of industrialization, which allowed states to grow and expand their territory. But he also notes that along with this expansion came a growing gap between the richest and the poorer nations within the international system. *In theory, globalization and the increased trade that came with it should help diminish this gap or division between countries. In reality, however, this has not been the case.*

In theory, then, the modern concept of globalization is tied to the notion that nation-states are interdependent and that progress in one will help others. Here we see the idea of the "rising tide lifting all boats," to use a cliché.

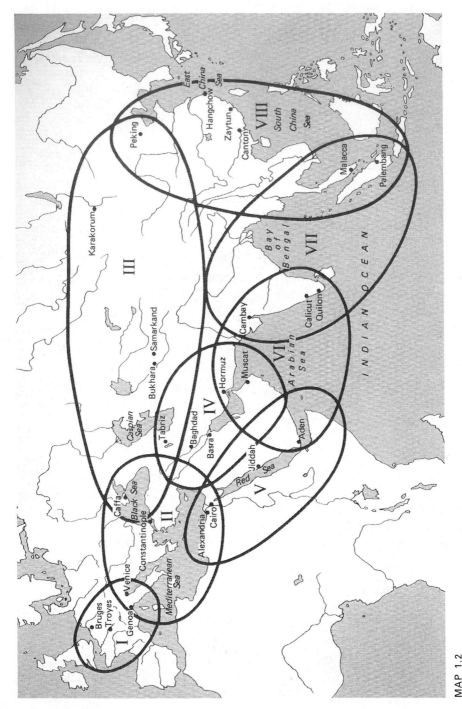

MAP 1.2
The Eight Circuits of the Thirteenth-Century World System

But Marks and others warn us that that has not been the case, and that the current round of globalization actually exacerbated the differences between and among nations, rather than closing them. He ties much of that to the concept of development, which should equal industrial growth. So as long as a country remained tied to traditional agriculture or resisted industrialization, as was the case with many countries in Africa or even China and India until relatively recently, they would continue to fall at the "poor" end of the international economic system.[15]

But it is also important to remember that many of these countries in Africa and Asia had been colonies of the major European powers. Even after they gained their independence, they remained tied to the colonial powers or were dependent on them for many reasons. This reinforced the patterns of trade tied to export of raw materials from the colony to the mother country, and the import of manufactured goods from the colonial power to the colony. This, in turn, led to the emergence of the so-called dependency theory, which posited that the poorer countries of the developing world (also known as the third world) would remain tied to and dependent upon the major developed countries and therefore could not develop or prosper on their own.[16]

Hence one of the goals of the movement toward development among many of these countries in Africa and Asia was to break that cycle of dependency. But that cycle is not easy to break, and it comes at a cost. Often (and we see this with China and India) the push toward development and industrialization comes at the expense of the environment, as countries see this as a necessary trade-off. These are often countries that tend to have agriculture-based economies, and even as they do move forward and develop, the majority of the population still lives on the land and depends upon it for food and sustenance. Peasant or rural economies depend upon a relatively large population—more children are needed to work the land—and so population growth continues without the economic base to sustain it, thereby perpetuating the pattern. Furthermore, the developed countries often had a vested interest in keeping the economic growth of the developing countries in check, lest it upset the entire and often delicate economic balance.

But what we are also seeing in a globalized world is how the impact of natural resources, such as oil, uranium, diamonds, or other precious substances, can alter that balance. For example, with the growing importance of and need for oil, some of the lesser developed countries started to become more prominent, both politically and economically. Thus, otherwise poor countries, such as Venezuela and Nigeria, have been able to exert relative power in the international system because of their possession of oil. This too has altered the balance of power within the international system and changed the perspective of "developed" and "developing."

When we look at the international system today, we see the emergence of a global free market that has allowed for the growth and prominence of countries like China, India, and Brazil, as well as the increasing role of countries such as Nigeria, Venezuela, and some of the countries of the Middle East, such as Iran. No one country can control the international economic system, any more than it can now control the international political system. The end of the Cold War and the subsequent emergence of more states and also more conflict has shown us that. While this also suggests that the theory is correct and that more countries are becoming economically strong, what the theories underlying globalization do not account for is the unequal distribution of wealth *within* any of those countries. So while some people within countries such as India or Nigeria are growing wealthy, others remain in a cycle of poverty that is virtually impossible to break. It is that aspect of globalization that has elicited protests.

As might be expected, those who take a more feminist approach to international relations have a different take on globalization and what it means. According to political scientist J. Ann Tickner,

> feminists call our attention to the fact that while women's positions vary according to race, class, and geographical location, women are disproportionately situated at the bottom of the socioeconomic scale in all societies; drawing on gender analysis, they point to the devaluation of women's work and the dichotomy between productive and reproductive labor as explanations of the relatively disadvantaged position of women and the growing feminization of poverty. . . . Globalization involves more than economic forces; it has also led to the spread of Western-centered definitions of human rights and democracy. Feminist scholars are questioning whether these definitions are gender biased.[17]

Thus, feminist theorists encourage us to explore all aspects of questions in IR, even areas that we might assume to be beneficial to all, such as human rights and democracy. For example, in her work, Tickner asks whether democracies really are friendly toward women, as feminists see the traditionally Western model of democracy and nation-states tied to a system that is patriarchal and traditional, which favored and privileged men's interests over women's. But she makes another important point that "since women have traditionally had less access to formal political institutions, the focus on state institutions by scholars of democratization may miss ways in which women are participating in politics—outside formal political channels at the grass-roots level."[18] In other words, Tickner directs us to look at the changes that have taken place at the level of the international system as a whole to see the impact they have had on women in general, and she admonishes us to look *within* the state to determine whether the spread of values such as democracy or even human rights has worked against women or has minimized the role that they play as actors in the international system.

The work of Friedman, Marks, and Tickner, among others, all suggest that the advent of globalization forces us to look at the international system in a new and different way. That means moving beyond the traditional theories and levels of analysis, as well as looking at the role played by primary actors other than the nation-state.

WHAT DOES GLOBALIZATION MEAN FOR THE STUDY OF IR?

In beginning our study of international relations by looking at globalization and the changes it has brought to the international system, we are moving beyond the traditional paradigms and approaches to the study of the field. What we are suggesting here is that in order to really understand international relations in the twenty-first century, we need to begin by understanding what the international system looks like *today*, if we are to understand all its component parts and how they have changed. That does not mean that we can ignore the traditional framework upon which the study of international relations is based. Quite the contrary. The theories, actors, and framework that have guided the study of international relations since it emerged as a discipline remain the building blocks for understanding the international system. Only by understanding those as our starting points can the contrasts with the world today really have meaning.

However, understanding IR in a globalized world also means going beyond the traditional state-centered approach that the field has often had. We need to be able to see the limits of that approach, and to expand our understanding and definitions in order to incorporate the roles of nonstate actors. But it is also important to remember that it is not possible to critique the theoretical perspectives or to offer new ones unless or until we have a good solid grounding in the fundamentals. Through the remainder of this book, our goal will be to provide those fundamentals so that we can, in turn, understand the weaknesses and look for alternative explanations and approaches.

With that introduction, we will now turn to the theories and framework that we will use to approach the field of international relations. After we have looked at these—theories, actors, and framework—we will return to our starting point of globalization and macrolevel questions in order to pull all the pieces together.

FURTHER READINGS

These additional readings are worth exploring and elaborate on some of the points raised in this chapter. This list is not meant to be exhaustive, but only illustrative.

Nancy Cleeland et al. "The Wal-Mart Effect." *Los Angeles Times*, November 23, 24, and 25, 2003 (available online).
J. David Singer. "The Levels-of-Analysis Problem in International Relations." *World Politics* 14, no. 1 (October 1961): 77–92.
J. Ann Tickner. "You Just Don't Understand." *International Studies Quarterly* 41, no. 4 (December 1997): 612.
"Treaty of Westphalia," at http://www.yale.edu/lawweb/avalon/westphal.htm.

NOTES

1. See Nancy Cleeland et al., "The Wal-Mart Effect," *Los Angeles Times*, November 23, 24, and 25, 2003.

2. See Hans J. Morgenthau, *Politics Among Nations: The Struggle for Power and Peace*, originally published in 1948. There are many more recent and abridged editions that have come out since that time.

3. As you will see later, the concept of the sovereign nation-state actually grew from the Treaty of Westphalia (also known as the Peace of Westphalia), which ended the Thirty Years' War in 1648. But it was after World War I that the map of Europe as we generally know it now was redrawn, with the emergence of new sovereign states. That process continued after World War II, as many then colonies were granted independence.

4. Joyce P. Kaufman and Kristen P. Williams, *Women, the State, and War: A Comparative Perspective on Citizenship and Nationalism* (Lanham, MD: Lexington Books, 2007), 12–13.

5. J. David Singer, "The Levels-of-Analysis Problem in International Relations," *World Politics* 14, no. 1 (October 1961): 77–92.

6. J. Ann Tickner, "You Just Don't Understand," *International Studies Quarterly* 41, no. 4 (December 1997): 612.

7. "Treaty of Westphalia," at http://www.yale.edu/lawweb/avalon/westphal.htm.

8. Some have argued that globalization is not a new concept, but that it actually dates back to the age of exploration in the fifteenth century or even earlier, a point that will be explored later in this chapter. See, for example, Thomas Friedman, *The World Is Flat: A Brief History of the Twenty-First Century* (New York: Farrar, Straus & Giroux, 2005), and Robert B. Marks, *The Origins of the Modern World*, 2nd ed. (Lanham, MD: Rowman & Littlefield, 2007).

9. Friedman, *The World Is Flat*, 9.

10. Friedman, *The World Is Flat*, 9.

11. Friedman, *The World Is Flat*, 10.

12. Marks, *Origins of the Modern World*, 33.

13. Marks, *Origins of the Modern World*, 33.

14. Marks, *Origins of the Modern World*, 35.

15. See Marks, *Origins of the Modern World*, especially "Introduction: The Rise of the West" and chapter 6, "The Great Departure," for more development of this idea.

16. For a concise definition of dependency theory, see J. Ann Tickner, *Gendering World Politics* (New York: Columbia University Press, 2001), 68. See also Marks, *Origins of the Modern World*.

17. Tickner, *Gendering World Politics*, 7.

18. Tickner, *Gendering World Politics*, 7.

2

Theoretical Overview

This chapter outlines the basic theoretical approaches that are the foundations of international relations and are critical to understanding the field. As a starting point, we will begin with Hans J. Morgenthau and his approach to realist/power politics, which has been one of the founding tenets of international relations since the end of World War II. (His seminal text, *Politics Among Nations*, was initially published in 1948.) Since then, the international political landscape has changed; new organizations tied to the notion of collective security assumed more idealistically that security could best be assured not by having nations increase their power, but by working cooperatively toward common goals and ends that would benefit all. Thus, a competing or (perhaps more appropriately) alternative theory of international relations was born, which challenged the basic principles of realism. This new approach focused more on cooperation between and among nations rather than competition for power, and it embodied many of the ideals earlier espoused by Woodrow Wilson. Referred to as "liberal theory," it incorporates economic ideas as well as political, and it has grown in prominence and importance since the end of the Cold War. Hence, the changes in the international system have contributed to a proliferation of other theories, all of which were designed to explain on a macro level, or more often on a micro level, some aspect of international relations.

In this chapter, we present a brief introduction to these various theoretical models (i.e., realism and structural realism, liberalism, constructivism, Marxism and its offshoots, and feminist approaches), with concrete examples of how each can be applied to understanding the international system and world events. Note that this is not meant to be a comprehensive study, as there are a number of approaches that we will not address in this short over-view, nor do we go into a lot of detail on the basic theories that we do ex-plore. If you are interested in learning more, there are a lot of readings you can delve into. Rather, what we want to do here is to offer an introduction to the major approaches so that you, the student, can determine which of these makes the most sense to you, and when and how you can apply each approach. This starting point will lead into the body of the remainder of the text.

WHAT IS THEORY, AND WHY IS IT IMPORTANT?

Before we can delve into IR theories, however, it is important to set out a few basic assumptions and to situate international relations within the broader field of political science. As noted in chapter 1, IR is the most macro level of all the subfields of political science. In contrast to the other subfields, such as American politics or comparative politics, international relations deals with the entire international system, which generally is made up of nation-states but also nonstate actors. Most nation-states have a political structure of some type, a culture and social organization that help define their values, and indi-viduals who influence the decisions that are made and are, in turn, affected by those decisions. Within each nation-state or nonstate actor, there are countless other groups that play a role in the decision-making process and interact with the political system in some way. This structure does not even begin to take into account the ways in which these broad entities, the nation-state or country, interact with and influence one another, although these too are legitimate questions for exploration within the area of international rela-tions.

Given this proliferation of actors and variables that can affect these actors and the international system as a whole, how can we begin to understand this complexity? That is the role of theory, which exists to provide the frame-work that can help guide our understanding of various events that occur within this complex system.

Theory and International Relations: Some Basic Assumptions

Every field of study has its theories or basic paradigms, as does interna-tional relations. These theories provide the framework that allows us to begin to simplify reality so that we can better address the complexities of the world.

Theory is a linked set of propositions or ideas that simplify the complex reality so that we can *describe* events that have happened, *explain* why they happened, and *predict* what might happen in the future. In the field of international relations, it is very difficult to predict with certainty, as there are so many variables that can affect the outcome of events. Unlike the "hard" sciences, where it is possible to work in a lab and to control the environment, in the social sciences in general and IR in particular, it is virtually impossible to control any single variable, let alone the interaction among these variables—although political scientists who employ various modeling techniques do try. This means that the theoretical perspectives are dynamic and evolve as situations change, as do the variables. Nonetheless, the main theories that have emerged allow us to identify general patterns that help us understand what has happened and why (i.e., describe and explain), and in so doing, give us some indicators of what might happen in the future under similar sets of circumstances (predict). So theories are important guides that allow us to navigate the complexity of the world.

Using these theories or paradigms can help us know how to ask and to answer some of the fundamental questions in the field. As a macrolevel field, IR tends to ask macrolevel questions—for example, what is war, and why do countries go to war? Why did a particular country act as it did, or respond to events in a particular way? How can one country influence another to engage in a particular pattern of behavior, or to stop it from behaving in a particular way? Why do some states appear to be cooperative, and others appear to be warlike? These are but some of the general questions that we see often in the field of IR, and that any number of theories and theorists have tried to answer. But how can we answer such questions in a world in which we can't identify all variables or hold things constant?

Political scientist Christine Sylvester provides some important clues when she writes: "In an international system filled with tensions, IR analysts are keenly interested in questions of *continuity* and *discontinuity*. States persist as key political entities, as does a world capitalist *system* of commodity production and exchange" (emphasis added). She continues, "Conventional wisdom has it that this is a world of states, nonstate actors and market transactions. It is a world in which neither men nor women figure *per se*, the emphasis being on impersonal actors, structures, and system processes."[1]

Sylvester seems to be telling us that in the traditional approaches to IR, people don't matter; IR is a field of actors, structures, and processes. But underlying this is another reality that Sylvester touches on later in her book, which gives us a more complete understanding of international relations—and that is *who* makes the decisions for these actors that result in the actions that we can see. Are states monolithic entities that operate on their own? Or put another way, what roles do individuals really play in steering the direction of a state?

This leads us to another component of our basic framework: the assumptions we have to make about nation-states and their behavior in order to arrive at generalizations (theories) about them. Whether they are accurate or not, making certain assumptions allows us to generalize, which in turn enables us to identify patterns as well as to draw conclusions based, in part, on studying cases that don't fit the patterns. These generalizations and patterns, and determining where there are deviations from these patterns and why, contribute to further information about and knowledge of the behavior of the international system.

To begin, we assume that states will behave as *monolithic* actors (that is, they will behave as if they were one single entity, rather than being made up of many individuals and groups) and that they will act in a *rational* manner (that is, they will make decisions based on a process that allows them to further their self-interest). States might be choosing to act in a certain way in order to maximize their power (the realist theoretical perspective), or because they feel that they will better achieve their interests by cooperating with other states (the liberal approach). But this also suggests that states have a way to identify what is in their *national interest* and that they will then act accordingly. Again, one can easily question this assumption, as any state has a number of competing interests, all of which can be argued to be in the best interest of the state. Nonetheless, for realists especially, it is important to assume that national interest can be identified and that states will pursue policies that help them achieve that interest.

Concept of National Interest

But what is *national interest* and how do countries actually achieve it? This is one of the critical concepts in IR, and one that is addressed in virtually every textbook on the subject. For example, according to political scientist Charles Kegley, "The primary obligation of every state—the goal to which all other national objectives should be subordinated—is to promote its *national interest* and to acquire power for this purpose" (emphasis in original).[2] Realist thinkers define national interest in terms of *power*, in the belief that only by acquiring power can a country achieve its primary goals. But some political scientists define national interest more broadly than simply the acquisition of power, such as protecting what the state sees as its core interests, which are those that involve the protection and continuation of the state and its people. For example, Barry Hughes sees core interests as those that "flow from the desire [of the state] to preserve its essence: territorial boundaries, population, government, and sovereignty."[3] From his perspective, core interest is more than simply security defined in traditional military terms, but it also means assuring a country's economic vitality, its values, and other components that are central to the essence of the state. One can argue that these are also essential to a country's security, but they fall outside the traditional definition, a point that we will return to later. So a country will pursue the policies that it deems to be in its national interest while also furthering its core interests.

Tied directly to the core interests/values and a country's national interest is the traditional notion of *security*, since one of the core values of any country is ensuring the safety and protection of the population. But this also leads to the dangers of the "security dilemma," which is a situation in which one state improves its military capabilities as a way of trying to ensure its own security. However, in doing this, the military buildup is seen by other states as an act of aggression and therefore a direct threat. Thus, each state tries to increase its own level of protection and hence its security to meet the perceived threat coming from another state, which contributes directly to the insecurity of others. The result is often an arms race, and no greater sense of security.

Generally, security is thought of in military terms. However, feminist theorists have challenged this preconception by expanding that definition to make a distinction between security defined in terms of the military and militarism and "human security," which refers to a broader set of issues necessary for human survival (core issues)—e.g., protection of the environment, eradication of diseases, freedom from hunger, access to potable water, and so on. In looking at these security issues, "feminists focus on how world politics can contribute to the insecurity of individuals, particularly marginalized and disempowered populations."[4] Put another way, "IR feminists frequently make different assumptions about the world, ask different questions, and use different methodologies to answer them."[5]

Feminist IR theorists would argue that only by broadening the approach to international relations as a field of study is it possible to get a complete picture of and accurate answers to many of the basic questions asked. As feminist theorist Gillian Youngs describes it, "In arguing that women and gender are essential to the field of International Relations, feminist scholars have had to address the *core* concepts and issues of the field: war, militarism and security; sovereignty and the state; and globalization" (emphasis in original).[6] In other words, while feminist theorists address the critical concepts, they inject a different perspective that should give us a more complete understanding of the issue studied.

This is not to suggest that one theory or approach is better or worse than another, or that one is right and another is wrong. What we do want to make clear, though, is that there are any number of approaches that can be used to understand international relations and that it is important to be clear about the questions that we want to ask and then to draw on the appropriate approach to answering those questions.

INTRODUCTION TO LEVELS OF ANALYSIS: A FRAMEWORK FOR UNDERSTANDING INTERNATIONAL RELATIONS

We noted above that international relations deals with the international system, which we can think of as being made up of nation-states but also non-state actors, each of which has a distinct political structure of some type, a culture and social organization that help define its values, and individuals who influence the decisions that are made and are, in turn, affected by those decisions. In effect, what we are referring to here are the *levels of analysis*. It is important to know more about what that concept means, as it is one of the primary building blocks for understanding international relations.

We can think of the levels of analysis as forming a pyramid. At the base is the *international system as a whole*, which is made up of nation-states, non-state actors, and international/multinational organizations. If we look within the international system, we can focus on the *individual nation-state*, the major component of the international system. Each nation-state, in turn, has a *government* and a *society*, which has its own *culture*, and then the *individuals* who make the decisions. (See figure 2.1.)

Put another way, we can start with the individual decision maker who emerges from the society and the culture of the nation and should reflect

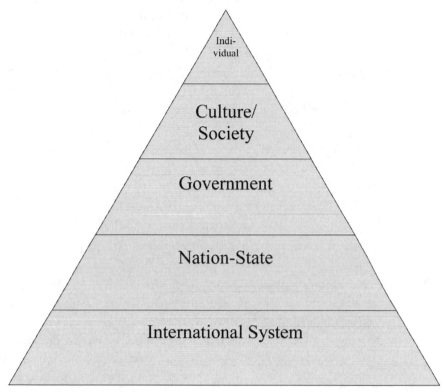

FIGURE 2.1
Levels of Analysis

those norms and values. Similarly, the government makes decisions for the nation-state and is tied directly to the society and culture. (In democratic societies, the government is elected, at least in part, by the members of the society.) Taken together, these are the primary component parts of the nation-state. Nation-states combine to create the international system. In fact, according to realist thinking, nation-states are the essence of the international system.

The logical question to ask here is: Why does this structure matter? It matters because it is important when asking a question about international relations to understand what level the question is really addressing so that it can be answered correctly.

For example, the Cuban missile crisis of October 1962 was one of the defining events of the Cold War. We can look at that incident and ask why

President John F. Kennedy made the decisions that he did. When asked that way, the focus of the question is the level of the individual decision maker, and it can be answered by reading about the processes Kennedy followed in order to make his decisions. What was he thinking? Whom did he turn to for advice?

But we can also ask how the American people reacted to what was going on at this time of heightened tension. To answer this question, we would have to look at the society and culture, which we can gauge through polls, newspaper accounts, and so on. Asking what role the formal governmental structure played gives us another insight into the crisis and how it was addressed. Was the Congress involved, and if so, in what ways? Or were decisions made by a small group of advisers to Kennedy, and what does that tell us about the role of government in crisis decision making and how decisions were made?

We can ask even more macrolevel questions, such as: How did the missile crisis change U.S. and Soviet relations during the Cold War? This is a question that can be answered by focusing on the nation-state level. At that level, we are looking at the United States and the Soviet Union as two major players in the international system and focusing on their reactions to one another, given their tense relationship during the Cold War. And finally, we can ask how the missile crisis affected the global balance of power. This question can best be answered at the macro level, by looking at the patterns of behavior of nation-states, what took place in the United Nations, and other macrolevel indicators.

The point here is that using levels of analysis as a framework makes it possible to ask specific questions and get the answers that are appropriate to the questions being asked. Each of the questions asked above is a valid one and can be answered. Using the levels of analysis allows us to focus on one level at a time, holding the others constant, in order to simplify the reality. This is the best way we can approximate what scientists do in a laboratory. It also allows us to look at a specific event and, using the basic framework for theory, *describe* what happened, *explain* why things happened as they did, and then *draw lessons* about what that might mean for similar events in the future. (Note that we are not saying that we can predict, but we can make educated guesses.) When the answers are taken together, it is possible to get a more complete picture of the event—what happened, how, and why.

The notion of using levels of analysis as a framework for approaching international relations goes back to the early 1960s and the work of political scientist J. David Singer. His article "The Level-of-Analysis Problem in International Relations"[7] draws on the even earlier work of Kenneth Waltz, who in his seminal book *Man, the State, and War* suggests that in order to really understand international relations in general and to address specific questions, such as why wars occur and whether there can ever be peace, it is necessary to understand human behavior (individual level), states (nation-state level) and how they are constructed (society, culture, and government levels), and finally to then address the international level.[8]

What Singer does in his article is to remind those of us who study international relations that until this point we have "roamed up and down the ladder of organizational complexity with remarkable abandon," which in turn has contributed to a failure "to appreciate the value of a stable point of focus."[9] After reminding us of the importance of a model or theory (to describe, explain, and predict), Singer illustrates the ways in which approaching international relations by using levels of analysis can provide a critical focal point for analysis. Furthermore, he alerts us to the fact that while the "big picture" might be lost by focusing on one level at the expense of another, what is gained is a picture that is richer in detail.

Singer describes for us the importance of being able to distinguish between levels, thereby aiding us in answering important questions. "So the problem is really not one of deciding which level is most valuable to the discipline as a whole and then demanding that it be adhered to from now unto eternity. Rather, it is one of realizing that there *is* this preliminary conceptual issue and that it must be temporarily resolved prior to any given research undertaking" (emphasis in original).[10] Thus, it is important to identify the appropriate level to be addressed early in the research process. But Singer also warns us of the dangers that can come with shifting between or among levels. "We may utilize one level here and another there, but we cannot afford to shift our orientation in the midst of a study."[11] When the answers are taken together and a number of levels analyzed, it is possible to get a more complete picture of the event—what happened, how, and why.

The "System" in the International System

In order to start applying these ideas and to be able to focus the theories most effectively, we also need to define what we mean by the concept of the *international system.* Here we can draw on the work of political scientist David Easton, who wrote in the 1960s about the concept of a "political system."[12] He drew on the ideas of systems theory to view political life as a "system of behavior" that has certain characteristics that can be defined, analyzed, and therefore understood. This approach makes certain assumptions that may or may not be accurate. However, it provides a good starting point for our understanding of international relations.

As Easton described it, political life can be seen as a pattern of behavior that exists within an environment that exerts influence on it and that it, in turn, influences. Components within this system are dynamic, and as each moves or acts, it affects the actions and behaviors of the other actors that also exist within this system. Since one of the primary functions of any system is to endure, the system as a whole will constantly be adjusting to changes within the environment. Another assumption is that these patterns of behavior have a certain regularity that can be identified, and therefore can be described and explained. And it is the role of theory to help us do those things.

But, we might ask, is there really such a thing as an *international system*? Clearly, there are political relationships that exist within the international community that can be identified, such as the United Nations or NATO, both of which are made up of nation-states. But do these organizations exhibit regular patterns of behavior? Do they ensure that nation-states will do so? The only way we can answer these questions and continue to build our theories of international relations is to make assumptions about the ways in which those entities or actors in the international system behave. We can then learn more by comparing the reality that we study with our assumptions, to see how well the theory describes the reality.

So, we can *assume* that there is an international system that can be identified, that it is made up of actors that exhibit some regular and identifiable patterns of behavior, that the nation-states that are the bases of international relations will act rationally (maximize gains and minimize losses), and that they act as monolithic entities. Without those assumptions, it would be impossible to understand or address the international system/international relations, let alone answer the complex questions that emerge in this field of study. And this brings us back to theory.

Theory provides the framework that allows us to begin to address the complexity by providing a way to simplify it. But it is also important to remember that theory does not emerge in a vacuum but must be tied to reality in some way, nor can it be so grounded in abstraction as to be virtually useless. Rather, good theory draws on concrete examples to arrive at generalizations that can help us explain real-world events. Ideally, a theory should be able to be tested in order to see whether it can be proved or disproved, and whether it holds up under a range of circumstances. It is in the attempt to do these things that the basic theories of international relations evolved.

Power

One of the assumptions of IR theories, especially realist thinking, is that nation-states will be motivated in no small part by a desire to increase their power. Hence, power is one of the most critical concepts in international relations. Simply put, power is the ability of one actor to influence the behavior of another in order to achieve its desired end. If we were to graph this very simply, it would look like this:

Country A wants Country B to do X.

Country A can then use its power to "persuade" (or encourage, motivate, or even coerce) Country B to take a particular action. That example assumes that Country A is the more powerful or has power over B, and that it can persuade Country B to take the desired action. But it is also important to remember that power is not necessarily unidirectional (Country A imposing its will on Country B) nor is it symmetrical. Or looking at it another way, Country A wants Country B to do X. Country B says that it will, but it wants something in exchange. In that case, there might be a negotiation that results in each country asking something of the other, and in that way, both can get what they want.

Another important point to remember when we introduce the concept of power is that it is a relative term. One country has power over another (A over B), meaning that it is relational; one has "power over" in relative terms. Although the feminist theorists have problems with this understanding of power, as noted below, it represents one of the easiest and most straightforward ways to think about this concept, and so we will continue with this basic approach. Given this relationship and understanding of power, a third country might be more powerful than both, in that it might have a greater number of weapons or resources than either of the two. These are the *capabilities* or materials and resources that a country has relative to others. And it is not only having the resources that makes a country powerful, but the willingness to use them, or its *credibility*. We will come back to these points in more detail below.

Countries have a range of policy options available to them that can be placed along a continuum from positive (rewards) to negative (punishment), which can be used between countries in order to get a desired outcome. In all cases, Country A decides which particular course of action to pursue by weighing the relative costs and benefits. Country B can then decide how to respond, based on what Country A is asking but also on what it is offering. Like Country A, Country B will engage in an evaluation of what it wants and needs, what it can get in exchange, and what is in its best interest. Thus, we are looking at a dynamic process.

A government, acting rationally, should choose the option that promises to give it the desired outcome at the least possible cost. In most cases, while a country might decide to offer or grant a reward to a country unilaterally, it generally will look to other countries to support it when the option chosen is negative. Threatening or imposing economic sanctions, for example, is a far more credible threat when more than one country agrees to abide by those sanctions. In deciding which option to pursue, the other thing any country must remember is that it must be credible, that is, it must have the resources and the will to follow through on the policy decision made.

Political scientist Joseph Nye identifies power as either *hard power* or *soft power*.[13] According to him, "Hard power rests on inducements (carrots) or threats (sticks)" whereas "soft power rests on the ability to set a political

Continuum of Actions

Positive (Cooperative)					Negative (Conflictual)	
Granting → rewards	Offering → rewards	Threats →			Imposition of → punishment	Armed conflict
	Foreign aid				Economic sanctions	
	Military technology				Boycotts	
	Military support				Recalling diplomats	
	Diplomatic recognition				Threaten force	
	Form alliances				Use of force	

FIGURE 2.2
Continuum of Actions

agenda in a way that shapes the preferences of others."[14] Generally, hard power is associated with military and/or economic strength, while soft power is tied to values. Nye later built on that starting point and included the concept of *smart power*, which he defines as "the ability to combine hard and soft power resources into effective strategies." And then he elaborates on this idea by adding, "Unlike soft power, smart power is an evaluative as well as a descriptive concept. Soft power can be good or bad from a normative perspective, depending on how it is used. Smart power has the evaluation built into the definition."[15] According to Nye, then, smart power is something that is available to all states, large or small, and is a function of the policies a country develops and the way in which a country chooses to use its resources.

Another author, Walter Russell Mead, divides power into four types: sharp (military), sticky (economic), sweet (culture and ideals), and hegemonic. Sharp, sticky, and sweet together contribute to hegemonic power, as they come together and create a whole that is bigger than the sum of the parts.[16] Clearly, power can be defined in any number of ways. A country is deemed powerful if it can use its power and the capabilities that make up that power (whether real or perceived) to influence the outcome of events. But this also assumes that County A knows what it wants to achieve, has an understanding of its own power relative to the needs and power of Country B, and can determine how best to use that power in order to achieve what it wants. That assessment governs many of the interactions in international relations.

It is important to note here that not all of the patterns between and among countries are conflictual. It should be clear from figure 2.2 above that sometimes the best way for a country to get what it wants is to find ways to cooperate and negotiate with other countries. Offering rewards, such as foreign aid or other inducements (i.e., "carrots") can sometimes be a more effective policy tool than threatening or imposing economic sanctions (i.e., "sticks"). But it is also important to remember that the particular policy chosen should grow out of an understanding of the situation, the desired goals, and the relative power of each of the countries involved.

In thinking about power and the international system, it is important to think about which countries have power and what gives them their power. As noted above, power is a relative concept, so when we talk about which countries are powerful, we mean relative to other countries with which it interacts.

There would be little dispute that the United States is a powerful country because of its economic and military strength. Similarly, China has clearly become a powerful country, not only because of its growing economic role internationally and its military strength, but also because of its size and its population; people are a *capability* that can enhance a country's power. So are a country's size and geography and topography. But if you were asked to make a list of other powerful countries, what would that list look like? What countries are powerful?

How about a country like Sudan—is it powerful? Generally, we would say that because of its lack of resources and relatively low level of economic development, it is not powerful. But it was able to perpetrate genocide in Darfur in defiance of the wishes of most other countries in the international system, including the United States. Does that mean it has power? If so, what is the basis for that power? What about a country like Nigeria? It is politically unstable, but it has oil. Does that make it powerful? Venezuela is a similar case—is it powerful?

In other words, we can argue and make lists of what countries are powerful, as long as we have established criteria for defining *power* and as long as we see power as relative, rather than in absolute terms.

When we talk about power, which clearly is one of the central concepts in understanding international relations, each of the theoretical perspectives has its own way of viewing the concept, and even of understanding how critical it is. For example, power is central to realist thinking, as we have noted. Liberal thinking and constructivist thinking focus less on power and more on other components of nation-state relationships, including cooperation and the structures that can hold them together rather than leading to competition. In contrast, feminist IR theorists inject some warnings into the discussion of power that are worth considering here. Specifically, they question the assumption that "power" equates with "power over," or "the ability to get someone to do what you want."[17] Feminist theorists are concerned that this approach to power "emphasizes separation and competition: Those who have power use it (or its threat) to keep others from securing enough to threaten them."[18] In effect, they argue that defining power in this way obscures critical aspects of relationships and does not take values into account. In contrast, they suggest that we need to think about a different definition of power that is less coercive and more about interdependence and relationships, less about zero-sum approaches and more about achieving a desired outcome through cooperation rather than conflict. In other words, it requires rethinking our definitions of basic concepts such as *security* and *power*. However, as Tickner and other feminist scholars note, "Imagining security divested of its statist connotations is problematic; the institutions of state power are not withering away."[19]

When we think of many of the basic concepts in IR, such as power, they tend to fall into the *public realm* (that is, they are considered part of the state, the government, and decision making), all of which tend to exclude women who exist in the *private realm* (that is, the home and the family). However, the feminist theorists remind us first of all, that more women are moving from the private realm to the public, thereby making women more visible. (We can see this with women such as Hillary Clinton and Condoleezza Rice, both of whom were U.S. secretaries of state.) But sometimes that might mean working at a grassroots or community level, rather than at the national or international level, where women can often have a marked impact. In general, though, this suggests that women are finding ways to have their voices heard and to play more of a role in political decision making. This was not something that was considered when the field of IR came into its own, and it was certainly not part of the thinking of the realist theorists.

There are many other concepts and definitions that will come into play as we continue our study of international relations. And we will review them as needed. But with the main concepts outlined, we will now turn to an introduction to the basic theories.

INTRODUCTION TO BASIC IR THEORIES

As noted above, the major role of theory is to provide a framework that will allow us to simplify a complex reality so that we can describe the events that took place in the past, try to explain them in causal terms ("this happened because that happened"), and in doing so, try to predict or at least anticipate what might happen in the future. Each of the major theoretical approaches attempts to do this. Remember that no one theory can explain all events or sets of circumstances. Thus, which theory is the most appropriate to use is partly a function of the question(s) asked, understanding the context for the particular event, and the assumptions we choose to use. Some IR scholars believe that one theory is inherently better at answering questions than another. But others take the viewpoint that the question(s) we ask should determine the theoretical approach we use to find the answer. The main point is that theory should provide a framework or a guide to help us understand the world.

Realism and Neo-/Structural Realism

As noted above, the major role of theory is to serve as a framework or a guide. In the words of one political scientist, "The realist tradition is certainly regarded by an overwhelming majority of scholars to be the definitive tradition in the field of international relations."[20] Because of the importance of realist theory in defining international relations, we will begin with that, and we will give a lot of attention to it. As you will see, many of the other modern theories grew up, at least in part, as reactions to realist theory. This means that realist theory should be our starting point.

The realist school puts the concept of *power* at the center of all the behaviors of the nation-state; the assumption is that nations act as they do in order to maximize their power so that they can better achieve their own goals. As described by Hans Morgenthau, the father of realist theory, "The main signpost that helps political realism to find its way through the landscape of international politics is the concept of *interest defined in terms of power*" (emphasis added).[21]

Although it is most associated with the work of Hans Morgenthau, realist thought can be found throughout history. Early versions of this description of the competition for power can be attributed to Thucydides, whose *History of the Peloponnesian War* is seen as one of the first examples of realist thinking. The "Melian Dialogue" between the Athenians (the stronger group) and the Melians (the weaker) describes a situation that took place during the Peloponnesian War, as the great city-states of the time were vying for power. There are important lessons to be learned from this history, written almost twenty-five hundred years ago.

The Melian Dialogue describes not only issues of power, but also the role of alliances as a strategy that states can use to maximize their power or to provide additional security. These are concepts that are central to the current understanding and application of realist thinking, and the same basic ideas can be and have been applied in modern times.

This idea of the importance of power and aggregating power is seen also in Niccolò Machiavelli's *The Prince*, which was written in 1505 and published in 1515.[22] Machiavelli came of age in Italy during a time of warfare among the Italian city-states and with external powers, such as Spain. This could not

BOX 2.1

THE MELIAN DIALOGUE

Written in approximately 400 BCE, the Melian Dialogue is an example of the belief that in the real world, basic ideals such as justice or freedom will fall to the demands of the powerful. In the dialogue, for example, the Athenians do not worry about whether they are acting in a way that is just or right. Rather, the Athenians argue that "you know as well as we do that right, as the world goes, is only in question between equals in power, *while the strong do what they can and the weak suffer what they must*" (emphasis added). In response, the Melians contend that "we speak as we are obliged, since you enjoin us to let right alone and talk only of interest—that *you should not destroy what is our common protection, the privilege of being allowed in danger to invoke what is fair and right*" (emphasis added).

And foreshadowing the idea of balance of power, in which one country aligns with another in order to balance the power of a superior one, the Melians also state, "You may be sure that we are as well aware as you of the difficulty of contending against your power and fortune, unless the terms be equal. But we trust that the gods may grant us fortune as good as yours, since we are just men fighting against unjust, and that what we want in power will be made up by the alliance of the Lacedaemonians, who are bound, if only for very shame, to come to the aid of their kindred. Our confidence, therefore, after all is not so utterly irrational."

In this case, the Lacedaemonians were a rival of the Athenians whom the Melians hoped to enlist as allies in their fight against the Athenians. However, the Lacedaemonians were engaged in their own battles and did not support the Melians, as the Athenians correctly anticipated ("and as you have staked most on, and trusted most in, the Lacedaemonians, your fortune, and your hopes, so will you be most completely deceived."). Ultimately, the outcome of the conflict was that the Melians were defeated by the Athenians.

Source: Thucydides, "The Melian Conference," in *History of the Peloponnesian War*, chapter 17, at http://www.mtholyoke.edu/acad/intrel/melian.htm.

help but affect his perceptions of politics and power as reflected in his writings. As noted in the introduction to one of the translations of *The Prince*, "From the pages of *The Prince* strides the figure of the autocrat, the new man, ruthless, efficient, and defiant, the literary forerunner of the new monarchs of the sixteenth century."[23] Yet, throughout the book, Machiavelli advocates for a strong state, with government based on the goodwill of the ruler, but with government also able to do whatever is necessary in order for it to achieve its ends. Or, put another way, "In the final resort he [Machiavelli] taught that in politics, whether an action is evil or not can only be decided in light of what it is meant to achieve and whether it successfully achieves it."[24] In other words, the ends justify the means. These sentiments and ideas certainly foreshadow much of the realist thought that would follow centuries later.

Thomas Hobbes, who wrote in the seventeenth century, also talked about the "state of nature," which is an anarchic world in which everyone pursues his or her own self-interest. Like Machiavelli, Hobbes was heavily influenced by his time—he wrote his famous work *Leviathan* while he was in exile—and he is best known for his discussion of the state of nature.[25] Like the realist thinkers, Hobbes begins with his understanding of basic human nature, which he believed required a strong government to keep people in check. For Hobbes, without that government, people would constantly be vying for power.

For modern realist political thinkers,

Hobbes's description of the state of nature has been viewed as analogous to the international system. Just as in the state of nature in which individuals stand alone, so too in the international system are states driven to maintain their independence. As in the state of nature, the international system is marked by constant tension and the possibility of conflict.[26]

Thus, there is historical precedent for the realist approach to understanding international relations and the idea of countries seeking to maximize their power using whatever means are necessary. In many ways, that understanding fits with the overall approach to the international system at a time when countries were vying for colonies, wealth, military superiority, and therefore, power. When countries did enter into alliances, they were transitory and often seemed to create more problems for the countries than they

BOX 2.2

THE LEVIATHAN, BY THOMAS HOBBES

Nature has made men so equal, in the faculties of body and mind as that, though there be found one man sometimes manifestly stronger in body; or of quicker mind than another; yet when all is reckoned together, the difference between man, and man is not so considerable, as that one man can thereupon claim to himself any benefit which another may not pretend, as well as he. For as to the strength of body, the weakest has strength enough to kill the strongest, either by secret machination, or by confederacy with others that are in the same danger as himself. . . .

Hereby it is manifest that, during the time men live without a common power to keep them all in awe, they are in that condition which is called war and such a war, as is of every man, against every man. . . .

To this war of every man against every man, this is also consequent: that nothing can be unjust. The notions of right and wrong, justice and injustice have there no place. Where there is no common power, there is no law.

Source. Thomas Hobbes, "Of the Natural Condition of Mankind as Concerning Their Felicity and Misery," in *The Leviathan*, part I, "Of Man," chapter 13 (Indianapolis, IN: Bobbs-Merrill, 1958), 104–9.

gained in security, which has become the more modern interpretation of an alliance. Thus, there were few opposing perspectives or understandings of the ways that states (city-states or nation-states) behaved beyond what we now know or think of as the realist tradition.

It was really after World War II, especially with the writings of Hans Morgenthau, that we saw the development of realist theory as we know it today. Realism presumes that the nation-state is the primary actor in the international system, that it will act rationally and as a unitary actor, that states are sovereign entities with sole responsibility to act within their borders, and that they will act to maximize their power. (We will explore the concept of the nation-state, its evolution, and the concepts such as sovereignty that are part of it, in more detail in the next chapter.) To Morgenthau, states act in a way that assures their survival, which in turn stems from maximizing their power; it is the phrase "interest defined as power" that embodies realist thought.

As Morgenthau assumes that the statesman and the state he[27] represents are virtually identical, it is logical that he would conclude that "statesmen think and act in terms of interest defined as power, and the evidence of history bears that assumption out."[28] Thus, while understanding motives would be helpful, he does not believe that is necessary in order to understand events. In fact, Morgenthau says that what is important to know "is not primarily the motives of the statesman, but his intellectual ability to comprehend the essentials of foreign policy, as well as his political ability to translate

---

BOX 2.3

MORGENTHAU'S SIX FUNDAMENTAL
PRINCIPLES OF POLITICAL REALISM

1. "Political realism believes that politics, like society in general, is governed by objective laws that have their roots in human nature."

2. "*The concept of interest defined as power.* This concept provides the link between reason trying to understand international politics and the facts to be understood" (emphasis added).

3. "Realism assumes that its key concept of interest defined as power is an objective category which is universally valid, but it does not endow that concept with a meaning that is fixed once and for all."

4. "Political realism is aware of the moral significance of political action."

5. "Political realism refuses to identify the moral aspirations of a particular nation with the moral laws that govern the universe."

6. "The difference, then, between political realism and other schools of thought is real, and it is profound."

Source: Hans J. Morgenthau, *Politics Among Nations: The Struggle for Power and Peace*, brief ed. (Boston: McGraw-Hill, 1993), 4–16.

what he has comprehended into successful political action."[29] And, according to realist thinking, that necessarily ties to power.

For Morgenthau and other realist thinkers, the principles of this approach are grounded in the belief that all relationships are ultimately rooted in power. To the realists, then, the ongoing struggle for power, whether between individuals or nations, means that conflict is inevitable. It is in this basic approach to and understanding of human nature that other theorists—liberals and constructivists especially—deviate from the realists. But realism also advocates that alternative political actions must be weighed, with their consequences assessed and evaluated and placed within the specific political and cultural environment. This means that the concept and conditions for the uses of power can and will change, and that the change must be recognized by those who make decisions.

Morgenthau and realist theory gave rise to a number of important other political thinkers, such as Kenneth Waltz (who in turn was one of the earlier theorists of neorealist or structural realist refinement, below) and John Mearsheimer.[30] Realist theory also helped frame the approach of important policy makers such as George Kennan, who was the architect of the U.S. Cold War foreign policy of containment, and Henry Kissinger, who was secretary of state under President Nixon and helped frame the diplomatic opening between the United States and the People's Republic of China. Many would argue that until the end of the Cold War, virtually all of U.S. foreign policy was based on realist thinking—specifically, the constant assessment of U.S. power vis-à-vis Soviet power, and finding ways to ensure that power is balanced, at the very least.

Neorealism/Structural Realism

Realist thinking gave birth to other theoretical approaches in IR, notably *neorealism* (also called *structural realism*), as well as a number of theoretical perspectives that grew up in reaction to it. The latter group will be explored in more detail later in this chapter.

Neorealist thinking was led by Kenneth Waltz, who attempted to take realist theory one step further by asserting that there are general "laws" that can be identified to explain events in the international system. Waltz and other neorealists put the greatest emphasis on the international system rather than the nation-state as the primary unit of analysis. Neorealism also assumes that power within the international system will vary, and that states will seek to balance that distribution of power. Hence, the structure of the international system and the distribution of power within it become determining factors in the ways in which states behave. Many of the principles of alliance theory grow from the approach taken by the structural realists.

Waltz introduces the idea of neorealism or structural realism by critiquing realist theory. He writes: "The new realism, in contrast to the old, begins by proposing a solution to the problem of distinguishing factors internal to international political systems from those that are external. Theory isolates one realm from others in order to deal with it intellectually."[31] He continues to introduce his approach to solving this problem with the modification of realism that he has just identified.

> Neorealism develops the concept of a system's *structure* which at once bounds the domain that students of international politics deal with and enables them to see how the structure of the system, and variations in it, affect the interacting units and the outcomes they produce. International structure emerges from the interaction of states and then constrains them from taking certain actions while propelling them toward others. (emphasis added)[32]

Thus, the essence of neorealism lies in concentrating on the overall structure of the international system, as well as understanding its various parts, in order to arrive at what Waltz claims will be a more cohesive theory of international relations.

Like realist theory, the neorealists also look at balance of power, but they place this idea of balance within the structure of the international system as a whole rather than focusing just on the nation-state. The assumption of balance also contributes to the role that alliances play, as they affect the structure of the international system. One of the major assumptions of the neorealists is that peace is most assured as long as power is roughly balanced within the international system—a situation of *bipolarity*, that is, balance between two major powers.[33] To the realists, the Cold War, despite its tensions, was also a period of stability because of the perception of a balance of power between the United States and the Soviet Union.

In their way of thinking, least stable is a multipolar system, with a number of power centers and the dangers of countries shifting alliances. Thus, to many neorealists, the post–Cold War period is more dangerous and unstable than the Cold War was, with the ongoing power of the United States, but also the European Union and more recently the rise of China, as well as any number of other countries also seeking to gain more power and international prestige. It is the jockeying for power and position that makes a multipolar system inherently unstable.

A unipolar system with one major power (*hegemon*) potentially can be stable if the dominant country is strong enough to enforce rules and keep the lesser powers in check. However, realist political scientist John Mearsheimer warns that "great powers" are always vying with one another for power, as each strives to become the hegemon or dominant power. In the current international system, Mearsheimer warns, the dangers come not from global hegemons but from competition among regional hegemons, which could, in turn, lead to conflict or war.[34] We can see that with the rise of China in Asia and its aggressive behavior in the South and East China Seas. According to this theory, China's actions are a result of its asserting itself as a power within its region. That assertion of power will lead to conflict, although not necessarily to actual warfare, as we can see with the increase in tensions between China and the United States vis-à-vis the South China Sea.

Clearly, realists and neorealists take power as the core concept of their theoretical approach to understanding international relations. Where they diverge is in identifying the principal actors and the underlying assumptions governing their behavior.

Limitations and Critique of Realism and Neorealism

In looking at realism and its offshoots, we can argue that both realism and neorealism offer insights into understanding some aspects of international relations. Both approaches clearly put forward their assumptions and the central role that power plays. Both make it clear that they are not really looking within the nation-state, but rather only at the *decisions* made by or the policies of the nation-state, and trying to deconstruct the reasons behind those decisions. And both assume prescriptions for foreign policy decisions. One of the other advantages of the realist and neorealist approaches is that they are relatively straightforward and easy to understand.

That said, both approaches have weaknesses or limitations as well. Both of them are premised on the importance of power, but power is a relative concept, not an absolute. In many ways, it is intangible and tied to perceptions as much as it might be tied to any actual measure. Whether pure realism or neorealism, the concept of national interest is assumed to be of great importance, although this too is an intangible that cannot be clearly identified or measured. As a result, as students of international relations we are left to wonder how we know that a state really acted in its own self-interest. For example, was the U.S. decision to go to war with Vietnam in its own interest? What about the U.S. invasion of Iraq in 2003?

Furthermore, there are questions about how applicable realist or neorealist thinking is in a globalized, post–Cold War world in which countries are increasingly interdependent economically. As we saw in chapter 1, a globalized world suggests the need for countries to work together, which speaks to the liberal approach, rather than seeing nation-states compete with one another, as would be suggested by the realist approaches to international relations. Also associated with the application of Realpolitik,[35] many see realist politics as having a negative connotation, as it suggests that states will do anything in order to gain power. However, rather than thinking of it in that way, as either negative or positive, it is more important to think of the realist perspectives as offering one explanation as to why states act as they do.

Finally, feminist IR theorists, such as Tickner, would argue that neither the realist nor the neorealist approach takes gender into account, claiming that "virtually no attention has been given to gender as a category of analysis," nor has any attention been paid to "how women are affected by global politics or the workings of the world economy."[36] If realism is tied to certain assumptions of human nature and behavior, are they truly generalizable to all men, let alone women? This is not to suggest that women or women's experiences need to be injected into all aspects of international relations theory. But it does mean that we need to be aware of the ways in which these theories are framed if we are to understand their weaknesses.

These critiques or limitations do not mean that realism and/or neorealism cannot be applied to help us understand some aspects of international events. And in fact, they can and do help us explain some of the actions that states take. The warnings mean that we must be aware of the assumptions, and we must apply these theoretical approaches carefully.

Liberalism as a Theoretical Model

We just looked at realism and neorealist theory, both of which posit a world and an international system in which power is one of the primary driving forces, if not the single force, that determines how states behave and why they act as they do. We are now going to turn to other theoretical models that enhance our understanding of the international system by approaching it, and the actors within it, differently. We will begin with the liberal model, also known as the pluralist or idealist approach. The liberal theoretical model should not be confused with the popular labels *liberal* and *conservative* pertaining to political ideology. Rather, in this case, the concept of liberal thinking grows out of early-nineteenth- and twentieth-century approaches to understanding international economics as well as politics. Thus, this theoretical approach blends economics and politics, which is one of the reasons it seems to fit well with our current globalized international system.

Within the field of IR, liberalism really emerged as an important theoretical construct in the 1970s as a critique of realism with its focus on power and conflict. "Liberal scholars pointed to the growth of transnational forces, economic interdependence, regional integration, and cooperation in areas where war appeared unlikely—trends and issues not amenable to realist analysis."[37] Thus, liberal thinking grew up to fill the theoretical void emerging in an increasingly globalized and interdependent world. This approach relies heavily on the confluence of economics and politics in its belief that everyone and all states will benefit from the flourishing of free markets and open exchange of ideas. In many ways, liberalism is tied heavily to a belief in the importance of both capitalism and democracy, and the notion that free trade will create interdependence among states that will result in greater benefit for all.

Liberalism, also known as *idealism*, starts with different assumptions about the world than does realism, and it believes in pursuing policies that can be termed to be in the common good, rather than what is good for the individual state. In fact, early hints of this idea of idealism can be found in the description of the Peloponnesian War, referenced above under "Realism and Neo-/Structural Realism." However, in this case, it was the Melians who called upon the Athenians to practice "what is fair and right," and, in the spirit of cooperation, they asked the Athenians "to allow us [the Melians] to be friends to you and foes to neither party, and to retire from our country after making such a treaty as shall seem fit to us both."[38] Liberalism is also tied directly to twentieth-century ideas of idealism, and the belief that wars can be avoided if countries work together cooperatively. Because of its broad worldview and its acceptance of interdependence, there are many in international relations who think that the liberal model is more appropriate than realist theory in describing and explaining international relations in a globalized, post–Cold War world.

Like realism, liberalism has many offshoots. In fact, political scientist Michael Doyle, one of the preeminent liberal theorists, describes it this way:

> There is no canonical description of liberalism. What we tend to call *liberal* resembles a family portrait of principles and institutions, recognizable by certain characteristics—for example, individual freedom, political participation, private property, and equality of opportunity—that most liberal states share, although none has perfected them all. (emphasis in original)[39]

Like realism, liberalism builds on the work of earlier philosophers and theorists, including economist Adam Smith, and sees mutually beneficial exchanges, especially economic exchange, as central. But unlike realism, liberalism looks both within the nation-state to understand the impact of domestic politics and also at the system as a whole, in order to understand the growth and role of international organizations, for example. Taken together, they provide a more complete picture or understanding of a state's actions. Thus, liberalism covers more levels of analysis than realism does, while also making its own assumptions about the ways in which states behave and why.

Further, unlike realism, which starts with power as its major concept and assumes that states are motivated by a desire to increase their power, liberalism starts with the premise that the *individual* is the critical actor and that human beings are basically moral and good. Hence, liberalism injects a normative perspective into its basic starting assumptions. Because of this assumption, it follows that evils, such as injustice and war, are the products of corrupt institutions and/or misunderstandings or misperceptions among leaders. Thus, there is no assumption of the inevitability of international events, such as war. Rather, the assumption is that war and conflict can be eliminated or mitigated through cooperation, reform, or collective action initiated by individual leaders. In these assumptions, liberalism also draws on the work of eighteenth-century political philosopher Immanuel Kant, who argued that "a world of good, morally responsible states would be less likely to engage in wars."[40] This also assumes that international cooperation and engagement are possible, and that if all states adhere to basic global norms, war can be avoided and peace will result.

This approach to studying international relations also assumes that there will be multiple actors who interact in some way other than competing with one another. While liberal theory recognizes the importance of states, clearly it also sees other actors as important; within the nation-state (i.e., the individual decision makers, people within the political system), the broader international system and the various multinational organizations all play a role. Liberal theorists look at a world that they believe is truly global in order to account for actors that go beyond any single set of borders.

At the level of the individual, liberalism assumes that individuals are rational beings who understand and accept basic laws that govern human beings and society, and that in understanding these things, individuals can work to make them better. Thus, war is a product of people not understanding these basic laws or interactions, or not working to do anything to improve these conditions. Furthermore, this approach also assumes that individuals can satisfy their needs in rational ways, often by working together in cooperation so that all benefit. It is out of this approach that the idea of collective security and international organizations had its origins.

Also implicit in this theoretical approach, because of its focus on the individual and the inherent worth and goodness of individuals, is the assumption that democracy will be the best and most effective form of political system because it allows for individual freedom and choice. As noted above, economics is tied heavily to liberal political thinking, and the assumption is that capitalism, especially democratic capitalism, will help lead to peace. The political side of this approach is embodied in what has become known as Wilsonian idealism, the principles put forward by Woodrow Wilson that have become one clear stream of U.S. foreign policy. The desire to encourage countries to pursue democratic forms of government that was advocated by President George W. Bush is a recent example of this type of idealism put into practice.

Many of these same ideals can be found embedded in the charter of the creation of the UN, and they pervade major security alliances, such as NATO. The preamble to the treaty creating NATO states:

> The parties to this Treaty affirm their faith in the purposes and principles of the Charter of the United Nations and their desire to live in peace with all peoples and governments. They are determined to safeguard the freedom, common heritage and civilization of their peoples, founded on the principles of democracy, individual liberty and the rule of law. They seek to promote stability and well-being in the North Atlantic area. They are resolved to unite

WILSONIAN IDEALISM

President Wilson believed in the important role that values played (or should play) in determining the ways in which states act. In his speech in his declaration of the U.S. entrance into World War I, he said:

> The world must be made safe for democracy. Its peace must be planted upon the tested foundations of political liberty. We have no selfish ends to serve. We desire no conquest, no dominion. We seek no indemnities for ourselves, no material compensation for the sacrifices we shall freely make. We are but one of the champions of the rights of mankind. We shall be satisfied when those rights have been made as secure as the faith and the freedoms of nations can make them.[1]

This ideal was further embodied in the Fourteen Points, when Wilson addressed the Congress in January 1918 (during World War I) and said:

> We entered this war because violations of right had occurred which touched us to the quick and made the life of our own people impossible unless they were corrected and the world secure once for all against their recurrence. What we demand in this war, therefore, is nothing peculiar to ourselves. It is that the world be made fit and safe to live in; and particularly that it be made safe for every peace-loving nation which, like our own, wishes to live its own life, determine its own institutions, be assured of justice and fair dealing by the other peoples of the world as against force and selfish aggression. All the peoples of the world are in effect partners in this interest, and for our own part we see very clearly that unless justice be done to others it will not be done to us. The program of the world's peace, therefore, is our program; and that program, the only possible program, as we see it, is this. . . .

I. Open covenants of peace, openly arrived at, after which there shall be no private international understandings of any kind but diplomacy shall proceed always frankly and in the public view. . . .

XIV. A general association of nations must be formed under specific covenants for the purpose of affording mutual guarantees of political independence and territorial integrity to great and small states alike.[2]

NOTES

1. U.S. Declaration of War with Germany, April 2, 1917, at http://firstworld war.com/source/usawardeclaration.htm.
2. President Woodrow Wilson's Fourteen Points, January 8, 1918, at http://avalon.law.yale.edu/20th_century/wilson14.asp.

their efforts for collective defense and for the preservation of peace and security.[41]

Hence, liberalism stands in contrast to realism in its understanding of
human nature and human good, and how that gets translated into actions.
The underlying assumption is that when nations work together, the result
will be a more peaceful and cooperative world. This approach gained increased credibility after the Cold War ended for a couple of reasons. Partly it
is due to the spread of democracy and capitalism in the countries that had
formerly been under the wing of the Soviet Union. Liberal thinkers saw the
democratic and capitalist movements that swept the countries of Eastern Europe as vindication that the socialist/communist/Marxist approaches could
not be sustained. Rather, when given the chance, the will of the people was
to promote a democratic system of government coupled with a capitalist
economy. These furthered the integration of the former Soviet states into the
international political and economic systems to the benefit of the states and
the people within it. Tied to this, then, is the thesis that the integration of
these states contributes to globalization, which in turn assumes interdependence. This suggests that all will benefit if states work together for the common good. The Cold War world, with its boundaries between East and West,
communist and capitalist, precluded such an interaction.

Neoliberalism

Like realism, liberalism has also given rise to other perspectives, including
neoliberalism, which is a refinement of the liberal approach. Neoliberalism
recognizes the role of actors other than nation-states and places greater emphasis on the role that nonstate actors play in understanding international
relations. Like realists, neoliberal thinkers start with the assumption of the
state as a unitary actor that will act in its own best interest. However, here
the two approaches diverge. Rather than assuming that the inevitable result
will be conflict, as the realists do, the neoliberals conclude that cooperation
will be in the state's interest. Thus, even in an international system without
a single central authority, states will work together cooperatively because it is
in their best interest to do so. Using that logic, security can best be achieved
through the emergence of agreements, enhanced trade, and other cooperative
ventures that will benefit all states involved.

In another variation of liberal/neoliberal thought, *neoliberal institutionalists* also factor in the role that international and intergovernmental organizations play in world politics. They too look at security as an important variable, but they arrive at a different conclusion as to how best to ensure it. In this case, neoliberal institutionalists believe that security and cooperation can best be achieved through the creation of international *institutions*. In this variant, it is the international institutions that are created by individual leaders to represent states that ensure that there will be interaction on a range of issues—political, economic, security, environmental, and so on. The assumption here is that these institutions, which states enter into voluntarily, provide the framework for cooperative and peaceful interaction even in an anarchic international system.

Limitations and Critique of Liberalism

Like realism, liberalism and its variations also have their limitations. As noted above, liberalism and to a lesser extent neoliberalism assume the best of human nature, and they assume that this "good" behavior will ensure cooperative and beneficial relations among nations. This presumes that an individual can, in effect, steer a nation. While it is true that in some cases, the individual can have an impact, in most nation-states today governing or policy-making is the product of a group of people who comprise the government. In parliamentary systems, there is also the opposition. So, while there might be some general agreement as to ideology or the direction of the nation, it is determined by more than any single individual.

Moving beyond the role of the individual, the liberal perspective also assumes that nation-states will benefit from cooperation, which in turn will affect the ways in which they behave. Thus, countries will join together to create organizations such as the United Nations as a way to promote cooperation and stability in the international system. Yet a counterargument to that is the point that international organizations really exert only minimal impact on the behavior of nation-states. Or, put another way, nation-states will only remain in these organizations and conform to their policies if it is in their interest to do so, which takes us back to the realist idea. Thus, there are questions about how effective international institutions, which are the backbone of this approach, really are unless states give them the power to act. An international organization like the UN will only be as effective as countries allow it to be. And then one has to question whether—or how much—power states will surrender to these institutions. Thus, to critics (especially those in the realist school), it is virtually impossible to move beyond the basics of states and power.

The reality is that international organizations cannot force sovereign nation-states to behave in any particular way; rather, nation-states behave in a certain way because they perceive it is beneficial for them to do so—that is, in their national interest. Thus, questions remain about whether countries really will work together unless they perceive that it is in their own interest to do so. Or, put another way, will they really do something simply because they perceive that it is "good"? The liberal thinkers imbue states and individual leaders with making those moral judgments. But does that assumption really reflect reality?

Furthermore, some critics of liberalism say that it focuses on the areas of "low politics," such as human rights or the environment, rather than "high politics," primarily security. In a globalized world, countries have become more aware of the fact that decisions made within one country affect others, which reinforces the liberal perspective. In cases such as the environment that do not respect national borders, liberal theorists would say that *all* countries benefit from cleaning up their environments; it is in their common interest to do so and to cooperate. But the theory does not account for "free riders"—countries that do not take action but benefit from the action of others. Furthermore, ultimately a country's survival hinges on ensuring its security, which is a core interest and in the category of "high politics." Unless a country is assured of its own survival, then the other values become secondary.

Constructivism

Constructivism is one of the newer theoretical approaches, really coming into prominence in the 1990s. Also known as *social constructivism*, this approach focuses on international issues and questions as they exist within a larger set of social and political interactions and the ways in which those relationships help a state frame the answers. It also stresses the importance of ideas and the ways in which states socially construct reality and then act upon their constructions of reality. Alexander Wendt, one of the first political scientists to define and advocate for this approach, describes it as follows: "The irony is that social theories which seek to explain identities and interests do exist. . . . *I want to emphasize their focus on the social construction of* *subjectivity. . . . * I will call them 'constructivist'" (emphasis added). And he then notes how many of the theoretical approaches "share a concern with the basic 'sociological' issue bracketed by rationalists—namely, the issue of identity- and interest-formation."[42]

Wendt elaborates on some of these ideas in a later article, when he writes:

> Constructivism is a structural theory of the international system that makes the following core claims: 1) states are the principal units of analysis for international political theory; 2) the key structures in the state system are intersubjective, rather than material; and 3) state identities and interests are an important part *constructed by their social structures,* rather than given exogenously to the system by human nature or domestic politics. (emphasis added)[43]
>
> Thus, states form ideas about and understandings of the world around them based on the structures with which they interact, and they then act on the perceptions that they form. Wendt also writes, "A fundamental principle of constructivist social theory is that people act toward objects, including other actors, on the basis of the meanings that the objects have for them."[44]

States, like people, may have multiple identities. They will respond to the actions of other states depending, in part, on how the state views itself, as well as the ways in which it views the other state. Clearly, this is dynamic and will change over time, depending on the interactions between those states, and the ways in which they perceive themselves and the other country. So these perceptions will constantly be redefined as circumstances change. For constructivists, where institutions are relatively stable and set, relationships between states are more fluid.

For example, one can ask why the possibility of Iran's acquiring nuclear weapons is a threat to the United States. China has nuclear weapons already and, realistically, with its size and military might, should pose more of a threat than Iran. Yet, despite periods of tension between the United States and China, it is Iran that is seen as relatively more threatening and potentially destabilizing. Why?

To look for an answer to that question, constructivist theorists would look first at the relationship between the United States and China, which is built on economic interdependence and areas of mutual cooperation (for example, the two countries worked together to try to counter the possible threat from a nuclear North Korea), despite periods of tension. That stands in contrast to the difficult relationship that the United States and Iran have had since the Iranian Revolution in 1979 and the taking of hostages at the U.S. embassy in Tehran. In looking at these two cases, constructivists would argue that it is important to understand the full extent of the relationship, their identities, and their interactions, and to use that as the context for understanding the nature of the threat. In addition, constructivists would argue that China's behavior will be relatively constrained by international norms. China wants to be regarded as an important player internationally and therefore will adhere to basic international guidelines and structures. In contrast, Iran is seen as less rational and unwilling to accept those same norms, thereby making it potentially more dangerous and threatening. Thus, where realists would respond to this question by focusing on the destabilizing effects of Iran's nuclear weapons, constructivists would respond differently. Ultimately, their focus would be on the perceptions that the United States has of Iran and of the idea that Iran is acting in a way that is outside the accepted or appropriate mean of behavior in the international system. In other words, Iran's behavior flies in the face of established and/or accepted structural norms.

According to political scientist Karen Mingst, this approach "has returned international scholars to the foundational questions, including the nature of the state and the concepts of sovereignty and citizenship." According to her, it has also opened up the field to new substantive areas of inquiry, such as the roles of gender and ethnicity, which have been missing from the field.[45]

Like realists, constructivists see states as the principal units/actors in the international system, but what becomes most important about them is their interaction with other actors and structures that also exist within the international system. Thus, constructivists see the actors in the international system as existing within their environment, which influences them and changes them. The behavior of states, therefore, is shaped by a number of factors that are *socially constructed*, such as the attitudes and beliefs of the decision makers, social norms, and identities. Furthermore, it is characterized by the belief that these various actors not only respond to this constructed system but change it through their actions. Therefore, constructivism looks at a system that is inherently dynamic.

Although its focus is on the state, like the liberal perspective, constructivist theory crosses levels of analysis to look *within* the state, but it also suggests that what happens at one level, such as the individual or societal level, directly shapes the actions of the state. So as the interests or values of the components of the state change, ultimately the behavior of the state will change as well. Therefore, a new leader coming to power with a different worldview can alter significantly the behavior of a state. And like realism, constructivism acknowledges the importance of power as a concept, but it defines the term more broadly than just military or economic power. Rather, this approach sees power as tied to broad concepts and ideas that feed into the notion of "soft power" discussed above. Hence, negotiation and persuasion, rather than threats or acts of political violence, become important tools of foreign policy.

Limitations and Critique of Constructivism

Among the criticisms leveled at this approach is that it really is not a theoretical model, but it exists more as a set of concepts tied to individual ideas and understandings that can change. In fact, one of the basic premises of constructivism is the need to address structural change. Since the very basis of the approach is tied to dynamics, questions arise about how to account for these changes. Is it possible to generalize beyond any single case in order to build a model of behavior? And if change and dynamics are an inherent part of this approach, how can we use it to predict what might happen in the future? While constructivists value the social structures that make up nation-states and the international system, the approach raises questions about what changes these structures and what those changes ultimately mean for the international system.

If one of the goals of theory is to describe, explain, and predict, another critique that can be leveled at the constructivists is that if identities and perceptions can change over time, how can we predict what might happen? Constructivists might recognize the fact that identities and interests are always evolving through the process of interacting with others. But that makes this approach less useful to determining what might happen because of the number of variables. It also makes certain assumptions about the state, including the central role of the state's identities (plural, as there are many). Yet, while acknowledging that these are always in flux, the approach does little to help us understand where these come from or even how they evolve.

Where this approach has made an important contribution to the field, however, is in reinforcing the uncertainties and complexities of understanding international relations, acknowledging the fact that there are dynamics that can and do change, and providing certain guidelines and assumptions that help us in dealing with these many factors.

Other Theoretical Approaches: Marxism

Karl Marx (1818–1883) was a German philosopher and social theorist who saw the world in economic terms that have political implications. His emphasis was on the "dialectic," the often conflicting or contradictory patterns that emerged within societies. Much of his work was premised on the idea of unequal relationships that exist across economic classes, which would eventually lead to conflict both within and, ultimately, across states. Marx believed that the more powerful classes would oppress the less powerful, leading to some form of class warfare eventually, as the less powerful rise up against the established order and try to gain power for themselves. At an international level, Marxism sees relations between countries as similarly characterized by class struggle, with the richer oppressing the poorer, and the poorer struggling to gain power. This approach also suggests that domestic and economic factors shape the country's external relations, thereby blending both domestic and international attributes in a way that contrasts with most traditional IR theories. Hence, Marxist thought injects economics into our understanding of world affairs, specifically in its suggestion of capitalism as a dominant economic phenomenon and in its certainty that those who are oppressed by capitalism will rise up against it.

The underlying premise has to do with the control and distribution of wealth. While Marx developed his theory specifically to address what he saw going on within countries, it was then adopted as a framework for understanding relationships across countries. It can be seen in the development of socialism and communism, as political and economic systems within countries and then more broadly to explain the conflict between capitalist and communist systems across countries.

Marxist approaches have to do with the unequal distribution of wealth and power. From the perspective of IR, this approach gave rise to dependency theory (introduced in chapter 1) and the idea that the wealthy countries benefited at the expense of the poorer and less powerful countries that they colonized and exploited. Those less developed countries in Africa, Latin America, and Asia then became dependent upon the very countries that had colonized and exploited them. Or seen another way, the developed countries of the Northern Hemisphere gained their wealth at the expense of the less developed and exploited countries of the Southern Hemisphere, also known as the North-South divide. And this thinking helps explain the revolutions of the South as the workers (those without the wealth and power) rose up

BOX 2.5

EXCERPTS FROM *MANIFESTO OF THE COMMUNIST PARTY*, BY KARL MARX AND FRIEDRICH ENGELS

The history of all hitherto existing society is the history of class struggles.

Freeman and slave, patrician and plebeian, lord and serf, guild-master and journeyman, in a word, oppressor and oppressed, stood in constant opposition to one another, carried on an uninterrupted, now hidden, now open fight, a fight that each time ended, either in a revolutionary reconstitution of society at large, or in the common ruin of the contending classes. . . .

Our epoch, the epoch of the bourgeoisie, possesses, however, this distinct feature: it has simplified class antagonisms. Society as a whole is more and more splitting up into two great hostile camps, into two great classes directly facing each other—Bourgeoisie and Proletariat. . . .

The immediate aim of the Communists is the same as that of all other proletarian parties: formation of the proletariat into a class, overthrow of the bourgeois supremacy, conquest of political power by the proletariat. . . .

We have seen above, that the first step in the revolution by the working class is to raise the proletariat to the position of ruling class to win the battle of democracy.

The proletariat will use its political supremacy to wrest, by degree, all capital from the bourgeoisie, to centralise all instruments of production in the hands of the State, *i.e.*, of the proletariat organised as the ruling class; and to increase the total productive forces as rapidly as possible. . . .

In short, the Communists everywhere support every revolutionary movement against the existing social and political order of things.

In all these movements, they bring to the front, as the leading question in each, the property question, no matter what its degree of development at the time.

Finally, they labour everywhere for the union and agreement of the democratic parties of all countries.

The Communists disdain to conceal their views and aims. They openly declare that their ends can be attained only by the forcible overthrow of all existing social conditions. Let the ruling classes tremble at a Communistic revolution. The proletarians have nothing to lose but their chains. They have a world to win.

Working Men of All Countries, Unite!

Source: Karl Marx and Friedrich Engels, *Manifesto of the Communist Party*, at http://www.marxists.org/archive/marx/works/1848/communist-manifes to/.

against the existing order in order to break loose from the system and to establish themselves as the ones with the power. This can be seen to have happened in some cases, such as China under the leadership of Mao Tse-tung, who in effect led a peasant rebellion to overthrow the existing—and corrupt—order. However, in reality, it was not until China started to become a more market-oriented economy that it really started to develop economically.

Looking at it another way, the rhetoric of the inevitability of conflict between the capitalist economies, such as the United States, and the socialist or communist systems led to the Cold War between the United States and the Soviet Union. Rather than a class struggle, this became a political and military as well as an economic conflict that lasted for almost fifty years and defined many aspects of modern international relations.

In addition to dependency theory, Marxism also contributed to the growth of a number of other theoretical approaches that tried to explain international relations through the lenses of economics (especially capitalism) and the distribution of power relationships. All of these can fall broadly into what is generally called the "radical critique" or "radical perspective." Another offshoot of this approach is world systems theory, in which the world is seen as divided not just into rich and poor, developed and less developed, but into a core of strong and well-integrated states; a periphery, or states that depend largely on an unskilled, low-wage labor pool; and a semiperiphery of states that embody elements of both. This approach also assumes that the core group of nations exploits those at the periphery. But it also stresses the rise and fall of those at the core, as technological innovations and capital flows change the dynamics among the group.

From the perspective of IR, though, Marxism and the radical critiques it inspired continue to serve as an alternative to mainstream theories.

Limitations and Critique of Marxist Theory and Its Offshoots

In theory, as noted in chapter 1, globalization should have started to equalize the economic and then power divisions that exist among countries, as interdependence should have led to fairer exchanges among them. In reality, this has not been the case, thereby calling into question some of the premises of this group of theories. As long as countries remained agricultural and tied to the land and as long as the international economic system remained under the control of the developed (wealthy) countries, inequalities continued and there were "have" and "have not" countries.

Feminist theorists also raise the critique that the economic interpretations and assumptions of the Marxist and other "radical" theorists do not take gender into account as an explanatory factor.[46] While the other theories do not do so either, they also do not presume to speak for the powerless, which these variants do. Thus this becomes a significant omission limiting its explanatory power.

Theory Continued: Feminist Perspectives

Most of the traditional approaches to international relations theory "contain certain assumptions and lead us to ask certain questions, seek certain types of answers and use certain methodological tools."[47] What that means, in the words of political scientist Patrick Morgan, is that " 'our conception of [IR acts as a] map for directing our attention and distributing our efforts, and using the wrong map can lead us into a swamp instead of into higher ground.' "[48] Just as it is important to understand the levels of analysis and know which theoretical perspective is appropriate to help guide the answer to questions at different levels, by making certain assumptions and using certain tools we are ignoring or not taking into account whole areas of international politics. Thus, in order to get a more complete picture, we need to refocus our map so that it specifically includes women, and gender becomes a variable that is part of our ongoing understanding of international relations. In other words, we need to look at international relations through gender-sensitive lenses.

It is important to note that not all questions might involve gender, nor is it appropriate to artificially include gender or insert it into our analysis of international relations. However, what the feminist approach reminds us of from the beginning is that we need to be aware of the role of women, of the impact of decisions on the people within the nation-state, and the ways in which women and gender affect our theoretical understanding of the international system. If we then choose *not* to include gender in our questions or analysis, at least it becomes a conscious choice and not an oversight. Thus, in our overview of international relations theory, we are going to give some additional attention to this approach because it is so often overlooked in traditional international relations, and yet without consciously addressing women and gender, we cannot get a complete picture.

When we speak of gender and international relations, or "gendering world politics," what we are referring to is the introduction of the concept of "gender," which refers to "socially learned behavior and expectations that distinguish between masculinity and femininity. Whereas biological sex identity is determined by reference to genetic and anatomical characteristics, socially learned gender is an acquired identity."[49]

So what does this have to do with international politics? According to political scientists V. Spike Peterson and Ann Sisson Runyan, "The dominant masculinity in Western culture is associated with qualities of rationality, 'hardheadedness,' ambition, and strength. . . . Similarly, women who appear hard-headed and ambitious are often described as masculine." Also, the traits associated with masculinity "are perceived as positive and admired traits that are in contrast to less desirable feminine qualities."[50] Ann Tickner notes that a widely held belief is that

> military and foreign policy are arenas of policy-making least appropriate for women. Strength, power, autonomy, independence, and rationality, all typically associated with men and masculinity, are characteristics we most value in those to whom we trust the conduct of our foreign policy and national interest. Those women in the peace movements . . . are frequently branded as naïve, weak and unpatriotic.[51]

Therefore, generally when we look at qualities associated with international relations and foreign policy—power, politics, military might, strength—they assume that men are present and women are absent. Furthermore, they also assume that we can explain decisions by looking at the ways in which *men* are engaged in these activities.

By looking at the world through gender-sensitive lenses, we are able to understand how women are also present, even though they are often obscured by the focus on men. "Through a gender-sensitive lens, we see how constructions of masculinity are not independent of, but dependent upon, opposing constructions of femininity."[52] Understanding this can then give us a more complete picture about and understanding of international relations.

The introduction of the feminist perspective has its origin in the 1980s, and it has become more prominent in the last ten-plus years. To give you an idea as to how far we have come, remember that Morgenthau referred to "statesmen" in his book *Politics Among Nations*, and there is no entry for "women" in the index. Kenneth Waltz, who wrote *Man, the State, and War* in 1954, has one entry for women in the index: "Women, role in government." If you look at the entry, it is found within Waltz's discussion of peace and trying to understand human behavior in order to help understand what leads to war. This illustrates clearly the set of assumptions that have swirled around the study of international relations, which in many ways grow out of social beliefs about the nature of men and women: Men are warlike, militaristic, and competitive, while women are peace loving and inherently cooperative by nature. All of this obscures or muddles our understanding of international relations. So the real question becomes: What role *does* gender play in our understanding of international relations, how should we draw on it to help us describe/explain/predict, and where does the feminist perspective fit as a valid theoretical approach?

What Ann Tickner and other feminist thinkers have done is to force us to consider the presence and roles of women in international relations. They have allowed us to better understand how decisions are shaped by gender, and the ways in which political decisions affect men and women. This allows us to look at the roles women have played in various ways that affect the international system and at the contributions they have made. And it allows us to understand that it is no longer acceptable to study scholarly areas, especially those pertaining to important policy decisions, without acknowledging women and gender in some way.

So let us see how feminist theory fits within our understanding of international relations. Tickner begins by saying that we need to step back and really understand the way in which the world is constructed, to move beyond the stereotypes and assumptions and look at how women and gender fit within the field of international relations. But she also warns us that

> feminist theories must go beyond injecting women's experiences into different disciplines and attempt to challenge the core concepts of the disciplines themselves. . . . Drawing on feminist theories to examine and critique the meaning of these [key concepts, such as power, sovereignty, and security] could help us to reformulate these concepts in ways that might allow us to see new possibilities for solving our current insecurities.[53]

Tickner and other feminist thinkers argue that it is no longer possible to examine the new questions of security that we are now grappling with using the traditional theoretical approaches. The changes that have taken place in the international system since the end of the Cold War especially have led to the growth of new questions about what has been happening and why. And feminist IR thinkers argue that it is time to find theoretical approaches that are more appropriate for answering these new questions.

Tickner provides examples of the types of questions feminists would ask—and then how to answer them. For example, she notes that

> whereas IR theorists focus on the causes and termination of wars, feminists are as concerned with what happens *during* wars as well as their causes and endings. Rather than seeing military capabilities as an assurance against outside threats to the state, militaries are seen as frequently antithetical to individual security, particularly to the security of women and other vulnerable groups. (emphasis added)[54]

Like liberalism and constructivism, feminist approaches generally focus within the state, looking at the role of the individual within the social structure. They look at questions such as the ways in which an unequal structure constrains or affects women's as well as men's lives, and how this inequality can be addressed. They ask how women's voices can be heard within a political system that is generally patriarchal as well as hierarchical, and how the lack of women's voices affects the decisions that are made. This must move beyond the notion of "peace as a women's issue" to focus instead on how any country can best use and represent *all* its citizens and be aware of the impact of decisions on those citizens as well.

When we discuss feminist IR and understanding the role that gender plays in the field, it is also important to note that not all work that deals with women is inherently feminist, nor do we need to assume that all women's political action is feminist. For example, there are groups of women who work for peace at the community level in countries in conflict, such as Northern Ireland or Israel and Palestine. When asked, these women do not think of their work as "feminist" action per se. They simply look at it as working to make their community and their country a better place in which to live and to raise their children. However, looking at their activities seriously takes into account the fact that women have an important role to play in issues of peace and conflict without judging their motives.

Like the other theoretical approaches in the field, Tickner notes there are many strains of feminist thought within IR. There is *liberal feminism*, which claims that "discrimination deprives women of equal rights to pursue their self-interest; whereas men have been judged on their merits as individuals, women have tended to be judged as female or as a group."[55] This approach assumes that women have the potential to be participants in the political system, but that it would take work and restructuring of that system. Furthermore, liberal feminists do not necessarily agree that the inclusion of women would change the nature of the political system.

Radical feminists claim that "women were oppressed because of patriarchy or a pervasive system of male dominance, rooted in the biological inequality between the sexes and in women's reproductive roles, that assigns them to the household to take care of men and children."[56] Thus, women are blocked from participating in the public sphere, where policy is made, and are relegated to the realm of the private sphere, which is seen as far less important. Yet women have shown that they can have an impact and make a contribution to important policy discussions, such as about war and peace, by glorifying their roles as wives and mothers. While this runs the risk of "essentializing women" (that is, identifying them based on their traditional roles), it also acknowledges the contributions they can make.

The main point here is the acknowledgment that women's lives, roles, and experiences are different from those of men, who are the primary decision makers, and therefore that they must be considered if not as central to, certainly as part of our understanding of international relations. Therefore, understanding the structure of the state and the political system, and specifically introducing gender as a concept, should give us another and broader understanding of the state and therefore of the international system.

Limitations and Critique of Feminist Theory

One of the major critiques leveled against the feminist IR theorists is that there really is no single theory, but rather it is more a critique or series of critiques of the primary theories in IR. As noted above, even within the feminist perspective there are significant differences in approaches and understanding regarding the roles of women, specifically, the role of feminism as a motivator of women in the political sphere. Does it really matter whether women's political actions are a feminist statement or are the result of a desire to right a wrong? Are all women's political actions feminist by virtue of the fact that they are women? And more important, how do the answers to these questions help us understand international relations?

Another issue that needs to be considered in injecting the feminist perspective is whether doing so essentializes women. That is, women's actions are defined because they are women, or, put another way, it reduces them to a single common denominator. For example, in understanding issues of war and peace, it is easy to look at peace as a "women's issue" because of the underlying assumptions about women's nature, whereas men are presumed to be warriors and more warlike. This oversimplification minimizes the roles of *both* men and women in international relations.

SUMMARY

This chapter offered an introduction to ways of understanding international relations and some of the theoretical approaches and frameworks that help you understand the international system. As has been stressed throughout this chapter, it is important to remember that no one approach is right or wrong, and that no single approach will give you a broad or complete understanding of international relations. Rather, the point that we want to make is that the particular approach you choose should be dependent on the questions you want to ask. The theory, in turn, can then help guide you to an answer to those questions.

BOX 2.6

COMPARISON OF THEORETICAL APPROACHES

Theoretical perspectives	Realist	Liberal	Constructivist	Marxist	Feminist
Actors					
Within state					
Individual					
Culture/society					
Government					
Nation-state					
International system					
Explanatory capability?					
Predictive capability?					

Box 2.6 provides a grid that gives some guidance to each of the theoretical approaches and what they can tell you. Remember that the answer to any question you ask is only as good as the material and approach you use to answer it.

FURTHER READINGS

These additional readings are worth exploring and elaborate on some of the points raised in this chapter. This list is not meant to be exhaustive, but only illustrative.

Michael Doyle. "Liberalism and World Politics." *American Political Science Review* 80, no. 4 (December 1986): 1151–1169.

J. David Singer. "The Level-of-Analysis Problem in International Relations." *World Politics* 14, no. 1 (October 1961): 77–92.

Jack Snyder. "One World, Rival Theories." *Foreign Policy*, November 1, 2004, 52–62.

Kenneth Waltz. "The Stability of a Bipolar World." *Daedalus* 93, no. 3 (Summer 1964): 881–909.

———. *Man, the State, and War: A Theoretical Analysis.* New York: Columbia University Press, 1954.

Alexander Wendt. "Anarchy Is What States Make of It: The Social Construction of Power Politics." *International Organization* 46, no. 2 (Spring 1992): 391–425.

———. "Collective Identity Formation and the International State." *American Political Science Review* 88, no. 2 (June 1994), 384–96.

Gillian Youngs. "Feminist International Relations: A Contradiction in Terms? Or: Why Women and Gender Are Essential to Understanding the World 'We' Live In." *International Affairs* 80, no. 1 (2004): 75–87.

NOTES

1. Christine Sylvester, *Feminist International Relations: An Unfinished Journey* (Cambridge: Cambridge University Press, 2002), 161.

2. Charles W. Kegley Jr., *World Politics: Trend and Transformation* (Belmont, CA: Wadsworth Cengage Learning, 2009), 28.

3. Barry Hughes, *Continuity and Change in World Politics: The Clash of Perspectives*, 2nd ed. (Englewood Cliffs, NJ: Prentice Hall, 1994), 79.

4. J. Ann Tickner, *Gendering World Politics: Issues and Approaches in the Post–Cold War Era* (New York: Columbia University Press, 2001), 3.

5. Tickner, *Gendering World Politics*, 3.

6. Gillian Youngs, "Feminist International Relations: A Contradiction in Terms? Or: Why Women and Gender Are Essential to Understanding the World 'We' Live

In," *International Affairs* 80, no. 1 (2004): 77. In a footnote attached to the title of the article, Youngs also states that "The aim [of the article] is to stimulate productive debate about the nature and contribution of feminist approaches to International Relations." Youngs, "Feminist International Relations," 75.

7. J. David Singer, "The Level-of-Analysis Problem in International Relations," *World Politics* 14, no. 1 (October 1961): 77–92.

8. Kenneth N. Waltz, *Man, the State and War: A Theoretical Analysis* (New York: Columbia University Press, 1954).

9. Singer, "The Level-of-Analysis Problem," 78.

10. Singer, "The Level-of-Analysis Problem," 90.

11. Singer, "The Level-of-Analysis Problem," 90.

12. See David Easton, *A Systems Analysis of Political Life* (New York: Wiley, 1965).

13. See Joseph S. Nye Jr., *The Paradox of American Power: Why the World's Only Superpower Can't Go It Alone* (New York: Oxford University Press, 2002).

14. Nye, *Paradox*, 8–9.

15. Joseph S. Nye, *The Future of Power* (New York: Public Affairs, 2011), 22–23.

16. See Walter Russell Mead, *Power, Terror, Peace, and War: America's Grand Strategy in a World at Risk* (New York: Knopf, 2004).

17. V. Spike Peterson and Anne Sisson Runyan, *Global Gender Issues*, 2nd ed. (Boulder, CO: Westview Press, 1999), 53.

18. Peterson and Runyan, *Global Gender Issues*, 53.

19. Tickner, *Gendering World Politics*, 17.

20. Brian C. Schmidt, *The Political Discourse of Anarchy: A Disciplinary History of International Relations* (Albany: State University of New York Press, 1998), 27.

21. Hans J. Morgenthau, *Politics Among Nations: The Struggle for Power and Peace*, brief ed. (Boston: McGraw-Hill, 1993), 5.

22. See Machiavelli, *The Prince*, trans. and ed. George Bull (Baltimore: Penguin Books, 1970).

23. Machiavelli, *The Prince*, 20.

24. Machiavelli, *The Prince*, 24.

25. See Thomas Hobbes, *The Leviathan*, at http://www.oregonstate.edu/intrsucts/phl302/texts/hobbes/leviathan-a.html.

26. Paul R. Viotii and Mark V. Kauppi, *International Relations and World Politics: Security, Economy, Identity*, 4th ed. (Upper Saddle River, NJ: Pearson Prentice Hall, 2009), 59.

27. It must be remembered here that virtually all references to states*men* are tied to the assumption that diplomats and generally decision makers will be male. In fact, in Ken Waltz's *Man, the State, and War*, women are only mentioned once and in a rather gendered way: "And J. Cohen, another psychologist, believes that the cause of

peace might be promoted if women were substituted for men in the governing of nations." Waltz, *Man, the State, and War*, 46.

28. Morganthau, *Politics Among Nations*, 5.

29. Morganthau, "Six Principles of Political Realism," *Politics Among Nations*, 6.

30. John Mearsheimer is a prolific author who remains one of the most prominent realist thinkers in political science today. His published works are too numerous to list here. For more detail, see his website, at http://mearsheimer.uchicago.edu/index .htm (accessed August 14, 2012).

31. Kenneth N. Waltz, *Realism and International Politics* (New York: Routledge, 2008), 73.

32. Waltz, *Realism and International Politics*, 73–74. It is well worth reading Waltz's entire essay, "Realist Thought and Neorealist Theory," for his critique of realist theory and as a way to better understand the evolution of his thinking regarding neorealism. See "Realist Thought and Neorealist Theory," in *Realism and International Politics*, 67–82.

33. See Kenneth Waltz, "The Stability of a Bipolar World," in *Realism and International Politics*, 99–122.

34. See John Mearsheimer, *The Tragedy of Great Power Politics* (New York: Norton, 2001).

35. *Realpolitik* is a German term that refers to foreign policy tied primarily to power. When he was secretary of state, Henry Kissinger was known for pursuing U.S. foreign policy based on Realpolitik.

36. J. Ann Tickner, *Gender in International Relations* (New York: Columbia University Press, 1992), 14.

37. Tickner, *Gendering World Politics*, 24.

38. Thucydides, "The Melian Conference," in *History of the Peloponnesian War*, chap. 17, at http://www.mtholyoke.edu/acad/intrel/melian.htm.

39. Michael W. Doyle, "Liberalism and World Politics," *American Political Science Review* 80, no. 4 (December 1986): 1152.

40. Viotti and Kauppi, *International Relations and World Politics*, 92.

41. Preamble to the North Atlantic Treaty, April 4, 1949, at http://www.nato.int.

42. Alexander Wendt, "Anarchy Is What States Make of It: The Social Construction of Power Politics," *International Organization* 46, no. 2 (Spring 1992): 393.

43. Alexander Wendt, "Collective Identity Formation and the International State," *American Political Science Review* 88, no. 2 (June 1994): 385.

44. Wendt, "Anarchy Is What States Make of It," 396–97.

45. Karen A. Mingst, *Essentials of International Relations*, 4th ed. (New York: Norton, 2008), 72.

46. Tickner, *Gender in International Relations*, 16–17.

47. Peterson and Runyan, *Global Gender Issues*, 1.

48. Quoted in Peterson and Runyan, *Global Gender Issues*, 2.

49. Peterson and Runyan, *Global Gender Issues*, 5.

50. Peterson and Runyan, *Global Gender Issues*, 7.

51. Tickner, *Gender in International Relations*, 3.

52. Peterson and Runyan, *Global Gender Issues*, 7.

53. Tickner, *Gender in International Relations*, 18.

54. Tickner, *Gendering World Politics*, 4.

55. Tickner, *Gendering World Politics*, 12.

56. Tickner, *Gendering World Politics*, 13.

The Nation-State Level

With the broad theoretical frameworks outlined, we are now going to move through the various levels of analysis in order to focus on the major actors that can help us better understand the international system. In doing so, it is also important to remember that *levels of analysis* is just a framework; it is not an inclusive guide to understanding all aspects of international relations or events in the international system. In fact, in going through this, one of the things that should become clear is where there are weaknesses or failings in this approach.

As we go through the levels, it will also be important to think about how to apply your understanding of the level to current international events and which theory would be most appropriate to help describe and explain that event. Learning a theoretical approach is not helpful unless you can apply it, since that is the way in which you can determine how useful the theory really is.

In this chapter, we are going to begin by focusing on the nation-state level, which is the primary actor in international relations. After defining the concept and putting it into historical perspective, we will move into an analysis of it, including understanding some of the major questions that have influenced the field of IR and that pertain to the nation-state: issues of peace and war. As we do this, it will be important to bear in mind the different theoretical approaches we raised in the previous chapter (i.e., realism, liberalism, constructivism, Marxism, and feminist IR) so that you can better understand how each can help explain aspects of the behavior of the nation-state within international relations. We will conclude the chapter with a discussion of war and peace—understanding what they are, why nations resort to war and how they end, and what the concept of "peace" really means.

DEFINITION OF *NATION-STATE*

As we saw in chapter 1 and our overview of globalization, the current international system has evolved over time from one in which empires interacted based on trade and economics, to the emergence of the nation-state and the quest for colonies that resulted in another stage of globalization as the world started to get smaller, to the truly globalized and interdependent world that we know today. Included in the changing structure of the current international system are the concepts of *integration* and *disintegration*. *Integration* suggests the merging of ideas and policies so that individual sovereign states start to blend into a unified whole. Although each state keeps its individual identity, it is also part of a single larger bloc. An example of this is the European Union (EU), which as of this writing is composed of twenty-seven sovereign states, each with its own government and political system, that agreed to merge into a single entity with a parliament and a president, which arrives at a single set of policies on a number of issues. Although the countries agreed to join and develop policies together, some have adopted the euro as a common currency, while others (such as the United Kingdom, Denmark, and Sweden) chose not to do so. How can twenty-seven states each remain sovereign and still be part of a larger bloc with a single set of policies? How can seventeen of those integrated states agree to adopt the euro while ten refuse to do so? Confused? We will return to this apparent conundrum in a bit.

Similarly, the end of the Cold War has witnessed examples of the *disintegration* of single sovereign states to create any number of others. In this case, the notion of disintegration refers to the breakup of a single nation-state into two or more entities that seek statehood. Some of this has been done peacefully; for example, in 1993, the country of Czechoslovakia split into two countries, the Czech Republic and Slovakia, in what was known as "the Velvet Divorce" because of the absence of bloodshed. In 1991, the Soviet Union broke up into fifteen nations, and although the initial disintegration was relatively peaceful, fighting continues in Chechnya with ongoing conflict among a number of other republics. At the other extreme, the country of Yugoslavia was racked by civil war and ethnic violence from 1991 until 1996, and violence escalated again in 1999 over the status of the autonomous province of Kosovo. Kosovo's situation remains unresolved, with some countries in the international system, including the United States and the European Union countries, recognizing it as an independent sovereign nation. However, other countries (Serbia and those allied with it, including Russia) do not. In the case of those countries that don't recognize Kosovo, the fear is that by doing so, any breakaway republic/nation could declare itself to be independent, thereby threatening the very nature of the state.

The real underlying question here is: Why do some countries choose to integrate with others, thereby forming a larger bloc, while other countries break apart? To answer those questions, we need to have a better understanding of the *nation-state* as a concept. It is important to note that as we explore some of these questions, our focus is on the nation-state itself, and not on the individual leaders or the impact of the policy decisions on the people within the state. That will come later.

Given the central role of the concept *nation-state*, it is important to begin with a definition. When we look at a nation-state, we are looking at two separate yet interrelated concepts, both of which have emerged as especially relevant in the international system today. *Nation* denotes a group of people with common history, background, and values, all of whom accept the sanctity of the state. The *state*, in turn, represents the formal trappings of the political system, such as the government and defined borders, and it, in turn, accepts certain responsibilities for the people who live within those borders. Hence, a *nation-state* is an entity that we usually think of as a country, made up of groups of individuals who live within a defined border and under a single government. Even though there might be different groups of people with their own cultures and ideas, they form a single society that has certain values and beliefs in common.

Along with the emergence of the nation-state came another core principle, that of *nationalism*. Nationalism ties the identification of the group with a common past, language, history, customs, practices, and so on. Author Fareed Zakaria sees the concept this way:

> When I write of nationalism, I am describing a broader phenomenon—the assertion of *identity*. The nation-state is a relatively new invention, often no more than a hundred years old. Much older are the religious, ethnic, and linguistic groups that live within the nation-states. And these bonds have stayed strong, in fact grown, as economic interdependence has deepened. (emphasis added)[1]

Hence, Zakaria believes that the globalization that we see in the world today has contributed directly to the growth of nationalism, or to the importance of "core identities," as he calls them, which has replaced loyalty to the nation-state as a whole. This is one of the contributors to conflict, as different nations seek recognition or *self-determination*, the belief that each group of people should be allowed to determine who is responsible for leading or governing them. This in turn can lead to the disintegration of the nation-state into various parts, as noted above—peacefully or, more often, as a result of civil conflict (ethnic, religious, tribal, etc.) as different groups within the country seek to establish their independence and autonomy separate from the larger state structure and establish a state of their own.

Another concept that is important in this discussion is the notion of *legitimacy*, which grows from the idea articulated in the seventeenth century by philosopher John Locke that political power ultimately rests with the people, rather than the leader. According to Locke, the political leader derives his or her power from "the consent of the governed," which became part of the *social contract*. It is this acceptance that grants legitimacy to a government.[2]

Much of contemporary international relations theory is tied to the nation-state, known as a country, as the primary actor. Furthermore, as noted in chapter 2, there are assumptions made about the ways in which this unit behaves and reacts to other nation-states that can help explain major concepts such as why countries go to war, or how countries seek to influence the behavior of one another. Realism and structural realism explicitly address the nation-state as the critical actor in international relations. Liberalism also focuses on the nation-state as a primary actor, but it also looks within the state as well in order to get a more complete picture of the state's behavior. Constructivism focuses on the nation-state, but as an entity affected and constrained by the social and political structures within which it interacts. The critiques of these theories are often tied to flaws that are perceived as coming from the use of the nation-state as the primary unit of analysis.

In fact, one of the problems with the nation-state as a central concept of international relations is that there are often many nations or groups of people who live within a state and do not necessarily recognize the legitimacy of that single state. This suggests some of the weaknesses in focusing on the nation-state as the basis for international relations. As we will see in chapter 5, the problem becomes more acute when we look at nonstate actors and stateless peoples. An example of the flaws of this can be seen with a group such as the Palestinians, who are in effect a "stateless people." That is, they have some of the trappings of statehood, including a governmental structure and a single dominant nation, but they do not have a defined state. Therefore, there is no logical place for them to fit within the levels of analysis, yet they cannot be discounted as important players internationally. The Kurds, who straddle a number of different countries (Turkey, Iraq, and Iran, primarily), are another example of a single group that seeks its own state. How to account for such groups is one of the dilemmas facing students of international relations today.

Despite some of these structural issues, understanding the nation-state and the central role it plays in international relations is critical to understanding IR theory.

HISTORY OF THE NATION-STATE

The approach to understanding the nation-state level and the basic concepts that are inherent in it (such as sovereignty) is derived from the 1648 Treaty of Westphalia (or Peace of Westphalia). Here the treaty itself serves as an important resource, and it is easily accessible online.[3] (It is difficult to wade through, but it is interesting to see how the modern nation-state and concepts such as sovereignty have their origins here. Its impact is felt to this day.) What is critical about the document is that it outlines the concept of the *sovereign nation-state* and reminds all states of the importance of recognizing the sanctity of national borders. Since the time of that treaty, we have not only the emergence of the modern sovereign nation-state, which is the primary actor in the international system, but also the emergence of nonstate actors, which have also come to play a major role in international relations. In order to understand what is meant by a nonstate actor, we need to focus first on the idea of the state. That is going to be our starting point here.

As we look back in history prior to 1648, we see a world that was made up not only of city-states but also empires. The Greek city-states that Thucydides wrote about in his *History of the Peloponnesian Wars*, which we talked about in chapter 2, were at the height of their power around 400 BCE. These city-states were characterized by relatively small populations with limited territory, usually found behind city walls. Although they existed in close proximity, each was independent. Inevitably, some became more powerful than others. Over time, Sparta and Athens emerged as the two major city-states, thereby creating a *bipolar system* in which power was roughly balanced between the two. Under the leadership of Athens, many of the Greek city-states united in what became known as the Delian League, an early idea of *collective security* that brought the Greek city-states together so that they could defend themselves from the Persian empire, which had been trying to expand into Greek territory.

Relations between Athens and Sparta deteriorated, ultimately leading to armed conflict between them. A truce was reached after six years, with each recognizing the power of the other and acknowledging domination over their respective spheres of influence. This truce was short-lived, however, and its failure led to the outbreak of the Second Peloponnesian War, which was documented by Thucydides, as noted in chapter 2.

Why is this ancient history important? The creation of the Delian League, designed to protect against the perceived aggression of Persia, was one of the earliest documented examples of what was later known as *collective security*. What took place during the Peloponnesian War was also an example of realist politics and the balance of power, both of which we will return to later in this chapter. And since so much of what happened then has been repeated since that time, it is an important lesson about the behavior of states.

Following the period of the domination of the Greek city-states, we really see the emergence of the age of empires. An *empire* (as opposed to a nation-state or a city-state) can be defined as an entity composed of separate units, all of which are under the domination of one single power that asserts political and economic supremacy over the others, which formally or informally accept this relationship. Thus, the separate units or groups have some independence, but they remain under the domination of a supra-entity. One of the major goals of an empire, like any system, was to ensure that it perpetuated itself and continued to expand its domain and therefore its wealth. Because of its size, often the ruler of the empire had to depend upon local officials to carry out his or her bidding.

There were a number of empires throughout history, including those in Europe, such as the Holy Roman Empire and the Austro-Hungarian, and in Eurasia, such as the Persian and later the Ottoman. In Asia, the Chinese empire was in place from 221 BCE to 1911 (with some periods of disruption) and was characterized by centralized rule with allegiance paid to the emperor in Beijing. The Chinese empire was especially enduring.

The end of the Roman empire in approximately 500 CE led to what became known as the Middle Ages in Europe. During this time we see the growth of the Christian church, which melded political power and religion to solidify its empire. In Europe in the twelfth and thirteenth centuries, we also start seeing a flourishing of municipalities that functioned like the old Greek city-states. Venice, Florence, Paris, Oxford, and so on each became established centers of law and behavior, focused primarily on universities. Many became the center of important trade patterns and commerce, as well as diplomacy. Eventually this also led to a clash between secular rule and the church, and by the late Middle Ages, we start seeing the rise of what we now refer to as *nationalism*, specifically, commitment to a central identity or consciousness rather than loyalty to the ruler or state. We also see the emergence of strong monarchs who reigned over their domain, sometimes with the support of the church and sometimes in opposition to it, such as Henry VIII in England. This was also the start of the age of exploration and colonization, as states looked for ways to expand their wealth and fortunes by going outside the limited territory of Europe, leading to the early era of globalization. And in a Marxist interpretation of events, this was also the start of the exploitation of colonies by the major powers of the time.

But as we also saw earlier, the growth of the city-states contributed to competition and eventually conflict between and among many of these states, especially regarding the role of religion and political power within the area that was known as the Holy Roman Empire. Eventually this led to the Thirty Years' War, which lasted from 1618 to 1648. The war "devastated Europe; the armies plundered the central European landscapes, fought battles, and survived by ravaging the civilian population. But the treaty that ended the conflict had a profound effect on the practice of international relations."[4]

Treaty of Westphalia

The Thirty Years' War ended with the signing of the Treaty (or Peace) of Westphalia in 1648. This treaty established some of the basic principles that govern international relations today, as well as firmly establishing the nation-state as the primary actor in the international system with certain responsibilities and powers. The treaty established the European political system that we are familiar with (although the borders of some of the specific countries have since changed and new ones have been created). It ended the Holy Roman Empire and replaced it with a system of sovereign states. It made the monarch the primary political leader with authority over his people, supplanting the role of the church. Thus, as a result of this treaty, secular rule superseded the rule of the church. This in turn led to the notion that each national leader has the right to maintain his own military in order to protect himself and his territory. This also contributed to the growth of centralized control of the political system, since each monarch now had an army to support it, not only as protection from external threats but to maintain internal order, collect taxes, and so on. In fact, the monarch had a monopoly on the use of force for both domestic and external purposes.[5] Thus, the individual state and the monarch or leader of the state became more powerful, with that power backed up by the use of force. In addition, the Treaty of Westphalia led to a redrawing of the map of Europe so that a core group of states became dominant, primarily Austria, Russia, Prussia, England, France, and the northern area that would become Belgium and the Netherlands.

Along with the legacy of the modern nation-state, the Treaty of Westphalia also gave us some of the major concepts that govern the relationship between and among nation-states. Paramount among those is the concept of *sovereignty*. K. J. Holsti, in his classic text on international relations, notes that

> the principle [of sovereignty] underlies relations between all states today. . . . The principle of sovereignty is relatively simple: Within a specified territory, no external power . . . has the right to exercise legal jurisdiction or political authority. This establishes the exclusive domestic authority of a government. That authority is based on a monopoly over the *legitimate* use of force. (emphasis added)[6]

Holsti then notes in a corollary to his definition that "no state has the right to interfere in the domestic affairs of another state. This prohibitive injunction has been breached frequently, but it is assumed and observed most of the time by most states."[7]

Although, as Holsti notes, there have been frequent violations of this norm, on the whole it provides the basic framework for relations between and among nation-states (i.e., international relations). Yet, it is the breaching of this concept that provides for some interesting questions and discussion. For example, are there times when one country has the right, even the obligation, to intervene in the affairs of another sovereign state—for example, to stop genocide or other human rights abuses? Should countries have intervened to prevent or stop the genocides in Rwanda or Bosnia or Darfur? What about the U.S. invasion of Iraq in March 2003? Was this a justifiable violation of the sovereignty of that country, since evidence showed that Iraq had no responsibility in the 9/11 attacks, which was one of the alleged reasons for the invasion? These types of questions can both help us understand the behavior of a country and provide the grist for important discussions that will contribute to a better understanding of the application of the theories.

The important point to remember is that the current international system grew from events that took place almost four hundred years ago. Although some specifics have changed as new countries were created and as different political systems, such as democracies, evolved to replace the monarchy that was then the norm, the basic structure and concepts governing the nation-state and its actions in the international system remain in place. And questions such as the sanctity of sovereignty and if and/or when it should be violated remain very much a part of the discourse of international relations today.

BALANCE OF POWER AND ALLIANCES

We have just been looking at the evolution of the nation-state from a historical perspective in order to understand how the current international system and the reliance on the nation-state as the primary actor evolved. Now we are going to move from the historical perspective to the present time and look at the nation-state system today, specifically looking at concepts such as balance of power and the role of alliances. Both of these concepts have come to play a prominent role in contemporary international relations.

We initially alluded to the concept of balance of power in the discussion above about the Delian League and the ways in which the Greek city-states united as a way of protecting themselves from Persia, which was a larger and more powerful empire. (We also saw this in chapter 2, in the excerpt from the "Melian Dialogue," which explicitly references the idea of enlisting allies.) The idea was that if the Greek city-states worked together, they could counter the power of Persia and deter it from trying to attack. Or if Persia did decide to attack, they would work together to respond. In effect, what they did was try to balance the power of one of the *hegemons*, or major powers, of the time. According to realist theory, if unchecked, countries will seek to increase their power. So the dilemma facing countries is how to make sure that the power of the hegemon is balanced.

Interestingly, the concept of balance of power is steeped in realist thought. Yet the concept of alliances, which was applied often in the Cold War period, has a serious liberal and constructivist core. Again we see an apparent contradiction here. On the one hand, realist theory assumes that countries will always seek to maximize their power—"interest defined as power," in Morgenthau's terms. Therefore, countries will do whatever they need to, including making temporary alliances with other countries, if that will help them maximize their own power. To the realists, then, alliances are pragmatic policy decisions that will enable them to get something they need (more power) that is greater than what they could achieve on their own. On the other hand, the liberal theorists would say alliances bring countries with common interests together in order to pursue policies that are in their collective best interest. Thus, they *all* benefit from working together. Similarly, the constructivists would place alliances into a broader structural framework of the international system and would offer the policy decision for countries to join together as a response to structural constraints and realities.

With this quick overview, we will now look at the idea of balance of power and the concept of alliances from a variety of theoretical perspectives in more detail, as another way of understanding the behavior of nation-states in the international system.

Balance of Power

The realist perspective

portrays world politics as a struggle for power in anarchy by competitive rivals acting for their own self-interests (and *not* for moral principles and global ideals such as improving the security and welfare of *all* throughout the globe). International politics to realism is a war of all against all, to increase national power and national security by preparing for war and seeking advantages over rivals such as by acquiring superior military capabilities. (emphasis in original)[8]

Inherent in this is the idea not only of acquiring power, but of balancing the power of hegemons in order to ensure the country's own security. Or that's the way it's supposed to work, in theory.

The classical balance-of-power system is generally traced back to approximately 1815 and the Congress of Vienna, which contributed to the changing role and power of the major countries in Europe. During that time, there were a number of powerful states that were emerging. The belief was that the only way to balance or constrain their power, and therefore to ensure security, was for countries to join together and align against it, thereby countering its power. In effect, this was an updated version of what we saw earlier in the case of the Greek city-states. So, for example, Britain and Russia joined together to counter the perceived growing power of France. The idea was that *if countries joined together, their combined power would offset the power of any one dominant nation and thereby hold it in check.* In doing so, the stability of the system would be ensured, as evidenced by an absence of conflict.

Britain was often seen as playing the role of balancer, because of its economic and military (naval) strength. That means that it shifted its allegiances to make sure that there was a general perception of balance among the states of Europe. Not only did this allow Britain to maintain an important position internationally, but Britain's military might also ensured that other states did not interfere in the European conflicts, at least not in Europe proper. Instead, the European countries in effect divided up the rest of the world, and after the Spanish-American War, the United States became an important player as well.[9] Thus, we see the major countries each with its own sphere of influence.

Most political scientists see the classic balance-of-power system as coming to an end at the start of the twentieth century, when Britain broke from its role as balancer to join Japan in its war against Russia (the Russo-Japanese War of 1902). This was the first time a major European country had aligned with an Asian country against another European ally (in this case, Russia). This is an indicator of how much smaller the world was getting, but also of the difference in the ways in which countries were perceiving their role: internationally and not just regionally.

It was the outbreak of World War I that really ended the balance-of-power system that had dominated European politics for about a hundred years to that point. The war also pointed out the dangers in this system. Some see World War I as the result of a struggle between competitive alliances "made all the more dangerous by the German position. . . . Germany still sought additional territory," even if that meant redrawing the map of Europe.[10] With the assassination of Archduke Ferdinand, the heir to the throne of the Austro-Hungarian Empire, in Sarajevo in 1914, Germany encouraged Austria to fight Serbia. But by that time, since virtually all of Europe was involved with one alliance or another, once one country went to war, the whole continent was in effect brought into the war. And therein lies one of the dangers of alliances.

By the end of World War I, under the leadership of U.S. president Woodrow Wilson, the quintessential liberal thinker who believed that war could best be averted in the future if all countries worked together (collectively), the idea of the League of Nations was born. Even though it proved to be unsuccessful, it served as a model, and the concept of *collective security* remained an important one.

In effect, the idea of *collective security* was premised on the notion that "if one country behaved aggressively . . . other states had a legal right to enforce international law against aggression by taking collective action to stop it."[11] Rather than focusing on the realist idea that countries would seek to maximize their own power, this approach was steeped in the liberal notion that cooperation was in all countries' best interest and therefore that countries would work together to pursue their goals. But this only works if countries behave as anticipated. When the United States, which was one of the most powerful countries at that time, did not join the League of Nations, it undermined the entire concept. When Japan went into Manchuria in 1931, the League was powerless to stop it, since any action required unanimous approval, which was virtually impossible to achieve. Similarly, when Italy invaded Ethiopia in 1936, although both countries were members of the League of Nations, that organization proved unable either to control Italy or to protect Ethiopia. Hence, one of the lessons was that collective security would work only if the countries involved all bought in and were willing to take a stand.

Clearly, the notion of collective security did not stop the outbreak of World War II. However, the weaknesses of the collective security concept that were exposed through the failures of the League and then the outbreak of World War II gave way to a system of *collective defense*, which was a modification of the earlier concept. One distinction that can be drawn between the two concepts is that "*collective security* is based on international law-enforcement obligations whereas *collective defense* is merely a form of balance-of-power politics" (emphasis added). Thus, collective defense presumes the creation of alliances "that pool power or capabilities of state members to balance . . . the power of other states, alliances, or other coalitions."[12] However, often the two concepts are used interchangeably.

Collective Defense, Alliances, and the Cold War

This updated notion of balance of power was embodied in Article 51 of the UN Charter and Article 5 of the NATO Treaty and became especially

---

BOX 3.1

COLLECTIVE DEFENSE.

The notion of collective defense was embodied in the Charter of the United Nations, where Article 51 explicitly states: "Nothing in the present Charter shall impair the inherent right of individual or collective self-defense if an armed attack occurs against a Member of the United Nations."[1]

It is similarly embedded in Article 5 of the treaty that created the North Atlantic Treaty Organization (NATO):

> The Parties agree that an armed attack against one or more of them in Europe or North America shall be considered an attack against them all and consequently they agree that, if such an armed attack occurs, each of them, in exercise of the right of individual or collective self-defense recognized by Article 51 of the Charter of the United Nations, will assist the Party or Parties so attacked by taking forthwith, individually and in concert with the other Parties, such action as it deems necessary, including the use of armed force, to restore and maintain the security of the North Atlantic area.[2]

NOTES

1. "Charter of the United Nations," Article 51, at http://www.un/org/en/documents/charter/chapter7.shtml.

2. "The North Atlantic Treaty," Article 5, at http://www.nato.int/cps/en/natolive/official_texts_17120.htm.

---

important during the Cold War. Much of the Cold War was premised on the need to maintain a rough balance of power between the United States and its allies, and the Soviet Union and its allies. The perception at the time was that if there were a rough approximation of balance, then neither side would be willing to attack the other, and therefore peace (or a balance of terror, as it was often known) would be maintained. The balance was tied to each country's capabilities, especially its nuclear arsenal, and its ability to inflict grave damage on the other side should an attack occur. The assumption here was that both countries not only had the weapons (*capability*) but also the willingness to use those weapons should it become necessary (*credibility*). It was the combination of these two factors—having the weapons and the perceived willingness to use them—that ensured that balance was maintained and that neither side would attack the other.

It is also important to note that much of this balance was tied to the idea of *perceptions*, specifically the perception that the two sides were roughly balanced in number of weapons as well as willingness to use them. While it was possible to get a rough count of things like number of aircraft or submarines deployed, it was the perception that their weapons arsenals were roughly balanced and would be used against the other side that became especially important. Or in the world of international relations, perceptions became reality as they were translated into policy decision.

Throughout the Cold War (from roughly 1945 until the Soviet Union ended in 1991), much of international relations was tied to the need to maintain this perceived balance of power between the two major blocs, each anchored by a single nuclear nation-state (the United States or the USSR). In addition to asserting dominance by building up their respective nuclear arsenals and alliances, both countries also engaged in arms control negotiations, which is a cooperative strategy. In this case, the goal was for the two sides to agree on a level of weapons that would ensure that there would be stability and predictability, rather than relying on relations based on an increasing arms buildup. Such a buildup would only contribute to insecurity (the security dilemma, referred to in chapter 2) rather than making countries feel safer.

Now that the Cold War is over, one can ask whether alliances remain important. Clearly they do, because countries still enter into alliances, albeit for more than just security or defense reasons, although those continue to remain important. But countries now recognize that aligning or uniting with other countries can bring them more benefits than just security; increased trade and other economic benefits have contributed to various alliance relationships. Thus, nations continue to work together and to enter into formal relationships for any number of reasons.

Why do we need to understand alliances in the context of understanding the nation-state? As noted above, alliances are part of understanding the ways in which nation-states behave. In addition, they straddle a number of important theoretical perspectives, and they have played an important role in the international system in virtually all of modern times.

UNDERSTANDING NATIONAL INTEREST

In theory, all interactions between and among nation-states are designed to further the *national interest*. This means that there needs to be an understanding of what is in the national interest and how to protect and preserve it. In this discussion, it is important to remember that defining national interest is done by an individual leader or members of the government (within the nation-state). Yet, it is the policies of the nation-state as a whole that become the focus for our understanding of national interest and the types of actions states engage in to further that national interest.

Generally, a nation-state begins with a clear statement of its own goals, that is, what is in its perceived "national interest." National interest might be protecting the country from external aggression (security), enhancing trade with other countries (economics), or cleaning up the environment and protecting the population from the spread of disease (human security). From that starting point, there are a range of possible options open to countries as they seek to protect the national interest. Since these all deal with one country's relationship to other countries, these are called *foreign policy orientations*. The particular option chosen should reflect the country's needs at that particular time. What that means in theory is that the national leader(s) understand what the country's priorities are, and how those priorities and needs can best be met through its interactions with other countries. The goal, then, would be to formulate policies that help a country move toward achieving its defined national interest through its interactions with other countries and actors in the international system.

Clearly, these needs and priorities can change as both domestic and international circumstances change, which means that countries are constantly evaluating and adapting their policies, while always bearing in mind what is in the national interest.

Foreign Policy Orientations

Countries have various foreign policy orientations or options that are available to them. All involve making a decision within the country that requires or affects its interaction with another nation-state or actor beyond its borders.[13] Theoretically, the option chosen should reflect what is in the country's national interest within the context of the time during which the policy is formulated.

One option for a country is to pursue a policy of *isolationism*, the desire to turn inward and to minimize political or military involvement with other countries. Or, put another way, isolationism is a policy decision to be removed from the international system. Often the only exception to this policy is in trading or economic relationships; even the most isolationist country, such as North Korea, recognizes the need to trade and interact economically with a small number of countries beyond its own borders, albeit in a limited way. A complement to this is the policy of *unilateralism*, the policy that the United States engaged in from its founding until the First World War. Similar to isolationism, unilateralism advocates a policy of political and military detachment from other countries, but unilateralism explicitly acknowledges the need to interact with other countries in a range of areas, such as economics and trade. Thus, this policy of unilateralism gave the United States the freedom to engage openly with other countries economically while keeping it out of formal alliances or agreements that could have dragged it into foreign wars.

A country can choose to be *neutral*, which means it does not commit its military forces or engage in a military or security alliance with other countries. This does not mean that a neutral country is removed from the international system; rather, neutral nations are often quite engaged because the status of neutrality gives it certain rights and responsibilities in the eyes of the international system. For example, Switzerland, a neutral nation, has become an international banking center as well as the location for many international negotiations.

Or depending on its national interest, a country can choose to become *engaged* internationally. This too can take on a number of characteristics, depending on the country and the international circumstances. For example, countries can choose to enter into military alliances or security arrangements of various types. These can be bilateral (between two countries) or multilateral (among three or more). Often the goal underlying the creation of these alliances is the belief that countries acting together can wield more power internationally than any country can acting alone. NATO is one example of a multilateral alliance; it was created in 1949, early in the Cold War period, to join the countries of Western Europe with the United States as a way to deter Soviet aggression. It remains in place today and has expanded its mandate to include missions outside its formal area, including the war in Afghanistan. The European Union (EU) represents a case in which twenty-seven diverse countries throughout Europe have united to pursue common economic, political, and security interests while still maintaining the sovereignty of each of the member states. This requires a constant balancing act as the goals of each individual member state must be weighed against the priorities and policies of the whole group. We will return to this point again in chapter 5.

In general, a country will choose which foreign policy to pursue in order to best assure its own national interest and security. However, countries also have to determine how best to respond to any particular set of actions taken by other countries in the international system. Again, they may choose to act unilaterally, bilaterally, or multilaterally. In most cases, however, the greater the number of countries acting together, the more effective a policy decision will be, although the more difficult it might be to reach agreement.

Here we need to inject our understanding of the theoretical perspectives as they apply to the nation-states and their foreign policy orientations. Realist thinkers will address foreign policy defined in terms of power. President Nixon and Henry Kissinger, who served first as Nixon's national security adviser and then as secretary of state, are both seen as quintessential realist decision makers who used the threat—or application—of military force to achieve U.S. foreign policy goals when they deemed it necessary. But they were also masters at knowing how to play one actor (the Soviet Union) against another (China) to the advantage of the United States. In that case, they used the United States as a balancer nation to exact concessions from both sides.

The foreign policies advocated by Woodrow Wilson are clear examples of the application of liberal thinking to foreign policy decisions. Wilson's advocacy for an organization, the League of Nations, that would thwart expansionist tendencies of other countries was steeped in classic liberal ideals or cooperation. President George W. Bush, with his belief in the importance of spreading the values of freedom and democracy, is another more recent example of this way of thinking. In this case, the emphasis was not as much on cooperation as it was on perpetuating liberal values that, in theory, should result in a more peaceful world.

These cases are illustrations of the ways in which a leader applies a particular theoretical perspective that results in the policies of a particular nation-state regarding other states—i.e., international relations.

Negotiation as a Tool of Foreign Policy

When we talk about the nation-state, one of the critical questions is: How do nation-states talk to one another? That is, how do they communicate in order to avoid a conflict or to resolve one that is under way? That is the role of diplomacy and negotiation, two important tools that are used by nation-states in the international system.

Diplomacy and *negotiation* represent alternatives to the use of force in the settlement of potential or actual disputes between countries. Negotiation between and among the various parties is often used to help avoid a conflict before it starts or escalates, or to resolve a conflict once it is under way. International negotiation is a phased process predicated on expectations of reciprocity, compromise, and the search for mutually beneficial outcomes. All parties to a negotiation must prepare their positions carefully, looking for a balance between national (domestic) considerations and political realities.

Negotiation is one tool of foreign policy available to countries as a way of addressing their concerns. According to realist international relations theory, countries will behave in a way that maximizes their national interest; theoretically, every country will pursue policies that enable it to further national interest, however that is defined. But the notion of negotiation, which is premised on the idea that countries can and will cooperate because all will benefit from doing so, is steeped in liberal thinking.

Generally, when entering into any negotiation, a country will begin by ensuring that its core values are maintained. Those values are the ones that guarantee continuity and a country's security, militarily and economically, and are often not negotiable. A country's national interest, however, might also include protecting its heritage and its history, its culture and traditions. What we are seeing increasingly in the post–Cold War world, however, is that there are variations within a country as to what these are or how they are interpreted. Hence, ethnic or religious conflict can result when different groups within a country have conflicting interpretations of what its national interest is or how it can be defined and protected.

Negotiations can be among allies or adversaries. Generally, negotiating with allies is easier because the countries start with common values. But this does not necessarily mean they will be easy. For example, the United States alienated some of its NATO allies by its decision to invade Iraq in March 2003, and no amount of negotiations or discussion could get France or Germany to agree with the U.S. position. In that sense, sometimes negotiating with an enemy or adversary might be a more straightforward task. For example, the bilateral arms control negotiations that took place throughout the Cold War between the United States and the Soviet Union—political and military adversaries—were seen as having a positive outcome. Even when the two sides didn't reach an agreement, the very process of negotiating ensured ongoing communication, which meant that they were talking to one another. The belief was that the more they communicated, the less likely the two sides were to go to war. Thus, in that case, the *process* of negotiating had a beneficial impact regardless of whether or not an agreement was reached, one product of negotiations.

Thus, another lesson of negotiation as a tool of communicating between and among nation-states is to understand what the negotiation is really about. Is it about the product, or getting a defined outcome, or the process—specifically, making sure that there is ongoing communication, which is especially important when the negotiation is between or among adversaries?

Negotiations can be used to avoid a conflict by having states discuss areas of disagreement to see if they can arrive at a compromise, or at least a point at which they can agree to disagree. Examples of this might range from trade disputes to trying to keep North Korea or Iran from building a nuclear weapon. Or they can be used to reinforce a positive relationship, such as the 2008 agreement between India and the United States facilitating nuclear cooperation. This agreement went beyond just providing assistance from the United States to India to aid its civilian nuclear energy program. It also strengthened the ties between the two countries, which had often had an uneasy relationship. This was seen as important to both countries politically.

As outlined in chapter 2, countries have a range of policy options available to them that can be placed along a continuum from positive (rewards) to negative (punishment) (see figure 2.2). In all cases, the country decides which particular course of action to pursue by weighing the relative costs and benefits. A government, acting rationally, would be most likely to choose the option that promises to give it the desired outcome at the least possible cost.

Thus, *negotiation* is a tool of foreign policy that can be and is used at all points along the continuum. In "normal" (i.e., noncrisis) situations, negotiations can be quite routine and might involve nothing more than determining the ways in which two or more countries can implement an ongoing agreement. However, in times of crisis, negotiations can be used to help manage the situation and to avoid armed conflict. Even during times of war, negotiations can be involved as a way to bring the conflict to a halt, to dictate the terms of a cease-fire, and to determine what happens after the conflict ends.

The specifics of crisis decision-making will be discussed in more detail in chapter 4.

One of the major challenges facing any government involved in a negotiation, however, is separating out the diplomatic from the political. *Diplomacy* is the formal process of interaction and is usually carried out by diplomats who are asked to *implement* a government's policy or policies. This is different from the work of politicians or government bureaucrats, many of whom are also engaged in negotiations of various types but whose main job is to *formulate* policy (rather than carry it out). Both of these play an important role in the world of international negotiations, although the functions are different.

One of the other challenges in any negotiation lies in understanding the culture and perspective of the country or countries with which you are negotiating. Different countries have different negotiating styles, and these must be considered in formulating a position and in determining how to approach another country.[14] In addition, there is a strategy involved with any negotiation: whether to begin the negotiation or wait for another country to respond; how much to reveal about your own position and at what point; how much you are willing to compromise in order to reach an agreement; and most important, what your own desired outcome of the negotiation is. These must be determined by each country in advance of the negotiation so that it will know how to begin and/or how to respond to another country's overtures.

That said, ideally, all countries approach negotiations by bargaining in good faith. This means that they have a sincere desire to compromise so that an agreement can be reached. But there are cases where that has proven to be impossible. For example, the country of Cyprus has been divided into two parts, Greek (south) and Turkish (north) since 1974, with the United Nations patrolling the border, known as the Green Zone. Despite many attempts at negotiations to unite the island, they have all failed, in part because neither side would make any concessions. Thus, the island remains divided and in a state of low-level conflict, thereby making it an intractable problem that could not be solved by negotiating. What the negotiations were able to do, however, was to make clear what the issues are and to have imposed some ongoing procedures that can help ensure that the conflict does not escalate into a case of armed violence.

Thus, negotiations are important ways for countries to communicate either bilaterally or among a group (multilaterally) as a way for them to pursue policies that are in their national interest. Before we move beyond this section and our understanding of negotiations, two other points are important to stress. First is that negotiations should always be used to further national interest, which suggests that the nation-state has clearly defined priorities and sees negotiations as an important and cooperative way for it to achieve that end. The second point ties directly to the first, and that is that negotiation is a foreign policy tool. Those who negotiate are often diplomats who do not necessarily make policy but help implement it. This is a fine distinction but an important one.

If negotiation is one foreign policy tool that countries can use to try to avert conflict, then why do so many countries seem to go to war? And what is war, anyway?

WAR AND PEACE

In order to understand international relations and the nation-state level of analysis, it is essential to understand and tackle big questions. Among the biggest questions that we explore in international relations are issues of war and peace. Wars tend to be between states (inter-state) or increasingly, within states, such as civil war. We are going to look at the concepts of war and peace, beginning with definitions of each, and then move into the particular cases of intra-state or civil wars, which are often tied to questions of nationalism and self-determination, and thereby threaten the traditional concept of the nation-state.

What Is War?

Different theoretical approaches and most political scientists have their own definition of war. One definition of war is "organized armed conflict between or among states (*interstate war*) or within a given state or society (*civil war*)" (italics in original).[15] Another definition of war is "a condition arising within states (civil war) or between states (interstate war) when actors appear to use violent means to destroy their opponents or coerce them into submission."[16] A third defines "general war" (as opposed to more limited types of war) as "armed conflict involving massive loss of life and widespread destruction, usually with many participants, including multiple major powers."[17] Morgenthau, the great realist thinker, makes the point that "both domestic and international politics are a *struggle for power*, modified only by the different conditions under which this struggle takes place in the domestic and international spheres." He also notes that "most societies condemn killing as a means of attaining power within society, but all societies encourage the killing of enemies in the struggle for power which is called *war*" (emphasis added).[18]

In his classic book *Man, the State, and War*, Kenneth Waltz, a neorealist, writes that "the locus of the important causes of war is found in *the nature and behavior of man*. Wars result from selfishness, from misdirected aggressive impulses, from stupidity" (emphasis added).[19] Here Waltz equates state behavior with human behavior: Both can sometimes behave badly and sometimes not. But if the natural state of the international system is anarchy, which is what most realists think, then there is nothing that can stop the bad behavior of either states or people from prevailing, resulting in war. In another piece written many years later, Waltz draws on the work of Immanuel Kant when he says, "The natural state is the state of war. Under the conditions of international politics, war recurs; the sure way to abolish war, then, is to abolish international politics."[20] Hence, Waltz notes, "To explain war is easier than to understand the conditions of peace. If one asks what might cause war, the simple answer is 'anything.'"[21]

You can arrive at your own definition that would probably be as descriptive or even explanatory. But, generally, *war* as a concept involves acts of armed conflict or violence involving two or more parties designed to achieve a specific objective. The objective could be political, economic (over and for resources), competition for the acquisition of territory, even ascendancy of ideas—all of these or none of these. So while there are certain traits that are common to the definition or categorization of war, there are countless possible objectives or reasons for it—or, as Waltz notes, the cause can be "anything."

Before we continue this discussion, it is also important to make a distinction among the following concepts: *conflict, armed conflict*, and *war*. The realists would say that *conflict* is an inevitable part of any interaction, which is often a struggle for power. But it is also important to note that not all conflicts lead to armed violence. So too in international relations there is often conflict between and among states, or even among different individuals or groups of people within states. But most are resolved peacefully, without escalating to violence, armed conflict, or on a larger scale, war.

Carl von Clausewitz, the Prussian general, military theorist, and author, worked on developing a major theory of war and the use of force. He served in both the Russian and Prussian military fighting against France in the Napoleonic wars, which ended in the defeat of France in 1815. His most famous piece, *On War*, was published in 1832, one year after his death. He opens the book with his definition of war, seeking to distill it to its simplest and most basic form. According to him, "War is nothing but a duel on an extensive scale . . . [where] each strives by physical force to compel the other to submit to his will: each endeavors to throw his adversary, and thus render him incapable of further resistance. *War therefore is an act of violence intended to compel our opponent to fulfill our will*" (emphasis in original).[22]

Clausewitz's definition of war grows out of his basic philosophy and understanding of international relations. He is very clear that *the conduct of war is a military opinion, but the decision to go to war is a political one*: "War is a mere continuation of policy by other means. . . . We see, therefore, that War is not merely a political act, but also a real political instrument, a continuation of political commerce, a carrying out of the same by other means."[23] In other words, in his formulation war is another way nations engage with one another; it is a means to achieve a policy option that has not been accomplished in any other way. It is not an end! Put another way, war should not be a policy goal, but an action only of last resort when all else has failed.

As a general, Clausewitz had his own understanding of war and its relationship to policy (the decision to go to war) and strategy (the conduct of war). According to him, a country is justified in going to war when other policy options fail. But there are other ways to approach the decision to go to war that are tied to moral values. In other words, when is war the *right* thing to do? Is it ever the correct and moral decision?

That aspect of war and the decision to go to war is embedded in theology and not necessarily just in politics.

Just War Doctrine

It is virtually impossible to study war, and especially war as an instrument of policy, without talking about *just war doctrine*. Given what we have been talking about regarding war, then the question becomes whether going to war is ever a rational decision for a country to make and, if so, under what set of circumstances? At what point *should* a country resort to war (a normative

question)? When is it justified? How does a country know that all other policy options, as advocated by Clausewitz, have been exhausted and this remains the only one? In answering these questions countries have long been
guided (at least in theory) by the concept of *just war*, another idea that must
be placed into historical context.

The classical idea of *just war* is normative in scope and is steeped in Western and Christian doctrine and morality. Just war doctrine, interpreted most
broadly, pertains to the moral criteria that states *should* use when justifying
armed aggression or war against another state. The precepts of just war doctrine are most often attributed to St. Augustine, who wrote in the fourth century about the apparent contradictions between Christian morality and
beliefs ("Thou shall not kill") and the violations of that commandment by
the state authorizing killing in its name. In the thirteenth century, St. Thomas
Aquinas outlined his concept of what has become known as traditional just
war theory in his *Summa Theologicae*. In this, he discusses the justification
for war, but also the kinds of activities and behaviors that are permissible in
the course of war.

Those ideas in turn, led to the work of Hugo Grotius, a Dutch reformer
who wrote during the Thirty Years' War. His *Law of War and Peace*, originally
published in Latin in 1625, outlined the moral and basic principles that we
now think of as the laws of war. These can be further broken down into
component parts that distinguish between "the rules that govern the justice
of war, that is, when a country can go to war (*jus ad bellum*), from those that
govern just and fair conduct in war (*jus in bellum*), and the responsibility
and accountability of warring parties after the war (*jus post bellum*)."[24] These
precepts have led to a series of accepted principles known collectively as *just
war*.

Many of the ideas of conflict, and especially of combat, that grew from
our modern understanding of just war doctrine, such as protecting civilians,
were embodied in the Geneva Conventions of 1949 and its various proto-
cols.[25] But it is also clear that many of the distinctions outlined clearly in
just war doctrine have broken down with the advent of weapons of mass
destruction, as well as the occurrence of civil conflicts of various types. Furthermore, although the United Nations has taken a stand at various times
when there have been violations, the international system really has no mechanism to enforce the principles, nor to punish states that violate them.

BOX 3.2

BASIC PRECEPTS OF JUST WAR DOCTRINE

Jus ad bellum (justice of war):

- War can only be waged as a last resort, after all other alternatives have been exhausted;
- War can only be waged by a legitimate government or authority;
- War can only be undertaken to correct a wrong, and never for revenge; or, it can be waged to restore justice after an injury has been inflicted;
- War must have a reasonable chance of succeeding;
- War can be used to defend a stable political order or a morally just cause against a real threat.

Jus in bellum (conduct of war):

- Negotiations to end the conflict must be continuous;
- Civilians are never legitimate targets of war. Population, especially noncombatants, should be protected;
- The damage incurred by the war must be in proportion to the injury suffered.

Jus post bellum (after the war):

- The ultimate goal of the war is to reestablish peace. "The peace established after the war must be preferable to the peace that would have prevailed if the war had not been fought."

Rather, it is up to the states and the governments to determine when—or whether—a war is just.

This highlights one of the failings of current international law. For example, when U.S. president George H. W. Bush authorized the use of U.S. troops in response to Iraq's invasion of Kuwait, a U.S. ally, he made it clear that this was an act of aggression that "would not stand." A range of diplomatic options were tried to resolve the situation through the United Nations, and only after those failed and Iraq still did not withdraw from Kuwait was military action deemed necessary.[26] The U.S. ability to pull together a "coalition of the willing" to help fight the war suggests that other countries agreed with the necessity of the use of military force.

This example stands in contrast to the circumstances surrounding the invasion of Iraq authorized by U.S. president George W. Bush in 2003. In this case, the evidence that Iraq was developing weapons of mass destruction, which justified the invasion, was ambiguous at best. Some of the U.S. NATO allies, most notably France and Germany, opposed the decision, causing a rift in the alliance. And the decision to use military force was made in defiance of the United Nations. Hence, in this case there were none of the moral imperatives that were present in the case of the first Gulf War. Nonetheless, the war went forward and the international community was virtually powerless to prevent it.

Feminist Theory and War

As you might expect, feminist theorists address issues of war and peace in great detail. Charles Tilly in his book *Coercion, Capital, and European States* reminds us that the modern nation-state was born from war and that the military was integral to the continued success of and even existence of the state.[27] But according to feminist IR scholars, it is the militaristic essence of the state that builds into it a gendered perspective, especially because of the connection between masculinity and war. It is in this discussion that we can really get a clear understanding of the feminist perspective and how it changes the discussion in international relations.

Governments often garner support for war by appealing to masculine characteristics but resorting to symbolism associated with women, such as the need to fight for the "motherland."[28] Women, as members of the society, are directly affected by war but are generally excluded from the decision to go to war. Especially in the civil and ethnic conflicts that have proliferated since the end of the Cold War, not only are women increasingly likely to be killed as more civilians are targeted, but war takes other tolls on them: They are often displaced by war; they are violated physically, psychologically, and emotionally; and the social structure that they inhabit is totally disrupted.

There is a high incidence of sexual violence against women, as rape has become one of the weapons of war. Furthermore, even if the women themselves are not literally wounded by the violence, many will have lost family members—husbands, sons, fathers—during the war. Thus, war has a direct effect on women as individuals and as members of the society of a nation at war.

There are other impacts of war on women. Any society in war goes through economic and social disruptions and dislocation. Women might lose their jobs, or conversely, what we often see is women having to take on new roles and responsibilities during war to keep the society going. But they then have to give them up and return to secondary status after the war ends and the men return home. At that point, society returns to the "natural" order, which displaces women once again.

However, the effects of war are often felt by women long after the conflict ends. For example, there is a direct correlation between conflict and domestic violence against women. Incidents of domestic violence increase during but especially after war, which is a consequence of a militarized society. Since that violence takes place at home, which is seen as private space, it is not always perceived as a consequence of conflict or war, but feminist authors have documented the relationship.[29]

War destroys the natural environment, resulting in environmental degradation that has health consequences for women and children long after the conflict ends. And of course, if government is spending money to fund a war it is not supporting the social services that many women depend on—that is, "guns versus butter." Thus, while the decision to go to war, the conduct of it, and often the reconstruction of society after the war ends is often left to men as decision makers, the impact of all these decisions is felt by women.

The impact of war or violence is felt especially by women during civil conflict, or war that takes place within the state (intranational conflict), which pits one group against another within a single nation. Thus, the growth of ethnic, religious, tribal, and national conflicts within a single state means that those who had lived together within a culture and society turn on one another; former friends can quickly become enemies, and even family members who are from different ethnic or religious groups can become adversaries.[30] Not only does this put women into positions where they must choose sides, but it can also give them the greatest opportunities to become politically active as they work for conflict resolution and peace, or as combatants supporting one side or the other.

On the other hand, because civil conflicts take place close to home, they give women greater opportunity to make a difference, whether at the national or, more likely, the grassroots or community level. Although the fact that women have been active in working for causes pertaining to peace is not a new phenomenon, civil conflicts can accelerate this process, often drawing on women's traditional roles as wives and mothers as the basis for commonality that allows women to be active participants. And the literature has also documented the fact that women not only work for peace but are also engaged as combatants during civil and ethnic conflict in which, like men, they feel it is their responsibility to fight for a cause they believe in.[31]

Thus, understanding women's roles and their relationship to war and conflict adds another and broader dimension to our understanding of the reasons countries go to war, how it pertains to their national interests, and who is affected by war—all important questions in international relations.

ISSUES OF PEACE AND NATION BUILDING

We have talked a lot about issues of war and conflict, including when and whether countries are justified in going to war. We have also talked about negotiations as an instrument of policy and particularly how difficult it is to end a conflict, especially one that is considered intractable, such as the Israel-Palestine situation that is often in the news, or the case of Cyprus, the island nation that has been divided into two parts since 1974.

Yet, if conflict is an inevitable component of international politics, as the realists argue, then one can justifiably ask where the concept of peace fits in the framework. The liberals would argue for the importance of cooperation in pursuit of the greater good, such as peace. Constructivists focus on normative structures and the beliefs of the value system of the elites to lead the nation into the right path, which is assumed to be peace. But the realists make little accommodation for understanding peace within their theoretical framework.

What we are going to explore here are the large issues of how conflict can be resolved to create conditions of peace, and then what are the various steps related to peace (e.g., peacemaking, peace building, and peacekeeping), and we will also look at the relationship between peace and nation-building.

What Is Peace?

When we talk about war, we also need to talk about peace. It is important to define the various terms as we use them—as we did with the definition of *war*, starting with what we mean by the concept of *peace*. At the most simplistic level, the term *peace* can be defined in the negative—that is, the absence of war. However, in order to get a full understanding of the term, we need to broaden the definition considerably. From an academic perspective, Peterson and Runyan look to the period during the Vietnam War and the rise of the subfield of peace studies, which as a group asked what peace is— "because surely it must be more than simply the time between wars."[32] At a workshop on peace through human rights and international understanding held in Ireland in October 1986, the workshop record summarized the results of a discussion group built around the question of "What is peace?" as follows: "Peace does not mean a lack of conflict—conflict cannot be avoided, but can be resolved. Conflict arises from a fear of losing that in which one has a vested interest. Removal of fear [i.e., creation of trust] brings peace."[33] The UN-sponsored Third World Conference on Women, held in Nairobi in 1985, arrived at a definition of peace that includes "not only the absence of war, violence and hostilities at the national and international levels but also the enjoyment of economic and social justice, equality and the entire range of human rights and fundamental freedoms within society."[34] And a range of feminist authors "define peace as the elimination of insecurity and danger" and as "relations between peoples based on 'trust, cooperation and recognition of the interdependence and importance of the common good and mutual interests of all peoples.'"[35]

What all these definitions have in common is the broad understanding that peace must be seen as more than the absence of violent conflict, but that it should also address broad issues such as equality, social justice, and ensuring basic freedoms and fundamental rights for all people in society. And while conflict is in many ways unavoidable, it can be addressed before it becomes violent or can be resolved through trust and communication. Thus, the concept of peace pertains not only to a situation characterized by an absence of hostility, but in a more positive sense, it is a situation of trust, sense of security, and cooperation among peoples. It is this larger understanding of the concept of peace that has allowed the concept to be seen as a "feminine" or "feminized" notion, which is all too often dismissed as unrealistic and unattainable in the "real world."

Peace can be achieved through the process of *peacemaking*, which can be defined as "the process of diplomacy, mediation, negotiation or other forms

BOX 3.3

THE NORTHERN IRELAND WOMEN'S COALITION

The Northern Ireland Women's Coalition (NIWC) stands as one example of the ways in which women have worked together not only to help bring about peace (i.e., an end to violence) but also to address the underlying causes of that violence within the society. The NIWC was created in 1996 as "a cross-community party, founded on human rights, inclusion and equality."[1] But what is more important, it was created specifically to help give women a voice in the process of negotiating an end to the violence in Northern Ireland known as "the troubles." One of the things that set the NIWC apart in the negotiations was the belief that "solving the political problems are only one part of addressing the broader issues plaguing Northern Ireland and especially those within the society who have suffered the most, primarily women."[2] Hence, while the other groups involved with the negotiations believed that getting the groups to put down arms (decommissioning) would lead to peace, the members of the NIWC wanted to address the structural issues that led to the divisions within the society and to the violence.

The Belfast (Good Friday) Agreement, which brought an end to the violence, was signed in April 1998. Once the agreement was signed and the troubles that had plagued the country since the early 1960s ended, the NIWC was no longer able to win any local elections. The NIWC held its final meeting on May 11, 2006, and then disbanded.

NOTES

1. http://www.niwc.org (accessed June 13, 2007).
2. Joyce P. Kaufman and Kristen P. Williams, *Women, the State, and War* (Lanham, MD: Lexington Books, 2007), 183.

of peaceful settlement that arranges an end to a dispute and resolves the issues that led to conflict."[36] This definition obviously involves two separate but interrelated pieces. First is ending the dispute. But the second, which in many ways is the more critical, pertains to resolving the issues that contributed to the conflict in the first place. It is in the latter case that the role of women becomes most important. While men often look at peacemaking as ending the fighting, including disarming the belligerents, women strive for addressing the issues that contributed to the conflict initially, also known as "structural violence."[37]

As articulated by Norwegian Johann Galtung, the concept refers to the idea that

> violence is built into the structure and shows up as unequal life choices. . . . *Resources* are unevenly distributed, as when income distributions are heavily skewed, literacy/education unevenly distributed, medical services existent only in some districts and for some groups only, and so on. Above all, *the power to decide over the distribution of resources* is unevenly distributed. (emphasis in original)[38]

The point that Galtung is trying to make is that as long as there is an unequal distribution of resources and unequal access to power that distribute those resources, then there will always be an element of conflict within the society. So although the society might not exist in a situation of armed violence or conflict, it is really not "at peace." As a result of this structural violence, in general, when working for peace, women see it as an opportunity to address those inequalities that will help remove some of the factors that contributed to the conflict in the first place.

In addition to *peacemaking*, we can look at a number of other concepts directly related that pertain to finding ways to make sure that peace is maintained and future conflict avoided. Here we have two more concepts. One is *peace building*, which pertains to "postconflict actions, predominantly diplomatic and economic, that strengthen and rebuild governmental infrastructure and institutions in order to avoid renewed recourse to armed conflict."[39]

The third concept that is important to understand is that of *peacekeeping*, which involves active efforts by third parties, such as the United Nations, to keep the warring parties apart so that they do not resort to hostilities. Often peacekeeping forces can be inserted during the process of negotiating an end to a conflict. However, the danger here is that once they are in place, if an agreement cannot be reached, the forces remain. The UN is currently involved with fifteen peacekeeping operations around the world.[40] But, as we can see, having a peacekeeping operation in place is no guarantee that there will continue to be peace.

Ending a War?

Often the future of a country following a conflict depends heavily on how the war ended and peace occurred. This is especially critical in cases of civil/national/ethnic conflict, where groups within a single nation-state are at war with one another. The challenge then becomes how to knit the society back together, if that is at all possible, in order to once again establish a stable nation-state. Part of that will depend on how the war ends.

Political scientist Monica Duffy Toft identified different ways in which wars might end. As we will see below in the examples, the different ways in which wars end have implications for what follows the war. According to Toft, "The most common type of ending is when one side wins so you have a military victory."[41] This is not unlike Japan's surrender after World War II. The United States prepared for the military victory by sending in an occupation force under General MacArthur, who had the troop strength to keep the peace but also helped put into place a political structure for a democratic Japan that would continue after the U.S. forces left. Ultimately, the U.S. occupation force was able to leave and the groundwork for a stable democratic Japan was in place.

Toft continues, "The second most common is negotiated settlements, and that's when the two parties agree to stop hostilities and form a common government."[42] A negotiated settlement is like what happened with the Dayton Agreement that ended the war in Bosnia, which was the result of the major leaders coming together and meeting together under U.S. leadership. As a result of the agreement, Bosnia-Herzegovina was divided into two parts, the Serb Republic and the Muslim-Croat Federation, two entities that exist together within a single state. So, in that case, the way to end the conflict and deal with the ethnic divisions that led to it was to divide the country into two parts, each of which was made up primarily of one nation or ethnic group. And, for Toft, the third way a conflict or war might end would be a ceasefire or stalemate. In that case, "the violence ends but the war itself, we don't talk about it having ended, because it could re-ignite at any moment."[43] Thus, we are looking at something that might be a temporary cessation of hostilities, although that situation could last for a very long time.

The third example of a ceasefire or a stalemate can be seen in Korea, where the Korean War ended in 1953 with an armistice that drew a line between North and South. That armistice largely brought a halt to the armed conflict, with the demilitarized zone (DMZ) dividing the two belligerents patrolled by UN forces to this day. In that case, no one won and no side lost; rather, the status quo was codified. The divided island of Cyprus is another example of this, where the "green line" that divides the Turkish north from the Greek south remains in place today. Despite the talk in both of these cases of how there will one day be a unified Korea or a unified Cyprus, the real question remains: How might that be possible?

In 2008, the PRI radio show *Marketplace* did a series on "how wars end."[44] What this show concluded was fascinating, and it raised many examples of how *not* preparing for peace contributed to future conflict. For example, it looked at the case of Iraq, after the U.S. invasion in March 2003 and the subsequent fall of Saddam Hussein and his regime. Baghdad fell to U.S. troops, and President George W. Bush declared victory. Since "regime change" was one of the reasons given for the U.S. invasion of Iraq, then the war should have been over, with an authoritarian government replaced by a democratically elected one. But, as we can see, ten years later, that was not the case. To that we can ask why.

One answer given is that the United States did not plan for the peace, or what would happen after the invasion.[45] The focus was on the conflict, not on what would happen after the United States "won." This means not only preparing for a new government, but preparing to win over the population in the country that was at war. Rather than accepting defeat, the Sunni forces initiated an insurgency that bedeviled the United States for years. The lesson here is in the importance of preparing for the peace during the war.

In another example, while the end of the First Gulf War in 1991 looked like a great success, many would argue that the way that war ended actually contributed to the subsequent problems in Iraq. From the U.S. perspective, that war in 1991 ended quickly with a relatively low loss of life. However, it looked different from the Iraqi perspective. Then president George H. W. Bush encouraged the Iraqi people to rise up and overthrow President Hussein, which some of the Iraqi Kurds and Shiites tried to do. But even with forces in Iraq, the United States did not come to their aid. Hussein's forces crushed the rebellion, and tens of thousands died. So even though this was a military victory for the United States in that Iraq left Kuwait, which was the justification for the invasion, Hussein was still in power with military forces like the Republican Guard backing him, which allowed him to take retribution against his own people. In many ways, the lack of preparing for that peace set the stage for the war against Iraq that actually took place years later. President Bush, without UN approval and over the objections of NATO allies France and Germany, authorized an attack against Iraq in 2003. Under the Status of Forces Agreement signed in November 2008, the last of the U.S. combat troops withdrew in 2009, but U.S. forces remained in Iraq until 2012. Although the country currently is under Iraqi government control and there are signs that it is rebounding, it is too early to tell what the longer-term prognosis is.

There are any number of examples of how ending a war does not guarantee that peace will follow, nor that there will be a real peace. In fact, the way the war ends might actually pave the way for more conflict. For example, it can be argued that one of the reasons for the NATO war against Serbia over Kosovo in 1999 was that the Dayton Agreement that ended the war in Bosnia did nothing to address the underlying ethnic problems already festering in Kosovo, thereby making another conflict inevitable.[46] The armistice that ended the war in Korea remains in place, but with ongoing tensions between the North and the South remaining. And the various agreements that have been negotiated to end the conflicts between Israel and its neighbors have not assured peace in the Middle East or security for Israel.

There are important lessons to be learned here, not least of which is that if there is to be a real peace, the groundwork needs to be started during the period of war. And for a nation-state in conflict, the reconstruction and re-building process will determine whether the state will continue to endure as a stable entity.

SUMMARY

This chapter focused on the nation-state level of analysis, beginning with a definition of *nation-state*. It is important to understand the nation-state and the concepts that govern state behavior, such as sovereignty, by putting them into historical context and understanding the evolution of the state. That was the starting point for our discussion of this level of analysis.

Also looking from a historical perspective, we talked about issues of *balance of power*, what that means, and how that concept has been realized using the different theoretical perspectives. Thus, we see the realists who look at all relations in terms of power and, therefore, to the inevitability of conflict, and the liberal thinkers who look at cooperation as the most effective foreign policy tool. Constructivists look at the ways in which the existing social and political structures affect the relationships among nation-states and ways to alter those structures for more positive ends. And the feminists would admonish us to look not only at the states, but at the impact of the actions of those nation-states.

We also talked about some of the "big questions" pertaining to the nation-state level: What is war, and why do countries go to war? What is peace, and how can peace be realized? How do countries communicate, and what options are available to countries as they are determining their foreign policy or their relations with other nations? These are all big and important questions to think about, and they make up an important element of international relations.

However, understanding international relations means understanding *all* of the critical levels of analysis. In the next chapter, we will start looking within the nation-state at the component parts: the *nation,* and what that means, and the *state,* or the trappings of the government. When we look at the nation, we also have to look at the people, the society, the culture, and ultimately the individuals. By understanding these, we can better understand how and why nations behave as they do, but also why so many nation-states break up or end up in civil, ethnic, or religious conflict. These are all critical pieces of understanding international relations.

FURTHER READINGS

These additional readings are worth exploring and elaborate on some of the points raised in this chapter. This list is not meant to be exhaustive, but only illustrative.

Galtung, Johann. "Violence, Peace, and Peace Research." *Journal of Peace Research* 6, no. 3 (1969): 167–91.

Jones, Anne. "Wars Abroad Continue at Home." http://www.tomdispatch.com/blog/175053/tomgram:__ann_jones,_wars_abroad_continue_at_home.

"Treaty of Westphalia." http://avalon.law.yale.edu/17th_century/westphal.asp.

NOTES

1. Fareed Zakaria, *The Post-American World* (New York: Norton, 2009), 38.

2. Locke's belief in the inherent goodness of man stands in marked contrast to the ideas of Thomas Hobbes, outlined in chapter 2, and makes Locke one of the founders of modern liberalism. See John Locke, especially his two *Treatises of Government* and his *Essay Concerning Human Understanding*, in which he outlines his understanding of human nature and the role of government. Both are widely available.

3. See "Treaty of Westphalia," http://avalon.law.yale.edu/17th_century/westphal.asp.

4. Karen A. Mingst, *Essentials of International Relations*, 4th ed. (New York: Norton, 2008), 24.

5. In describing the origins of the modern state, Charles Tilly asserts that it was born from war, and that the military was integral to the continued success, or even existence, of the state. Specifically, Tilly places "the organization of coercion and preparation for war squarely in the middle of the analysis, arguing . . . that state structure appeared chiefly as a by-product of rulers' efforts to acquire the means of war," and tied to that, "relations among states, especially through war and preparation for war, strongly affected the entire process of state formation." Charles Tilly, *Coercion, Capital, and European States, AD 990–1992* (Cambridge, MA: Blackwell, 1992), 14.

6. K. J. Holsti, *International Relations: A Framework for Analysis*, 7th ed. (Upper Saddle River, NJ: Prentice Hall, 1995), 46.

7. Holsti, *International Relations*, 47.

8. Charles W. Kegley Jr., *World Politics: Trend and Transformation* (Belmont, CA: Wadsworth Cengage Learning, 2009), 458–59.

9. As I note in *A Concise History of U.S. Foreign Policy*, "The Spanish-American War unambiguously made the United States an imperial power, rivaling the major powers of Europe." Joyce P. Kaufman, *A Concise History of U.S. Foreign Policy*, 2nd ed. (Lanham, MD: Rowman & Littlefield, 2010), 44.

10. Mingst, *Essentials of International Relations*, 32–33.

11. Paul R. Viotti and Mark V. Kauppi, *International Relations and World Politics*, 4th ed. (Upper Saddle River, NJ: Pearson Education, 2009), 70–71.

12. Viotti and Kauppi, *International Relations and World Politics*, 537.

13. For a more detailed discussion of foreign policy orientations, see Joyce P. Kaufman, *A Concise History of U.S. Foreign Policy*, 14–16.

14. For more detailed examples of the ways in which culture affects negotiations, see Raymond Cohen, *Negotiating Across Cultures: International Negotiation in an Interdependent* World (Washington, DC: United States Institute of Peace Press, 1997).

15. Viotti and Kauppi, *International Relations and World Politics*, 555.

16. Kegley, *World Politics*, 382.

17. Mingst, *Essentials of International Relations*, 218.

18. Hans J. Morgenthau, *Politics Among Nations: The Struggle for Power and Peace*, brief ed. (Boston: McGraw-Hill, 1993), 37.

19. Kenneth N. Waltz, *Man, the State, and War: A Theoretical Analysis* (New York: Columbia University Press, 2001), 16.

20. Kenneth N. Waltz, *Realism and International Politics* (New York: Routledge, 2008), 199.

21. Waltz, *Realism and International Politics*, 199.

22. Carl von Clausewitz, *On War*, ed. Anatol Rapoport (Middlesex, UK: Penguin, 1968), 101.

23. Clausewitz, *On War*, 119.

24. "Just War Theory," *Internet Encyclopedia of Philosophy*, at http://www.iep/utm/edu/justwar/print/.

25. Although the first Geneva Convention was adopted in 1864, the one that is generally referred to regarding protecting civilians is the fourth Geneva Convention, adopted in 1949. The principles embodied in this grew from the experiences of World War II; it was the first to deal explicitly with civilians. For a discussion of this and the other Geneva conventions, see "The Geneva Conventions of 1949," at http://www.icrc.org/Web/Eng/siteeng0.nsf/html/genevaconventions.

26. For President Bush's own account of the events, see George Bush and Brent Scowcroft, *A World Transformed* (New York: Knopf, 1998).

27. See Charles Tilly, *Coercion, Capital, and European States* (Cambridge, MA: Blackwell, 1992).

28. It should be noted that one of the few exceptions to this moniker was Hitler's Germany during World War II, where the fight was for the "fatherland."

29. See for example, Ann Jones, "Wars Abroad Continue at Home," at http://www.tomdispatch.com/blog/175053/tomgram:__ann_jones,_wars_abroad_continue_at_home; Cynthia Cockburn, *The Space Between Us: Negotiating Gender and National Identities in Conflict* (London: Zed Books, 1998); and Joyce P. Kaufman and Kristen P. Williams, *Women, the State, and War* (Lanham, MD: Lexington Books, 2007), 173–74.

30. Women in ethnically or religiously mixed marriages was one of the variables that we examined in *Women, the State, and War*. Marriage is one way that states gender citizenship and, as we saw in the cases we examined, generally it is the woman who suffers when she marries outside her group. She is often ostracized by her own family for marrying outside the group and is never really accepted by her husband's family because she is one of "the other." In some cases, as we saw in the case of former Yugoslavia, that led directly to violence against women. See Kaufman and Williams, *Women, the State, and War*, 96–103.

31. There are a number of authors who have studied women as combatants. For example, see Laura Sjoberg and Caron E. Gentry, *Mothers, Monsters, Whores: Women's Violence in Global Politics* (London: Zed Books, 2007); Miranda H. Alison, *Women and Political Violence* (New York: Routledge, 2009); Mia Bloom, *Dying to Kill: The Allure of Suicide Terror* (New York: Columbia University Press, 2005); and Joyce P. Kaufman and Kristen P. Williams, *Challenging Gender Norms: Women and Political Activism in Times of Conflict* (Sterling, VA: Kumarian Press, 2013).

32. V. Spike Peterson and Anne Sisson Runyan, *Global Gender Issues*, 2nd ed. (Boulder, CO: Westview Press, 1999), 179.

33. Workshop summary, "Workshop on Peace through Human Rights and Understanding," Navan, Ireland, October 12–17, 1986, 13. Accessed at the Women's Library, London, June 2008.

34. Inger Skjelsbaek, "Gendered Battlefields: A Gender Analysis of Peace and Conflict," PRIO Report (Oslo: International Peace Research Institute, 1997), 7.

35. Tami Amanda Jacoby, *Women in Zones of Conflict: Power and Resistance in Israel* (Montreal: McGill-Queen's University Press, 2005), 13.

36. Kegley, *World Politics*, 578.

37. Johann Galtung, "Violence, Peace, and Peace Research," *Journal of Peace Research* 6, no. 3 (1969): 167–91. Also see Galtung, *Peace by Peaceful Means: Peace and Conflict, Development and Civilization* (London: Sage, 1996).

38. Galtung, "Violence, Peace, and Peace Research," 171.

39. Kegley, *World Politics*, 578.

40. United Nations Peacekeeping Operations, at http://www.un.org/en/peace keeping/bnote.htm.

41. Quoted in "How Wars End," Part I, Introduction, October 6, 2008, at http://www.theworld.org.

42. Quoted in "How Wars End."

43. Quoted in "How Wars End."

44. October 6–10, 2008, at http://www.theworld.org.

45. For more detail on this point, see George Packer, *The Assassins' Gate: America in Iraq* (New York: Farrar, Straus & Giroux, 2005). See also Thomas E. Ricks, *Fiasco: The American Military Adventure in Iraq* (New York: Penguin, 2006).

46. See, for example, Tim Judah, *Kosovo: War and Revenge* (New Haven, CT: Yale University Press, 2000), and Joyce P. Kaufman, *NATO and the Former Yugoslavia: Crisis, Conflict, and the Atlantic Alliance* (Lanham, MD: Rowman & Littlefield, 2000).

4

Within the Nation-State

In the last chapter we looked at the nation-state—specifically, what it is, how it evolved, and the critical role that nation-states play in the international system. What we are going to do now is look *within* the nation-state, as we continue to move from the macro to the more micro levels of analysis. If the international system is the most macro level—it encompasses the entire system at its broadest—then we are moving toward the most micro level, the individual. Why is this important? Nation-states are the products of their component parts: the government and political system that run it; the cultures and societies of the people within it; and the individuals who make up the government, cultures, and societies. In fact, only by understanding all these interrelated parts is it really possible to understand why some nations (such as the United States) hold together despite the disparate groups of peoples it comprises, and why others (such as the former Yugoslavia) fall apart, often leading to bloody conflict. Understanding these pieces is critical to understanding international relations.

We will proceed in this chapter by going through the levels of analysis that are found within the nation-state, ultimately ending at the individual level. It is important to remember that even though we address these as if they were individual pieces, the reality is that they are parts of an integrated whole. For example, the parts of the nation-state include the government, culture, and societies, which are made up of individuals. Yet, in order to understand international relations, we do not need to know how every individual thinks. Rather, at the level of the individual, as we will see later in this chapter, what is most important is how individual decision makers think, since, ultimately, they are responsible for steering the course of the nation-state. That said, at a time of political transition in parts of the world, it is also important to think about how individuals, acting together, can change the course of political action in any one country, as they did in Tunisia, Libya, and Egypt, for example.

We will begin with an overview of government in general and of the role that government plays in international relations. From there, we will look at the "nation" part of the nation-state, with an eye toward understanding the culture and societies. Just as we examined large questions of peace and war when we talked about the nation-state level, there are important questions to be asked about conflict when we look within the nation-state. However, rather than looking specifically at wars between or among nation-states, here we will try to understand and get a better grasp of what causes civil or intra-state conflicts or wars. We need to look within the nation-state at the nations, culture, and societies in order to understand a little bit more about why one group within a country turns on another, and also, why these type of conflicts are often so difficult to resolve.

We will conclude the chapter with a discussion of the individual level and what role the individual plays in international relations under different sets of circumstances.

THE GOVERNMENT

Every nation-state has a government that is responsible for ensuring the collective well-being and security of the state and the people within it. Looking at it another way, for a government or the political system of the country to be considered legitimate, the people within the borders of the state (i.e., the nation) must feel an allegiance to the state. There are any number of different types of political systems or governments, some of which are considered more legitimate than others both by the people within its borders and by those outside the borders. The latter is an especially important point; if a government is not considered to be legitimate, then other countries and governments will not want to interact with it for fear of the appearance that doing so will be granting legitimacy. As you will see later, this affects whether or not a state is recognized by the other members of the international system.

This might seem confusing, so let's put this a different way. If a dictator takes power through illegitimate means such as overthrowing an established government, other countries will not want to deal with that leader, as a sign that they cannot support the methods used to take control. Hence, another country might not want to grant the country diplomatic recognition or will try to isolate it from interacting with other countries in the international system through measures such as imposing a trade embargo or economic sanctions. We have seen this with the imposition of sanctions against Iran as "punishment" for moving forward with its nuclear weapons program. Does that mean that the leader does not exist or will go away, or that the country (such as Iran) will change its policies? Not really. But it does send a signal regarding that country's place within the international system.

It has also been shown that even if a country opposes the policies of another or the means by which a leader took power, they might continue to work with the leader if they feel it's in the national interest. Here again, some examples might prove helpful. Although the United States did not support many of the repressive policies of Joseph Stalin, during World War II the United States and Stalin were allies against Hitler, who was seen as a greater threat. It was after the war ended and Hitler was defeated that there was a huge ideological and military divide between the two countries, which grew into the Cold War. More recently, we can look at the case of North Korea, which is a closed, isolationist regime—yet the UN Conference on Trade and Development estimates that "foreign direct investment in 2010 was $38m (£24m; 29m euros) and that the total amount invested in North Korea over the past few decades comes to $1.475bn (£940m; 1.13bn euros)."[1] Most of that investment was from China, due in part to the fact that North Korea has resources that China wants and needs for its own development. Neighboring South Korea has been investing in the North, and other countries, including Russia, India, and Germany, also see North Korea as holding potential for investment.

Countries will also isolate another country when a leader with whom they have problems ideologically takes power. For example, after then Chinese leader Mao Tse-tung officially declared the creation of the Peoples' Republic of China as a communist country on October 1, 1949, the United States would not recognize that country as "China," preferring instead to recognize the nationalist government on Formosa (Taiwan) as China. The United States had backed the nationalist leader Chiang Kai-shek against Mao during the civil war and preferred to make a statement about their allegiance to that leader, as well as against communism. It was not until many years later, in 1979, that the United States officially recognized what we now know as "China." U.S. nonrecognition of China did not mean that the country did not exist; clearly it did. But the policy sent a signal that the United States was continuing to support its ally, Taiwan—which in turn alerted China that should it decide to attack Taiwan and try to annex it, it would have to deal with the United States.

What does that tell us about the level of the government? It means that even though a government is something that exists within the nation-state specifically to govern the people, there are implications for the ways in which other states see the government of that country and interact with it. In other words, what happens within the country has implications for foreign policy, which is also international relations.

Clearly, there are many different types of governments and political systems. Some impose their will (and the hope of legitimacy) from the top down. These tend to be autocratic or authoritarian governments whose continuity within the country is often assured through means of coercion, such as the use of the military. Another type of government is a democracy, which is generally a participatory system in which the citizens have some say in choosing their leaders and, therefore, in the decisions that are made. Democracies are supposed to reflect the will of the masses (that is, the non–decision makers), since one of the characteristics of this form of government is that if the people are dissatisfied, they can throw out the decision makers in the next election. Democracies can be parliamentary systems, such as the United Kingdom, or presidential, such as the United States. Both of these variations *empower* their people.

It is also important to remember that holding an election does not ensure a democracy, as we can see in recent examples. For example, the elections that were held in Iran in June 2009 ensured the reelection of Mahmoud Ahmadinejad as president for a second term, despite accusations of fraud and the fact that the process was accompanied by violence. He remains in place as president to date. In Russia, former president Putin's role was formalized when he was again elected president in March 2012, succeeding Dmitry Medvedev, his hand-picked successor when Putin was "termed out" as president in 2008. But Putin's election in 2012 was not without controversy, leading to street protests that actually started even prior to the elections and grew violent at times. In many ways, the protests underscored how much Russia had changed in the period since Putin was last president. Although Putin "won" 64 percent of the vote this time, he was not recognized as the legitimate president by many in Russia. According to one report, "The election was neither open nor honest. . . . [And] by some estimates vote-rigging added at least ten percentage points to Mr. Putin's tally."[2] As also reported, the election results of more than 50 percent ensured that Putin did not have to face a run-off election and was a demonstration to the bureaucracy and security services that he remains in charge and can mobilize whatever resources he needs to stay in power. "Yet the fact that the Kremlin was forced to use more elaborate means to rig the election was also testimony to the growing pressure from civil society."[3] This serves as another case where an election does not equate to democracy and the will of the people.

In addition, the feminists would alert us to think about the concept of democracy through gender-sensitive lenses. Doing so alters the perspective still further. The feminist literature reminds us that even in democratic systems, generally women do not have the same access to power that men do, and that political agendas that benefit women are not always put forward. Even liberal definitions of citizenship are grounded in the social contract of seventeenth- and eighteenth-century Europe, which were based on "male, property-owning heads-of-households . . . [and] thus, democratic theory and practice have been built on the male-as-norm engaged in narrowly defined political activities."[4] We will return to the ways in which the state genders citizenship below. But the point to remember is that while we often think of democracy as a political form that the people can contribute to and benefit from, we still need to ask who participates and who benefits.

There are other forms of governments as well, such as monarchies, in which the power is vested in a king or queen who inherits that position. But a true monarchy, in which the monarch is more than a figurehead, is rare these days, although we do see them in some countries, such as Thailand and Saudi Arabia, where there is an inherited royal line and popular participation is limited. In democratic systems where there is a monarch, such as the UK or Spain, real power is vested in the parliament and the prime minister, although the monarch serves as the titular head of state—for example, formally opening the session of parliament.

We are not going to go into these different types of governments in depth here—that is really the purview of comparative politics—beyond noting that different types of governments have implications for international relations. Each political system has a different process for making decisions, including decisions on foreign policy. Since foreign policy is the process through which one nation-state interacts with another, foreign policy decisions and the ways that these are made have important implications for understanding international relations. It is that set of points that we will be exploring in more detail here.

Democratizing the State

One statistic suggests that "approximately thirty countries shifted from authoritarian to democratic systems during the 1970s and 1980s; this so-called 'third wave' of democratization, defined as a move toward competitive electoral politics, was most successful in countries where Western influences were strongest."[5] For example, this can be seen in the transition that took place in the countries of Eastern Europe, as they moved beyond Soviet-era communist systems to embrace both democratic political systems and capitalist economies. Ultimately, this was also manifested in their individual desire to join both NATO and the EU, as proof that they were indeed part of the family of "Western" countries.

This transformation to democracy spurred a greater interest in understanding democratization, especially as it was also connected to the growth of free market capitalist economies and an emphasis on improved human rights, both of which are tied to liberal values. Going back to our earlier discussions of theory, realists assume a unitary actor, which in turn makes assumptions about the behavior of states—specifically that they will always act in their own best interest to maximize power. On the other hand, liberal theorists are more interested in looking at the ways in which the transition to democratic systems has played out, not only economically, but also as it affects a country's foreign policy. This is especially important, as the liberal theorists see a direct connection between economics and politics. The constructivists would want us to understand the relationship between the various social and political structures and the country's policy decisions, and of course the Marxists see a direct link between economics and politics. Thus, each of the theoretical approaches would have something to contribute to this part of the discussion.

Accompanying the apparent move toward increased democratization has also been the assumption that democracy is a "better" form of government because of the apparent benefits derived: People have a vested interest; government will protect the "national interest"; human rights will be protected; theoretically, decisions will benefit the greater good or the collective; and so on. There is also the emergence of theories such as the "democratic peace," which makes assumptions about the supposedly peaceful nature of democracies explored in more detail below. This too has reinforced the idea of democracy as the "best" form of political system.

However, it is also important to remember that democracy brings with it certain responsibilities and requirements. Democracy assumes an educated citizenry, who are aware of the issues and willing participants in the process. In addition to voting, among a citizen's responsibilities are paying taxes; making their voices heard through the political process; serving in the military if required; obeying laws; and of course, owing allegiance to the government, among other things. The government in turn has its responsibilities, which include providing for the common defense; engaging with other countries (foreign policy); providing for "human security," such as clean air, food, and water; ensuring that the budget is apportioned wisely; and so on. Because of the range of responsibilities associated with democracy, it can be argued that it cannot be *imposed* on any state but must grow organically from within the state. Thus, the countries of Eastern Europe, which had been under Soviet domination, *chose* democracy as their preferred political system and pursued a capitalist market economy when they had the opportunity. This stands in contrast, for example, to cases like Iraq, where one of the stated reasons for the U.S. invasion in 2003 was to rid the country of a dictator and to encourage (impose) democracy in its place. This assumption that because it was the preferred form of political system and would contribute to a more peaceful world led to the liberal notion that democracy could be imposed on another country as a foreign policy goal.

The liberal belief in the primacy of democracy goes back to Immanuel Kant, who in 1795 argued that "the spread of democracy would change international politics by eliminating war."[6] In his view, the best way to ensure peace was to encourage the growth of republics, or representative democracies, which he felt would take international law more seriously than any other forms of government, which at that time were monarchies and empires. "The republican constitution, besides the purity of its origin (having sprung from the pure source of the concept of law), also gives a favorable prospect for the desired consequence, i.e., *perpetual peace*" (emphasis added).[7]

Democratic Peace

From this eighteenth-century notion about the peaceful nature of democracies grew one of the basic principles of international relations: *democratic*

BOX 4.1

PRESIDENT GEORGE W. BUSH AND
DEMOCRACY IN IRAQ

By looking a series of speeches made by the Bush administration (both Vice President Dick Cheney and President George W. Bush), it is possible to track the rhetoric leading to the war against Iraq, justified initially by the alleged presence of weapons of mass destruction, to the need for regime change and ultimately the hope of creating a democratic form of government in Iraq.

On September 14, 2001, at the request of President George W. Bush, the U.S. Senate and House of Representatives each passed a joint resolution authorizing a military attack against Afghanistan in response to the attacks of September 11. By early 2002, Bush made it clear "that the United States would not stop with the attack on Afghanistan but would expand the 'war on terror.' In his State of the Union speech in January 2002, Bush identified Iraq, Iran and North Korea as an 'axis of evil,' and he stated that 'some governments will be timid in the face of terror. . . . If they don't act, America will.'"[1]

While this foreshadowed the eventual attack on Iraq, the rationale for doing so continued to change. In August 2002, Vice President Dick Cheney, in a speech to the Veterans of Foreign Wars, set the stage by stating that "there is no doubt that Saddam Hussein now has weapons of mass destruction."[2]

By October 2002, President Bush addressed the country to prepare it for an attack against Iraq, now justified not only by the presence of weapons of mass destruction, but by painting Saddam Hussein as "a ruthless and aggressive dictator," "a threat to peace," and "a student of Stalin," who has "links to international terrorist groups." According to Bush, "*regime change* in Iraq is the only certain means of removing a great danger to our nation" (emphasis added).[3]

In December 2005, when the war against Iraq had been under way for almost three years, (the initial attacks began in March 2003), President Bush was speaking explicitly of the imposition of democracy in Iraq: "Today I am going to speak in depth about another vital element of our strategy: our efforts to help the Iraqi people build a lasting democracy in the heart of the Middle East."[4]

Under the Status of Forces Agreement signed with Iraq in November 2008, all U.S. forces "shall withdraw from all Iraqi territory no later than December 31, 2011."[5]

A paramount goal for both the United States and Iraq was to stress the importance of Iraq as a sovereign nation headed by a *democratically elected government* once the U.S. troops had withdrawn and a sense of "normalcy" returns to the country. When—or whether—that will happen remains uncertain.

NOTES

1. Joyce P. Kaufman, *A Concise History of U.S. Foreign Policy*, 2nd ed., Lanham, MD: Rowman & Littlefield, 2010, 146.

2. "Full Text of Dick Cheney's Speech," August 27, 2002, at http://www.guardian.co.uk/world/2002/aug/27/usa.iraq.

3. "President George W. Bush's Address Regarding Iraq, Cincinnati Museum Center," October 7, 2002, at http://www.johnstonsarchive.net/terrorism.bushiraq.html.

4. President George W. Bush, "The Struggle for Democracy in Iraq: Speech to the World Affairs Council of Philadelphia," December 12, 2005, http://www.presidentialrhetoric.com/speeches/12.12.05.html.

5. "Agreement between the United States of America and the Republic of Iraq on the Withdrawal of United States Forces from Iraq and the Organization of Their Activities during Their Temporary Presence in Iraq," at http://www.cfr.org/publication/17880/security_agreement_status_of_forces_agreement_us_and_iraq.html.

---

peace. This idea was introduced into IR thinking in the 1980s, put forward by Michael Doyle, among others. Doyle, an important liberal thinker in international relations, wrote in 1986 that "the predictions of liberal pacifists . . . are borne out: liberal states do exercise peaceful restraint, and a separate peace exists among them."[8] He drew on the work of Kant and also Joseph Schumpeter to conclude that although liberal states will fight when they must—when they are attacked and/or threatened in some way—they have established a "separate peace—but only among themselves."[9] This has contributed to the incorrect notion that democracies are more peaceful than other types of governments, which in turn has morphed into what appears to be a more accurate representation: that democracies do not fight one another. The reality is that democracies fight as many wars as authoritarian

BOX 4.2

EXCERPTS FROM ''PERPETUAL PEACE:
A PHILOSOPHICAL SKETCH,'' BY
IMMANUEL KANT

SECTION I. CONTAINING THE PRELIMINARY ARTICLES FOR PERPETUAL PEACE AMONG STATES

3. *"'Standing Armies (miles perpetuus) Shall in Time Be Totally Abolished'"*

"For they incessantly menace other states by their readiness to appear at all times prepared for war; they incite them to compete with each other in the number of armed men, and there is no limit to this. For this reason, the cost of peace finally becomes more oppressive than that of a short war, and consequently a standing army is itself a cause of offensive war waged in order to relieve the state of this burden."

SECTION II. CONTAINING THE DEFINITIVE ARTICLES FOR PERPETUAL PEACE AMONG STATES

"The state of peace among men living side by side is not the natural state (*status naturalis*); the natural state is one of war. This does not always mean open hostilities, but at least an unceasing threat of war. A state of peace, therefore, must be *established,* for in order to be secured against hostility it is not sufficient that hostilities simply be not committed; and, unless this security is pledged to each by his neighbor (a thing that can only occur in a civil state), each may treat his neighbor, from whom he demands this security, as an enemy."

FIRST DEFINITIVE ARTICLE FOR PERPETUAL PEACE

"'The Civil Constitution of Every State Should Be Republican'"

"The only constitution which derives from the idea of the original compact, and on which all juridical legislation of a people must be based, is the republican. This constitution is established, firstly, by principles of the freedom of the members of a society (as men); secondly, by principles of dependence of all upon a single common legislation (as subjects); and thirdly, by the law of their equality (as citizens). . . . Is it also the one which can lead to perpetual peace?

"The republican constitution, besides the purity of its origin (having sprung from the pure source of the concept of law), also gives a favorable prospect for the desired consequence, i.e., perpetual peace. The reason is this: if the consent of the citizens is required in order to decide that war should be declared (and in this constitution it cannot but be the case), nothing is more natural than they would be very cautious in commencing such a poor game, decreeing for themselves all the calamities of war."

SECOND DEFINITIVE ARTICLE FOR PERPETUAL PEACE

"'The Law of Nations Shall Be Founded on a Federation of Free States'"

"Peoples, as states, like individuals, may be judged to injure one another merely by their coexistence in the state of nature (i.e., while independent of external laws). Each of them, may and should for the sake of its own security demand that the others enter into a constitution similar to the civil constitution. . . . This would be a league of nations. . . .

"The practicability (objective reality) of this idea of federation, which should gradually spread to all states and thus lead to perpetual peace, can be proved. For if fortune directs that a powerful and enlightened people can make itself a republic, which by its nature must be inclined to perpetual peace, this gives a fulcrum to the federation with other states so that they may adhere to it and thus secure freedom under the idea of the law of nations. By more and more such associations, the federation may be gradually extended."

Source: Immanuel Kant, "Perpetual Peace: A Philosophical Sketch," at http://files.libertyfund.org/files/357/0075_Bk.pdf.

states do, *but not against other democratic states.* "No major historical cases contradict this generalization, which is known as the *democratic peace*" (emphasis in original).[10]

Political scientists continue to ponder why this is the case. Is this coincidence, or is there something inherent in the democratic system of government that is more peaceful, or at the least, less likely to engage in war as a means of settling disputes? Since democracies depend on "the consent of the governed," are they more hesitant to engage in war, which will not be popular at home, will require public support, and will result in loss of lives and great monetary expense? Or as democratic peace proponents argue, is it because the spread of democracy helps negate the inherent anarchy of the international system as understood by realists? Perhaps the existence of more democracies would help alleviate if not eliminate the "security dilemma," or the insecurity that comes with a buildup of weapons, thereby making war less likely.

New York Times columnist Thomas Friedman put forward a slightly different understanding in his thesis that "No two countries that both have a McDonald's have ever fought a war against each other." His "Golden Arches Theory of Conflict Prevention" suggests that "when a country reaches a certain level of development, when it has a middle class big enough to support a McDonald's, it becomes a McDonald's country, and people in McDonald's countries don't like to fight wars."[11] In other words, a country that can support a McDonald's, or any other major multinational corporation that requires a strong economic/middle-class base, has achieved a certain level of development economically and is probably integrated with the larger global community. Those characteristics alone mean that it is a country that is less likely to engage in war than a country that has not yet achieved those qualities. This also introduces an economic component to the understanding of democratic peace, which in many ways makes it a more complete package.

Militarizing the State

Political scientist John Mueller argues that it is not democracy that "causes" peace, but there are other conditions internal to a nation as well as external circumstances that contribute to *both* democracy *and* peace. For example, attitudes toward war have changed, such that "the appeal of war, both as a desirable exercise in itself and as a sensible method for resolving conflicts, has diminished markedly."[12] But in some countries, including the United States, there has also been significant militarization, which started during the Cold War and has continued. This has made it easier to move beyond peace to situations of conflict and war. The growth of the defense sector and its impact on the U.S. economy was something that President Eisenhower warned about in his farewell address to the nation:

> This conjunction of an immense military establishment and a large arms industry is new in the American experience. The total influence—economic, political, even spiritual—is felt in every city, every State house, every office of the

"DEMOCRATIC PEACE."

Liberalism has gained momentum with the emergence of the "democratic peace," the idea that countries that are democracies do not fight one another. Note, this does not suggest that democracies do not go to war, rather that *they do not go to war against one another!* So the question here is why that is the case. Some argue that shared democratic norms and values mean that democratic countries are not only less likely to have conflict, but that they are more likely to use peaceful means (negotiation) to resolve any differences.

Another possible reason can be drawn from Thomas Friedman's "Golden Arches Theory of Conflict Prevention," which suggests that countries that have McDonald's have never fought a war against one another.[1] This is not as silly as it sounds, for it reminds us that countries that have a McDonald's also have a certain level of economic development and that they are an integrated part of the international economic system. It would then be irrational for a country that is tied to other countries economically to go to war against them.

NOTES

1. See Thomas L. Friedman, "Foreign Affairs Big Mac I," *New York Times*, December 8, 1996, at http://www.nytimes.com/1996/12/08/opinion/foreign-affairs-big-mac-i.html. Friedman developed this idea further in his book *The Lexus and the Olive Tree: Understanding Globalization* (New York: Farrar, Straus & Giroux, 1999).

Federal government. We recognize the imperative need for this development. Yet we must not fail to comprehend its grave implications. Our toil, resources and livelihood are all involved; so is the very structure of our society.

In the councils of government, we must guard against the acquisition of unwarranted influence, whether sought or unsought, by the military-industrial complex. The potential for the disastrous rise of misplaced power exists and will persist.

We must never let the weight of this combination endanger our liberties or democratic processes. We should take nothing for granted. Only an alert and knowledgeable citizenry can compel the proper meshing of the huge industrial and military machinery of defense with our peaceful methods and goals, so that security and liberty may prosper together.

Akin to, and largely responsible for the sweeping changes in our industrial-military posture, has been the technological revolution during recent decades. (emphasis added)[13]

The changes that Eisenhower identified, which can be thought of as the *militarization of the state*, have continued, and as the technology has improved, the costs of war, especially the human costs, have changed. So while technology has allowed technologically developed countries like the United States to wage war using technology like drones to replace soldiers, the collateral damage to civilians has increased.[14]

Moving beyond the United States in particular to the international system in general, Mueller also argues that although there has been a proliferation of what he calls "local wars," there is also a marked diminishing of countries resorting to war as a means to settle disputes and differences. And he also makes the distinction between war and conflict, noting that although war has declined, "it certainly does not mean that conflict has been eliminated."[15] However, this also does not necessarily mean that war is the only means by which these conflicts can be resolved. In fact, looking at some of the NATO nations, for example, there can be very extreme disagreements about policy, such as the U.S. decision to go to war in Iraq, but they can be addressed without resorting to armed violence.

In examining the materials about democracy and the democratic peace, it does appear that from the perspective of international relations, this form of government has emerged as the most cooperative and beneficial not only to the individual nation, but to the direction of the international system as a whole. That said, the transition from another type of political system to democracy can be difficult and even violent. We know that it cannot be imposed from outside, but that the desire for this form of political system must originate from within and that the country must have the infrastructure (e.g., an educated citizenry, open access to media, a fair election process, etc.) to support it.

Democracy and Feminist Perspectives

In order to truly understand democracy, though, we also need to put on our gender-sensitive lenses and ask who makes the decisions and who is affected by the decisions even in a democratic system. As suggested above, feminist theorists, such as Ann Tickner, warn us that the movement toward democracy can actually have a detrimental effect both within and across states. Across states, decisions made by some of the more powerful democracies of the northern developed tier of states can limit the options available to the developing countries of the south. Often, the decisions of the major developed or industrialized states are made with consideration as to what is in their best interest, even if that means that the decisions will have a detrimental effect on the developing countries. For example, an environmental policy that was designed to improve the air or water quality of the developed countries can be more costly for a developing country to implement, or might even be irrelevant to a country struggling to feed its own people. The imposition of values by one country or group of countries onto another (something the countries of the developed West have increasingly been accused of doing) is often called *cultural imperialism.*

Within a country, while democracy promotes equality among all citizens in theory, the reality is that often these are patriarchal governmental structures, where power is concentrated in the hands of wealthy men who have the wherewithal to gain access to high office. Further, these same leaders often promote and mentor younger people who look and think just as they do. Thus, it can be argued, this is a system that can limit progress for women, rather than allowing them to advance.[16] So in order to really understand democracy in practice as well as in theory, we need to ask who has access to the system of governance and who participates in it.

Another point that Tickner and other feminists make—and it is one that keeps women out of decision making—has to do with the differentiation between the public and the private spheres, where politics is associated with the public, and the private sphere of running the household and the family is the domain of women. In fact, Tickner notes that "historically . . . terms such as *citizen* and *head of household* were not neutral but were associated with men."[17]

What this suggests is that no matter how democratic a political system might appear to be, it can exclude women from decision making and positions of power. This too has implications for the foreign policy decisions that a country makes, including issues of war and peace.

CULTURE AND SOCIETY

In chapter 3, we gave the definition of the nation-state as comprising two separate but interrelated concepts. The *nation* denotes a group of people with common history, background, and values, all of whom accept the sanctity of the state. The *state*, in turn, represents the formal trappings such as the government and defined borders, and it, in turn, accepts certain responsibilities for the people who live within those borders. In the section above on the government, we talked about the "state" part of the concept. We will now move into a discussion of the "nation" part, which is the people. It is the people as a whole who not only represent the nation but also define the culture and the society. While they might seem to exist outside the area of international relations per se, they are important for a number of reasons.

Ideally, any nation-state has one culture and one societal set of norms, or if there is more than one, they are compatible. These might be characterized by a common language, set of values, and traditions. Or in some countries, there might be more than one within a larger set of cultural and societal norms. For example, within the United States, the majority of people speak English (although a lot speak Spanish), but within the country there are ethnic enclaves, such as the Cajun areas of Louisiana, where the dominant language is a patois based on French. There are groups that hold on to their original ethnic heritage; they may speak Russian and worship in a Russian Orthodox Church, or live in Chinese enclaves and worship in Buddhist temples. The point is that although there are these subgroupings, they are found within a dominant cultural tradition that understands and expects certain behaviors that transcend any one cultural tradition and are "American." Thus, members of these various subgroups will all celebrate the Fourth of July or Thanksgiving as a common tradition, while they may also celebrate the Orthodox Easter or the Chinese New Year. Thus, various nations can live in harmony within one state.

These various "nations" need not be tied to ethnic background or traditions, religion, or culture but may be considered an artifact of "identity"— that is, issues of belonging. Sociologists, anthropologists, and other social scientists as well as political scientists have explored various aspects of this concept to try to get a broader understanding of what it is, what it means, and where it comes from. It might be tied to religion, ethnicity, culture, even region. But in many ways it is the broader understanding of a common identity that holds groups of people within the state together.

For our purposes, though, the question remains: How does this affect international relations? The fact of the matter is that it does affect it. For example, look at the strong pro-Israeli group within the United States, which has a powerful lobby that has had a direct influence on U.S. policy toward Israel.

This group of people advocates support for Israel as an important component of U.S. foreign policy. Although they are Americans, they also have a strong sense of identity with the Jewish religion and feelings of loyalty to the state of Israel, and therefore want the United States to support that country. This does not mean they want to leave the United States for Israel, but simply that they also feel strongly about the need to support Israel as a plank of U.S. foreign policy and are willing to argue for that policy. Or taking another example, we can look at the impact of the large number of Cuban émigrés who have settled in Florida. They might see themselves as Americans—one first-generation American whose parents left Cuba, Marco Rubio, was elected to the U.S. Senate from Florida—but they also feel strongly about their Cuban identity and follow events on the island, which translates into their interpretation of U.S. foreign policy. Not only has this group of émigrés had a marked impact on the domestic politics of the United States because of the strength of their votes, but they have also influenced U.S. foreign policy toward Cuba.

And the United States is not unique in this regard. Many of the former colonial powers in Europe, such as the United Kingdom, France, Belgium, the Netherlands, and Spain, not only have trade and political ties with their former colonies, but they also have relatively large immigrant populations who, if they don't directly affect the country's foreign policy, certainly affect its culture. Anyone who has traveled there has seen the large number of Indian restaurants in London or the North African restaurants found throughout Paris. Clearly, those immigrants bring with them their own cultural traditions that spill into and affect their adopted homeland in general, making it a culturally richer and more diverse place. But this also affects their sense of identity and belonging, not only to their new or adopted country, but also to what had been their home country. One of the benefits of a democratic form of government is the belief that these various identities are not contradictory.

However, this is not to suggest that assimilation of these immigrant groups into the dominant culture and society is always peaceful and/or easy. Witness the riots that broke out in France in 2007 and 2008 between immigrants from North and West Africa and the police, which in part were the result of anti-immigrant feeling. Or the anti-Muslim/anti-Arab feelings that emerged in England after the London bombings in July 2005—in a country that had previously been accepting of this group. The main point is that these groups exist *within* a larger cultural and social setting, and they are expected to conform to the norms of that larger culture. When they do not, or even a small and fringe group is perceived as not conforming, it can be threatening to the majority, and conflict can result.

One of the challenges facing all nation-states now is how to handle issues of the integration of different groups of people. Perhaps the old "melting pot" model is no longer appropriate in a globalized world, where no matter where people move internationally, they can easily retain ties to the home country, friends, family, culture, and traditions. The real issue then becomes what happens when a group's loyalty is to or their identity is with the *nation* as opposed to the state? That can lead to the growth of *nationalism*, which ultimately can lead to conflict. That has important implications for international relations.

Nationalism and Conflict

Nationalism can be defined as the promotion of national identity to the exclusion of other identities. It promotes the common characteristics of the group and allegiance to that group. In short, nationalism moves beyond patriotism (loyalty to the nation-state) to promote commitment to one's own group over others, including the broader interests of the state. This also alerts us to the fact that as students of international relations, it is important to look *within* the state if we are really going to understand the origins or root causes of intrastate civil conflict.

Nationalism is often tied to the principle of *self-determination*, which suggests that the peoples of a nation have the right to form a state and therefore to have control over their own affairs. But in this idea is an inherent theoretical conflict. If states are sovereign entities (a notion that goes back to the Treaty of Westphalia), then how can a group of people *within* the state declare themselves to be independent and able to make rules that govern only themselves?

Tied directly to this conundrum and to the idea of self-determination is the concept of *territory*. When the claim of nationhood is contested within a state, then who has primacy over the territory within which the "nation" resides? To address this, we can bring together different theoretical models or approaches, although none can really explain or address all sets of circumstances.

For example, the realists look at the international system as inherently an-archic, and as such, there are few rules as to how to deal with competing claims over territory. Therefore, in realist thinking, war will inevitably break out as a way to settle the dispute, and the group that is more powerful will win. By that logic, the conflicting claims that both Israel (a formal nation-state) and Palestine (a nation or stateless people) have to the land known as "Palestine" will inevitably lead to war, as there is no other way to settle the claim to the contested territory except by military might. The realist ap-proach would argue that there is no single system-level arbiter that these groups can turn to in order to resolve this conflict, nor can they really negoti-ate directly—especially since the role of the Palestinians, who do not have a state, does not fit neatly into the model of international relations, which pre-sumes that contact will always be state-to-state.

The liberal theorists would approach the issue differently. Initially, liberals would say that there are viable alternatives to settling disputes beyond war. The liberals especially would argue that the two sets of actors (Palestinians and Israel) *can* negotiate to see whether it might be possible to settle their dispute peacefully by beginning with what they might have in common, rather than their differences. Here the role of individuals can be important. For example, there are grassroots groups such as Women in Black, which started in 1988 when ten Israeli women held a vigil in Jerusalem to protest Israel's occupation of the West Bank and Gaza and to show their solidarity with the Palestinian people. As the movement spread, it started to incorpo-rate Palestinian as well as Israeli women, who were united by a common cause.[18] In this case, then, what started as a small group of women grew to encompass individuals around the world who have joined together to work for peace and justice and against violence. While this might not carry much weight officially nor influence government policy, it can draw public atten-tion to the issue, thereby building pressure on the government to settle the conflict.

At a more macro and official government level, working to settle the con-flict can be done by direct negotiations, or there can be a mediator or neutral third party involved, as we have seen so often in the Arab/Palestinian–Israeli case. In that case, the role of the mediator would be to hear each side's posi-tion and see if there is any common ground upon which they can build.

It was that mediation process that was used to arrive at the agreement that became known as the Camp David Accords, signed in September 1978 be-tween enemies Egypt and Israel. Mediated by the United States under the

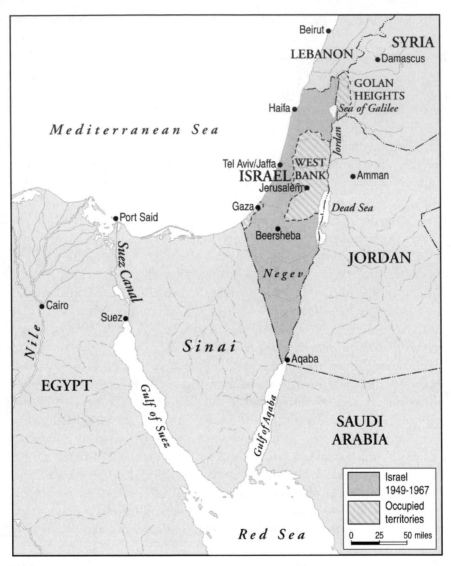

MAP 4.1
Israel's Borders, 2010

direction of then president Jimmy Carter, the result was the first major peace agreement between Israel and an Arab state (Egypt), and resulted in the resolution of the disputed territory of the Sinai, which Israel had taken in 1967 following the Six-Day War. In that case, consistent with liberal ideas, resolution was possible because of cooperation between the two countries, albeit with U.S. mediation, and because both countries saw peace as in their national interest. This confluence of views allowed both countries to arrive at an agreement that was consistent with the priorities of the members of the groups within the country, thereby ensuring support for the agreement both within and outside the country. However, not all within Egypt were pleased with the outcome. The then president of Egypt, Anwar Sadat, was assassinated in October 1981 by a group of fundamentalist officers who were opposed to his policies. Although the long-term international impact of the agreement was peace between Israel and Egypt, it cost the president his life and created rifts between the more fundamentalist members of the population and those who wanted peace. And there were groups within Egypt who similarly felt that it had given up too much in order to achieve an agreement. In the long term, however, the relationship between the two countries has been peaceful.

Intractable Conflicts

In some cases, a conflict is so intractable and deep seated that the issue of the disputed territory cannot be resolved by mediation or negotiation. The example of Jerusalem, a city claimed as sacred by all three monotheistic religions, is a case in point. Since both Israel and the Palestinians lay claim to the city as part of their dispute over land, and each feels that it has a legitimate right to Jerusalem, peaceful resolution seems impossible in this case. Further complicating the possibility of resolution is the fact that the Palestinians see Jerusalem as the capital of a future Palestinian state. Hence, here we have issues of self-determination and territory coming together.

What follows are three cases of these types of deep-seated intractable conflicts that are the result of nations seeking self-determination or statehood. Since all three are perceived as threatening the sovereignty of at least one existing state, resolution seems difficult if not impossible. There are many other examples of territorial disputes that are tied to nationalism and the desire for self-determination. This issue will also come up again when we talk about stateless peoples in chapter 5.

The Kurds

The case of the Kurds stands as one example of this type of conflict between nation and, in this case, a number of states. The Kurdish people share
a common language, culture, and so on, and increasingly support the creation of an independent state of Kurdistan. But as a people, they can be
found in parts of Turkey and Iraq primarily, but also in Iran and Syria. Each
of the states in which there is a significant Kurdish population refuses to give
up any part of its territory in order to create such a state, which they see as a
violation of their own sovereignty. This resistance became even more apparent with the uprising that became a civil war in Syria, where Syrian Kurds
have been fighting with the rebels against President Bashar al-Assad's government. Part of the rationale for their fighting is the hope of creating an autonomous Kurdish region in Syria as a step toward the creation of an

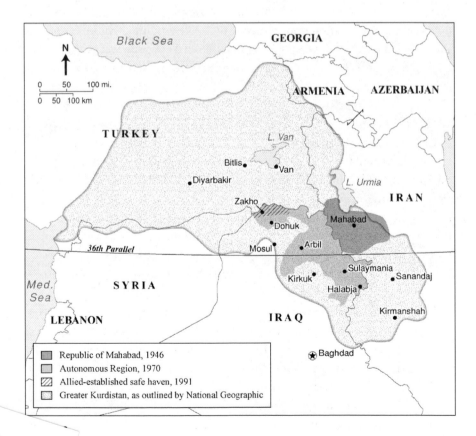

egions, 1946–Present

independent state of Kurdistan. But, as noted in one newspaper account, that hope "threatens to draw a violent reaction from those other nations [Iraq, Turkey, and Iran]. They have signaled a willingness to take *extreme actions* to prevent the loss of territory to a greater Kurdistan" (emphasis added).[19]

Within Iraq, the Kurds, who were brutally massacred under Saddam Hussein in an act of genocide, have been able or been allowed to maintain a degree of autonomy since the fall of Hussein in 2003. The Iraqi constitution of 2005 recognizes Iraqi Kurdistan as a federal region within Iraq, and it recognizes Kurdish as an official language of Iraq. Despite what appears to be a resolution of the issue, tensions remain over issues of borders and governance outside the formal boundaries of Iraqi Kurdistan, especially in Turkey. Turkey does not want to cede any of its territory to create a country of Kurdistan, and any movement in that direction is perceived by Turkey as a threat to its sovereignty and territory. Thus, while the situation appears to have been stabilized in Iraq, it remains far from resolved in Turkey. The Kurds' quest for self-determination at best and recognition of its identity within Turkey at a minimum has manifested as a low-level conflict with Kurdish guerilla forces, known as the PKK (Kurdistan Workers' Party), which was founded in 1974.

The issue of the Kurds and how they should be treated and recognized is not a new one, as the Kurdish people pre-dated the drawing of the current national boundaries that divided up the group. That situation becomes even more complicated when a semiautonomous group declares itself independent of its host state and seeks to create a new state. That is the situation both Iraq and Turkey fear about the Kurds, and it is the situation that we see with Kosovo.

Kosovo

Kosovo was an autonomous province of Serbia. Although it was under Serb control, the majority of the population was Albanian, and the Yugoslav constitution of 1974 granted this area the equivalent of republic status. It was made clear that although the area was not independent and sovereign, until the early 1980s it had a great deal of freedom. For example, Kosovo had its own political assembly, controlled banks and schools in the region, and was fairly free to set its own policies. By the late 1980s, the Serbs had restricted Kosovo's freedom considerably. Under Serbian leader Slobodan Milošević, who was an ardent Serb nationalist, the situation in Kosovo grew increasingly repressive. The increasing repression and apparent human rights violations

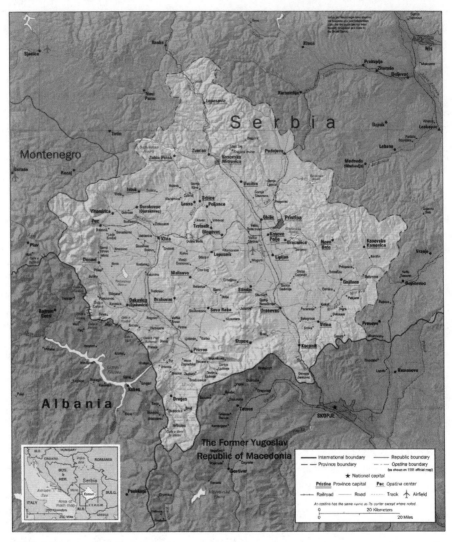

MAP 4.3
Serbia and Kosovo. *Source:* Central Intelligence Agency

finally caught the attention of the world, leading ultimately to the NATO
decision to take action against Serbia. NATO bombings lasted eleven weeks,
between March and May 1999, and resulted in a negotiated settlement. Ultimately NATO deployed peacekeeping troops to the area.

In June 1999, the United Nations passed a resolution that granted Kosovo
autonomy within the Federal Republic of Yugoslavia. Elections subsequently

took place, and a new government was created in that area. Then in February 2008, Kosovo declared its independence from Serbia. The United States, the UK, Germany, and other European countries quickly recognized Kosovo as a sovereign state. However, other countries, such as Russia and China, considered the declaration of independence illegal and would not recognize the country. Each of these countries, which has its own issues with minority groups seeking independence and self-determination, saw recognition for Kosovo as establishing a dangerous precedent that could ultimately be a threat to their own sovereignty.

In October 2008, the UN General Assembly requested that the International Court of Justice render an advisory opinion about Kosovo's declaration of statehood. On July 22, 2010, the court found that because there is no international law preventing declarations of independence, Kosovo's formal declaration of independence from Serbia in 2008 "did not violate general international law."[20] Under terms of international law, recognition by one hundred countries is required for full statehood; as of June 2012, ninety-one countries had recognized Kosovo.

As suggested above, the international ruling is very threatening to a number of existing countries. Russia, China, Spain, and other countries in which there are existing separatist movements refuse to acknowledge Kosovo's independence, seeing this as setting a dangerous precedent. By virtue of that, the ruling by the UN court in The Hague is bound to cause great consternation and possibly conflict within countries trying to preserve their territorial integrity and sovereignty in the face of resistant populations.

> Although the ruling is nonbinding, it is bound to give legal encouragement to Chechens, Kurds, Basques, Tibetans, and a host of other peoples from Africa to Asia seeking to break out on their own. Those countries include international heavyweights such as China and Russia, smaller democracies such as Spain, Greece, and Romania, and regions like the Middle East, where many of the Kurds who live in multiple countries want to form a single "Kurdistan."[21]

Russia and South Ossetia

The conflict between Russia and Georgia that broke out in August 2008 over the status of the republic of South Ossetia is another example of conflict between issues of sovereignty and the recognition of independent states that grew directly out of the Kosovo question. Both South Ossetia and Abkha are semiautonomous provinces of Georgia, a former republic of the old Soviet Union. Early in 2008, both requested that Russia recognize them as sovereign states. When Georgia moved to assert its authority over them, Russia came to their defense in opposition to Georgia, leading to a conflict between Georgia and Russia. Although the conflict ended, the situation between the two countries remains tense.

What these examples illustrate clearly is how difficult issues of self-determination are for the international system because they deal directly with sovereignty and the supremacy of the nation-state, two inviolate principles of international relations. Furthermore, they are extremely difficult to resolve, with tensions often festering for years. They also show how nationhood can conflict with the concept of nation-state. The end result can be armed conflict.

Ethnic Conflict

Nationalism can contribute to conflict in other ways. The concept of ethnic conflict is tied directly to the issue of nationalism. In countries in which there are a number of ethnic groups—nations—a leader often emerges who encourages the supremacy of one group at the expense of another. This can be carried to an extreme and has led to what we now call *ethnic cleansing*, or the systematic extermination of one ethnic group by another (i.e., genocide), often with the approval and support of the state. This is extremely difficult for the countries in the international system, since the issue pits the sovereignty of one state against the need to protect a group against human rights violations and, at its most extreme, genocide.

It was ethnic conflict that ripped former Yugoslavia apart, with Serbs, Croats, and Bosnian Muslims engaged in war over the area of Bosnia-Herzegovina. In this case, the ethnic cleansing was encouraged by nationalist leaders (Slobodan Milošević in Serbia, proclaiming the need for a "Greater Serbia," and Franjo Tudjman in Croatia), and it was directed primarily against the Bosnian Muslims.[22]

This can also be seen in Rwanda, where approximately 800,000 people were massacred in about a hundred days between April and June 1994. In Rwanda, the hatred against Tutsis had been building for decades and finally exploded in April 1994, following the death of Rwandan president Juvenal Habyarimana, a Hutu, when his plane was shot down above Kigali airport.

The blame for the rocket attack was placed on a Tutsi rebel leader, and within hours, the genocide started and quickly spread.[23]

There are other examples of such ethnic conflict and genocide, which seems to have become more commonplace. One of the ironies of ethnic conflict, though, is that often there is no ethnic difference between the groups. For example, in the case of Rwanda, "the two ethnic groups are actually very similar—they speak the same language, inhabit the same areas and follow the same traditions."[24]

In former Yugoslavia, Serbs, Croats, and Bosnian Muslims are ethnically the same, although their religions vary. Serbs tend to be Eastern Orthodox, Croats Catholic, and Bosnian Muslims obviously are Muslim. Yet the war in Yugoslavia was not about religion but about nationality commingled with "ethnicity." What that tells us is that often a conflict is attributed to one thing, such as religion or ethnicity, but there are other factors that actually are equally if not more important. So we must really look within the country in order to understand the full set of circumstances related to a civil conflict.

Northern Ireland: Religious Conflict?

Northern Ireland is an example of ongoing violent civil conflict that seems to have its root in religious differences. But in many ways, calling it a conflict between Catholics and Protestants becomes a shorthand that summarizes a host of other issues that really are at the heart of the divide between the two groups. Limiting it to a religious conflict also obscures some of the issues that would help us explain civil conflict in general: economic and political inequalities, issues of power, and what Johann Galtung would call "structural violence."[25] For example, the Protestants generally are tied to Great Britain and want to remain part of the UK. Historically, the Protestants, with their ties to England, were also the privileged group, and they were the land- and business-owners as well as the members of the government. As the land- and property-owners, they could discriminate against the Catholics. In contrast to the Protestants, the Catholics, who were tied politically to the independent Republic of Ireland, suffered economically. They were often discriminated against in housing and education, and they were not able to gain power politically. The root of "the troubles" that divided Northern Ireland from the 1960s until the signing of the Belfast (Good Friday) Agreement in April 1998 was economic and political as well as religious. The reality is that all three factors intertwined to work against the Catholics, who sought power through violence.

The lesson here is that when we try to understand the roots of violent civil conflict, we often have to look deep within the state if we are to really identify all the factors involved.

The Importance of Looking at Culture and Society

These cases all serve to remind us why it is important to look within the nation-state and to focus on the "nation" (culture and society), if we are really going to get a complete understanding of why a nation-state behaves the way in which it does. Especially since the end of the Cold War, we have seen a decline in the number of major wars but an increase in violent national, ethnic, and civil conflicts. If we are to understand the origins of those conflicts, we need to look at the cultural and social issues that exist within the nation-state as a whole.

The realists would claim that the decline in major wars within the international system is the result of the security commitment of the United States and its emergence as a global hegemon that has kept other countries in check. They would also argue that although we are seeing the emergence of other major powers, such as China, there is no conflict between the hegemons. Rather, each is asserting its presence in different places and parts of the world, so there is no conflict.[26]

The liberals argue that the decline in major interstate war is the result, at least in part, of the growth of democracies that are unlikely to go to war against one another (democratic peace). Not only are democracies less likely to go to war against one another, but the fact that they generally have capitalist economic systems and that they trade with one another means that they are also more economically interdependent. This too suggests that they are less likely to engage in war with one another.

The constructivists would claim that the relative decline in major war is due to a change in the predominant values of decision makers and the people within the nation from those that support war as a means of settling disputes to those that promote ideals of peace, as well as understanding that countries do not need to compete for material advantage. But this certainly does not explain the increase in intrastate war.

While the major theoretical approaches could all provide some explanation for the decrease in major wars, how well can they also explain the increase in civil wars? As noted above, the realists would simply argue that this is just another manifestation of the conflict for power. Different groups within the state all seek to maximize their power and position, even if that comes at the expense of another group. Marxists would attribute the growth of civil wars to economic inequities and to the desire of one group (the oppressed or less fortunate) to overturn the existing power balances. Liberals and neoliberals would probably argue that the growth of these wars is the result of failures of institutions and cooperative approaches, and the constructivists would similarly look at the failures of the structures that would otherwise have held these aggressive tendencies in check.

So in understanding the increase in the incidence of civil wars, one can look at the reasons as being the inherent competitive nature of the leaders, or the failures of the state and national structures that would emphasize cooperation among groups rather than facilitate conflict. But the important lesson is that in trying to get an answer to questions like why there is ethnic violence, or why there is conflict between groups within a country, it is important to look within the country at the various actors involved, their priorities and expectations, what the distribution of power actually is, and who is making the decisions.

It is also possible to examine this question from a broader levels-of-analysis perspective. For example, in focusing within the state on the emergence of national groups and the concomitant rise in nationalism, are we overlooking the possibility that we are witnessing the diminishment of the state as a major actor in international relations? As Charles Tilly notes, the state was born from war, and the growth of civil conflicts might mean that the militarized state carries within it the seeds of its own destruction.[27]

Regardless of which theoretical perspective seems most appealing, or how one would interpret the rise in conflicts as a lesson about the role of the nation-state, all would suggest at least some need to look within the country and understand the predominant cultures as well as the role and perspectives of the individual decision makers. It is to this last and most micro level of analysis that we will turn now.

THE ROLE OF THE INDIVIDUAL

We have been talking a lot about what goes on within the state and the role of government, culture, and society in order to understand some big questions in international relations pertaining to conflict. But one of the other

critical variables tied to understanding international relations, and particularly the behavior of any nation-state, is the individual or individuals who
actually make the decisions that affect foreign policy decision making. To do
this, we need to ask ourselves how much influence any individual has. What
gives these individuals power? Does a single individual really make a difference?

Here we need to distinguish between the individual decision maker, the
"average" person, and truly outstanding individuals, such as Nelson Mandela
in South Africa or Mahatma Gandhi in India. What about someone like now
deceased Mu'ammar Gadhafi in Libya or Hugo Chávez in Venezuela? Each of
them was a strong leader who directly influenced the policies of his country.
But Gadhafi was overthrown by his own people, and in 2012–2013, Chávez
faced a previously unheard-of election challenge, an election he won despite
being seriously ill at the time. How does an individual get—and keep—that
kind of power? And what changes could threaten that power?

Or let's put it another way: How much was Mikhail Gorbachev responsible for the end of the Cold War or the fall of the Soviet Union? Or what role
did Solidarity leader Lech Wałęsa play in leading to a change in the government of Poland, which in turn became a model for other Eastern European
countries' rebellions against Soviet domination? In all these cases, what we
are really asking is: What role did the individual play? Or how did the political and/or structural factors within the country and the changing international environment *coupled with* the role of a particular individual at that
particular time result in major change? Is it the individual alone who makes
the difference, or a strong and powerful leader who emerges when the environment is already starting to change, thereby providing a context for him
or her to facilitate change? These are difficult and important questions that
ask us to think about the role of an individual, but also to place that individual into a larger context if we are truly to understand the changes that have
taken place within a culture/society/government/nation-state.

The example of Gorbachev is especially interesting. The end of the Cold
War has been attributed to President Ronald Reagan's hard-line rhetoric,
which pushed an already significantly diminished Soviet Union to the brink.
Yet, when he was questioned about the role that he played in facilitating the
end of the Cold War, Reagan referred to himself as "a supporting actor."
According to one account, when Reagan was asked at a press conference who
deserved the credit for the changes in the Soviet Union that ultimately led to

the end of the Cold War, he replied, "Mr. Gorbachev deserves most of the credit, as the leader of this country."[28] The reality is that a number of factors came together at the right time to bring about an end to the Cold War, but both Reagan and Gorbachev were receptive to the ideological as well as political changes that affected both their countries.

For his part, Gorbachev had a broader understanding of the West than had previous leaders of the Soviet Union, and he saw Europe and Russia as sharing a common home. He articulated his ideas about *glasnost* (openness) and *perestroika* (economic restructuring away from a command economy) in his book *Perestroika*, which was readily available in the West.[29] And these ideas affected the direction in which he took the Soviet Union.

Reagan, in turn, was receptive to Gorbachev's ideas and was willing to work with him on implementing new policies.

> Reagan believed that a change in the direction of the Soviet Union would be in the best interests of the United States and therefore modified his own approach over time, becoming less "cold warrior" and more the diplomat whose primary goal was to encourage Gorbachev to continue down the road he had chosen. Doing this required *personal contact*, and *the two leaders met periodically to outline areas of common interest*. Reagan was so successful that by the time his administration ended, the Cold War was on a course to its inevitable end. (emphasis added)[30]

Thus, not only did the individual matter, but it was because of meetings between these two individual leaders that trust was established, leading to political change.

And if one is looking at this major change in policy through "gender-sensitive lenses," some insight can be gained by looking at the impact of both Raisa Gorbachev and Nancy Reagan, who each played important behind-the-scenes roles in influencing their husbands. Although each was, on the surface, a traditional wife, they played a part in the historical events unfolding.[31]

The important point here is that an individual can play an important role in influencing the direction of a country's policy and, in this case, of the international system. However, that individual can be helped considerably by other factors, especially the structures within which the leader acts. Within any given country, these might include the role of the military, an organized opposition (or lack thereof), the economy, and so on—all of which can either contribute to continued stability and legitimacy of an existing government or work in opposition to defy or even overthrow the individual leader.

In addition, as seen with the above example of Raisa Gorbachev and Nancy Reagan, an individual does not have to be the critical decision maker in order to have an impact on a country or even international politics. For example, feminist author Cynthia Enloe in her book *Bananas, Beaches, and Bases* notes:

> In the 1930s Hollywood moguls turned Brazilian singer Carmen Miranda into an American movie star. They were trying to aid President Franklin Roosevelt's efforts to promote friendlier relations between the US and Latin America. When United Fruit executives then drew on Carmen Miranda's popular Latinized female image to create a logo for their imported bananas, they were trying to construct a new, intimate relationship between American housewives and a multinational plantation company. With her famous fruited hats and vivacious screen presence, Carmen Miranda was used by American men to reshape international relations.[32]

Hence, in this case, Enloe would argue that an individual (Carmen Miranda) had a direct impact on international relations through symbolism, even if she was not a decision maker. But that symbolism played an important role in furthering U.S. policy interests.

But how representative is this case? How much does an individual influence the course of international politics? The individual level of analysis reflects the perceptions of individuals and the choices that they then make. Generally, this refers to leaders, who are in the best position to make decisions that influence international events. But as we have seen with the uprisings of the Arab Spring, individual citizens can have an impact, as can military leaders, people who can influence decision makers (such as lobbyists and members of various interest groups), and even the "ordinary" voter. But in thinking about the individual level, it is also important to remember that it is often difficult to pinpoint the exact impact that any one person has had. According to political scientists Paul Viotti and Mark Kauppi, "While individuals can have a tremendous impact on the short-term course of world events . . . it is extremely difficult to identify such individuals after their impact has been felt." In fact, they argue, "most people who want to influence

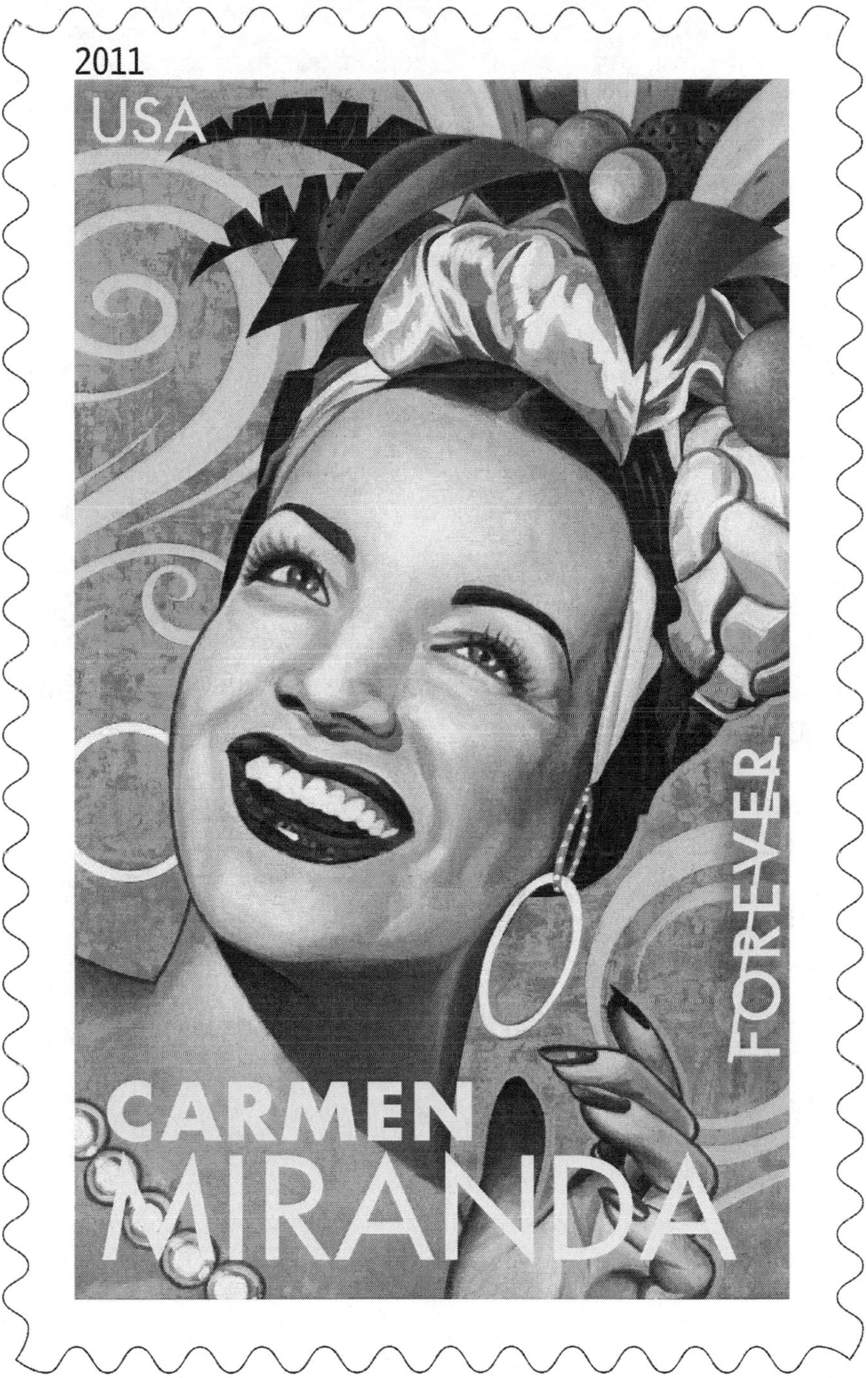

FIGURE 4.1

Carmen Miranda as a symbol. © 2011 United States Postal Service. All Rights Reserved. Used with Permission.

world politics do so in an indirect manner through collective actors such as states."[33]

The fact is that although we speak of "nation-states" and "governments" and "societies" and "cultures," all of these are collectives of individuals. States do not make the decision to go to war; the individuals within the government do. It is for this reason that political scientists argue that every international event ultimately is the result of decisions made by individuals. And most individuals, regardless of how powerful they are, still operate within and are subject to the constraints of the organization or government or structures of which they are a part.

Decision Maker as Rational Actor

When we do focus on the individual as decision maker, or on any individual who makes a decision that has some effect on a government, it is important to ask to what extent these decisions are *rational*. That means asking whether the decision was based on a logical process that includes an assessment and ranking of choices, understanding of the costs and benefits of the options, and review of alternatives before arriving at a final conclusion. In international relations, we make the assumption that decision makers will act rationally and that rationality will be reflected in their choices. This may—or may not—be a correct assumption, and it draws heavily on realist thinking. But simplifying the otherwise complex decision-making process in this way allows us to explain in general terms why a particular action was taken or a decision made.

In chapter 2 we talked about the importance of theory because it helps us describe, explain, and predict. The only way in which we can describe what happened and explain why it happened so that we can anticipate future events is to simplify reality. Similarly, when we talk about decision making, it is a complex undertaking that has many component parts. Hence, if we really are ever going to understand that complexity, we need to simplify it. Starting with the assumption of the rational actor is one way in which we can do so.

What is important to note is that decision makers are each distinct individuals who have differing beliefs, values, and unique personalities. Therefore, the decisions that they make are the result of their own experiences, belief systems, intellectual capabilities, personal styles, and so on. And here both liberal and constructivist theoretical approaches play a role. While national decisions are constrained by the political system and by precedent, there is also room for any individual to make his or her own mark. For example, you can ask yourself whether the outcome regarding the response to 9/11 would have been the same if Al Gore had been president in 2001 instead of George W. Bush. We know what the outcomes of President Bush's decisions were. But Gore would have approached the attacks differently, since he had different experiences as both vice president and a long-serving member of the Congress than Bush did who, before become president, had been governor of Texas and a businessman. In other words, how did the experience that each had affect the way in which he would have responded or did respond to this event?

But looking at decision makers as unique individuals also raises questions about the assumption of the rational decision maker, as every decision will be affected by the decision maker's own perceptions or (perhaps more important) misperceptions. Every person is selective in his or her perceptions, screening experiences and information, often drawing on those that are most consistent with his or her own existing beliefs. But the role of the decision maker is to filter the information received in order to arrive at a decision that also builds in bias. "*Information screens* are subconscious filters through which people put the information coming in from the world around them. Often they simply ignore any information that does not fit their expectations."[34] Thus, most decision makers will look for information or even "evidence" that supports what they already believe. Clearly, this will also change the outcome of any decision. Nor would all decision makers in the same set of circumstances do the same thing, because they would filter everything through their own information screen.

In terms of foreign policy decision making, what this means is that information can and will be screened as it passes from person to person. Remember the old game of "Telephone," in which one person whispers a secret to the next person, who passes it on to the next person, and so on? By the time it gets to the end of the chain, it is a totally different statement than the one that started. Similarly, when dealing with interpretation of events regarding other countries and cultures, not only do we have to deal with information screens and perceptions, but also with translation and cultural issues that can further skew or bias the information that is needed in order to make the decision. And of course, they will also affect the interpretation of any decision that is made.

But these are not the only biases or issues that can affect a decision maker and therefore a decision. There are also *affective biases*—that is, the impact of emotions. Regardless of how dispassionate or rational decision makers try to be, they will be affected by strong feelings that they have about the circumstances under which the decision has to be made and/or the person or state the decision will affect. This stands in contrast to *cognitive biases*, or "systematic distortions of rational calculations based not on emotional feelings but simply on the limitations of the human brain in making choices."[35] For example, individual decision makers will want to construct models that are consistent with their beliefs, so that they can reduce cognitive dissonance. This can lead a decision maker to make a decision on a goal or outcome that he or she has a greater chance of achieving, rather than a more grandiose or larger goal that, realistically, is unattainable. No decision maker wants to engage in an action that is likely to fail, nor to admit failure about any policy decision that he or she has made.

Here the work of political scientist Robert Jervis is important, because he not only warns us about the dangers or misperceptions that a decision maker will have, but he also recommends "safeguards" that can be followed by any decision maker who is aware of the possible dangers in decision making that come from biases and expectations.[36] Specifically, Jervis asks,

> Can anything then be said to scholars and decision-makers other than "Avoid being either too open or too closed, but be especially aware of the latter danger"? Although decision-makers will always be faced with ambiguous and confusing evidence and will be forced to make inferences about others which will often be inaccurate, a number of safeguards may be suggested which could enable them to minimize their errors.[37]

That is where the safeguards come in. To a student of international relations, this makes a great deal of sense. For example, in his first safeguard, Jervis notes that "decision-makers should be aware that they do not make 'unbiased' interpretations of each new bit of information, but rather are inevitably heavily influenced by the theories they expect to be verified." Jervis ultimately concludes that knowing their biases and how information is interpreted through these biases "should lead decision-makers to examine more closely evidence that others believe contradicts their views."[38] Or to put it another way, it is incumbent upon decision-makers to look at all points of view. Another safeguard would be to ask whether decision-makers' attitudes are consistent and logical, and whether they are based on evidence versus belief. All told, Jervis identifies five areas of possible danger, and the safeguards that can be used to guard against falling into those traps.[39]

But what a student of international relations also knows and understands about foreign policy decision-making is that analyzing the decisions after the fact is very different from the process that a decision maker actually goes through in order to make a decision while she or he is in office. We cannot always know what went on in the mind of any decision maker, nor whether she or he fell into any of the possible traps. This is especially true when decisions are made in times of crisis, when they have to be made quickly and a host of other variables come into play.

What all this tells us is that despite our attempts to arrive at the most rational models of decision making, there are a host of irrational and intangible factors that go into the making of a foreign policy decision *whether the decision maker is aware of them or not.* As students of international relations, if we really are to understand the decisions that are made, at the individual level we need to know who made the decision, something about his or background that might have influenced the decision, the circumstances surrounding the decision (e.g., crisis decision making or not), who else was involved with the decision-making process, and any other information that will provide insight into the variables and factors surrounding the decision. And we do this while holding the other levels constant—that is, we focus on one level at a time.

Crisis Decision Making: The Cuban Missile Crisis

The Cuban missile crisis stands as one of the best examples of foreign policy decision making under crisis circumstances. It is also a case where the situation can best be explained by looking at multiple levels of analysis. Taking place in October 1962 in the midst of the Cold War, it was one of the most dangerous confrontations, when the two superpowers were said to be "eyeball to eyeball."[40]

Graham Allison, who studied and wrote about the Cuban missile crisis, also reminds us that there are a range of approaches that can be used to explain the events that transpired and why, and that these can be found across a number of levels of analysis. His models, initially articulated in an article in the *American Political Science Review* and then developed further in his classic book *The Essence of Decision*, illustrate what he calls "alternative explanations of the same happening,"[41] which reminds us of the importance of looking at a range of explanations and how various models may be interrelated, all of which can contribute to our understanding of an event.

As the situation started to unfold, it evolved relatively quickly, and President John F. Kennedy, who was still recovering from an embarrassing foreign policy defeat in 1961 at the Bay of Pigs in Cuba, assembled a group of advisers around him to discuss what should be done about the missiles that the Soviet Union was deploying to Cuba, ninety miles off the Florida coast. The group of about twenty advisers, who became known as EXCOMM (for "executive committee") were members of the National Security Council and close advisers to the president, and included the secretaries of state and defense, Attorney General Robert Kennedy, the director of the CIA, the chairman of the Joint Chiefs of Staff, and others Kennedy trusted. Meeting regularly, the group charted the course that ultimately led to a peaceful resolution of the crisis and withdrawal of the Soviet missiles from Cuba. But what was most important was that the event was a turning point in the Cold War. No longer was Kennedy perceived as a young and inexperienced president, but as one who was able to face down the Soviet Union and win.

It was thirty years later, in 1992, when there was a conference in Havana that brought together former U.S., Soviet, and Cuban officials to explore the circumstances of the event in retrospect, when former secretary of defense Robert McNamara revealed that "the two nations [the United States and the Soviet Union] were much closer to nuclear conflict than previously realized."[42] McNamara also disclosed that he had learned at that conference that Soviet officials "had sent Havana short-range nuclear weapons and that Soviet commanders there were authorized to use them in the event of American invasion. . . . The short-range nuclear weapons were in addition to medium-range nuclear weapons that would have required authorization from Moscow to use." Given the new information, McNamara concluded that "the actions of all three parties were shaped by *misjudgments*, *miscalculations* and *misinformation*," and that "in a nuclear age, such mistakes could be disastrous" (emphasis added).[43]

As we talk about the role of individuals in foreign policy decision making, we have to ask about the Cuban missile crisis how the decisions were made and what happened, now that we know how close the world really was to nuclear catastrophe. Clearly, we have to begin with the role of President Kennedy, the individual decision maker who was a relatively new president and had already experienced a number of foreign policy failures, both in Cuba with the Bay of Pigs and also in Europe. The result of the confrontation between Kennedy and Soviet leader Nikita Khrushchev was the building of the Berlin Wall. Kennedy was also dealing with an insurrection in Southeast Asia that was escalating. So the missile crisis emerged amid a climate of confrontation between the United States and communist countries, most notably the Soviet Union, and the president had to make decisions relatively quickly.

In assessing the situation, Kennedy made sure that he had carefully chosen close advisers he could depend on. But this too carried certain dangers. First, we have to understand the psychology of *groupthink*, which clearly came into play. As articulated by Irving Janus, who studied the impact of this phenomenon on foreign policy decisions, the concept refers to "a psychological drive for consensus at any cost that suppresses dissent and appraisal of alternatives in cohesive decision making groups."[44] In this case, all were trusted advisers of President Kennedy who were pulled together as the crisis unfolded to try to arrive at a solution. They met intensively for days to arrive at a decision. Kennedy, aware of the potential problems associated with groupthink, periodically left the room to allow his advisers to have more open discussion. They finally arrived at a range of possible options, from doing nothing to invading Cuba, and settled on a naval blockade as the preferred option. In retrospect, this led to a desirable outcome from the perspective of the United States. But the episode stands as an excellent example of the issues associated with crisis decision making.

In addition to the dangers of groupthink, another point about crisis decision making is that the crisis situation itself alters the process by which decisions are made. The fact that the situation is perceived as critical, with the need for decisions to be made quickly, means that decisions will be made based on the information available at the time, even if it later proves to be incorrect, which was the case here. The time constraints also weigh in, for it means that decision makers will not screen information as carefully as they might otherwise, or they will discard information that is not consistent with their beliefs. Unlike the assumptions we mentioned above for rational actors, in times of crisis, choices might be limited, rather than all options being explored.

Further, the decision makers are affected by the stress of the situation, which further can cloud their rational judgment. In a classic *conflict spiral*, the decision makers often overestimate the hostility and intentions of the adversary, while underestimating their own hostility toward the adversary. Since so much of decision making depends on the perceptions of the individuals making the decisions, this too tends to alter the options that appear to be available.

As the situation unfolded over those few weeks in October, President Kennedy and his advisers arrived at a plan to place a naval blockade around the island of Cuba. Through back-channel negotiations, the situation was finally resolved peacefully, but not without an escalation of tension and the perception that the world was poised on the brink of nuclear catastrophe.

From a levels-of-analysis perspective, the three nation-state actors were the United States, the Soviet Union, and Cuba. But in this case, it is what happened *within* the nation-state level that is most critical. It was Kennedy (the individual) and his close advisers who made the decisions, with communication between the United States and the Soviet Union limited to discussions among a few trusted advisers on both sides. Government involvement was limited to the members of EXCOMM, most of whom represented the major executive agencies. There was little congressional involvement.

The public (culture/society) was kept informed through the media, but also through speeches made by Kennedy specifically to ensure the ongoing support and cooperation of the public, as well as to reassure them that he was in command of the situation. As noted in a press release from the Kennedy Library, the "public phase covered barely a week (October 22–28, 1962) . . . [and] is one of the key defining events of the Cold War in general and of John F. Kennedy's presidency in particular."[45] In assessing public opinion during and reactions to the missile crisis, the study commissioned by the Kennedy Library found that "similar to responses to other foreign crises both before and since, the Cuban missile crisis drew the country together as people rallied around the president. Presidential approval rose 13 to 15 percentage points, and the public backed the blockade and President Kennedy's resolve to have the offensive missiles removed." The study also found that following the peaceful resolution of the crisis, the public indicated lower fear of nuclear war than it had prior to the event. Thus, although the public was anxious and paid close attention to what was going on, "the public was neither traumatized nor paralyzed by events." And the public saw foreign policy as the most important area for evaluating Kennedy's presidency.[46]

The pattern seen in terms of public support for the president in times of crisis is a pattern that has been replicated in other crisis situations and is often referred to as the "rally-round-the-flag syndrome."[47] Similarly, the fact that the crisis itself galvanized the public has become an established pattern. The author of the Kennedy Library report in fact draws parallels between the missile crisis and the September 11 attacks, noting that

> they were both events of enormous importance that involved a clear and present danger to the country, galvanized the populace, and propelled the political leadership into decided and forceful action. . . . The American people . . . absorbed the shock, backed their leaders, and carried on with their lives. This may be the hallmark of the American people in times of greatest challenge.[48]

And, one can argue, the individual decision maker and those with whom he or she consults during a time of crisis could not do the job without the support of the public, at least not in a democracy.

In the case of the missile crisis, despite all the things that could possibly go wrong when we look at decision making in general and crisis decision making in particular, the situation was resolved peacefully. But it has become an excellent example of decision making, and why foreign policy decision making can be so difficult.[49]

SUMMARY

In this chapter we looked within the nation-state in order to understand how the range of internal factors—the government or political system, society and culture, and the individual—affect international relations and the decisions that are made by one country that affect another. What we learned is that one or all of these factors can have an impact on a nation-state's decisions about any number of factors that are relevant in international relations: going to war; how to avoid or, if it becomes necessary, respond to internal conflict; how to deal with divergent groups within the country; and how individual decision makers approach important decisions.

In the next chapter we are going to return to the macro level of the international system with a special focus on understanding nonstate actors. Although they are not explicitly included as part of the classic levels of analysis, they play an important role in affecting the international system and the nations that make up that system. And, as we will see, it is their very omission from this framework that points out one of the major weaknesses in the approach.

FURTHER READINGS

These additional readings are worth exploring and elaborate on some of the points raised in this chapter. This list is not meant to be exhaustive, but only illustrative.

Allison, Graham T. "Conceptual Models and the Cuban Missile Crisis." *American Political Science Review* 63, no. 3 (September 1969).

Doyle, Michael. "Kant's Perpetual Peace." *American Political Science Review* 80, no. 4 (December 1986).

Friedman, Thomas L. "Foreign Affairs Big Mac I." *New York Times*, December 8, 1996, http://www.nytimes.com/1996/12/08/opinion/foreign-affairs-big-mac-i.html.

Jervis, Robert. "Hypotheses on Misperception." *World Politics* 20, no. 3 (April 1968).

"Kennedy Library Releases New Report on Cuban Missile Crisis—Study Documents Impact of Crisis on American Public Opinion." October 16, 2002. http://www .jfklibrary.org/About-Us/News-and-Press/Press-Releases/Kennedy-Library-Re leases-New-Report-on-Cuban-Missile-Crisis-Study-Documents-Impact-of-Crisis-on-Amer.aspx#.

NOTES

1. Lucy Williamson, "Made in North Korea: Business in a 'Communist Monarchy,'" *BBC News Magazine*, February 12, 2012, at http://www.bbc.co.uk/news/magazine-17046941.

2. "Russia's Presidential Election: Moscow Doesn't Believe in Tears," *The Economist*, March 10, 2012, 62.

3. "Russia's Presidential Election," 62.

4. J. Ann Tickner, *Gendering World Politics: Issues and Approaches in the Post–Cold War Era* (New York: Columbia University Press, 2001), 105.

5. Tickner, *Gendering World Politics*, 96.

6. Karen A. Mingst, *Essentials of International Relations*, 4th ed. (New York: Norton, 2008), 121.

7. Immanuel Kant, "Perpetual Peace: A Philosophical Sketch," at http://www .mtholyoke.edu/acad/intrel/kant/kant1.htm.

8. Michael Doyle, "Kant's Perpetual Peace," *American Political Science Review* 80, no. 4 (1986), 1156.

9. Doyle, "Kant's Perpetual Peace," 1156.

10. Joshua S. Goldstein and Jon C. Pevehouse, *Principles of International Relations* (New York: Pearson Longman, 2009), 72.

11. Thomas L. Friedman, "Foreign Affairs Big Mac I," *New York Times*, December 8, 1996, at http://www.nytimes.com/1996/12/08/opinion/foreign-affairs-big-mac-i.html. This idea was developed still further as part of Friedman's book, *The Lexus and the Olive Tree: Understanding Globalization* (New York: Farrar, Straus & Giroux, 1999).

12. John Mueller, "Is War Still Becoming Obsolete?" paper presented at the Annual Meeting of the American Political Science Association, 1991, 2.

13. President Dwight D. Eisenhower's farewell address to the nation, January 17, 1961, at http://avalon.law.yale.edu/20th_century/eisenhower001.asp.

14. For a more complete description of the militarization of the United States, see Andrew J. Bacevich, *Washington Rules: America's Path to Permanent War* (New York: Henry Holt, 2010).

15. Mueller, "Is War Still Becoming Obsolete?" 19.

16. Tickner, *Gendering World Politics*, 104–6.

17. Tickner, *Gendering World Politics*, 106.

18. See Women in Black, official website, at http://www.womeninblack.org/en/vigil.

19. Tim Arango, "Kurds to Pursue More Autonomy in a Fallen Syria," *New York Times*, September 29, 2012.

20. "Court Settles Legal Question of Kosovo Independence, but Not the Political Issue," *Christian Science Monitor*, July 22, 2010, at http://www.csmonitor.com/layout/set/print/content/view/print/315711.

21. "Court Settles Legal Question of Kosovo Independence."

22. There are a number of sources documenting the genocide and other atrocities committed during the war in Bosnia-Herzegovina. Some that deal specifically with the acts of ethnic cleansing and the nationalist/ethnic struggle include Tom Gallagher, *The Balkans after the Cold War: From Tyranny to Tragedy* (London: Routledge, 2003); Davorak Ljubisic, *A Politics of Sorrow: The Disintegration of Yugoslavia* (Montreal: Black Rose Books, 2004); and Vjeksolav Perica, *Balkan Idols: Religion and Nationalism in Yugoslav States* (New York: Oxford University Press, 2002).

23. For a quick background see BBC News, "Rwanda: How the Genocide Happened," December 18, 2008, at http://news.bbc.co.uk/2/hi/1288230.stm. For more detailed background of the conflict see, for example, Romeo Dallaire and Samantha Power, *Shake Hands with the Devil: The Failure of Humanity in Rwanda* (New York: Carroll & Graf, 2004); and Scott Straus, *The Order of Genocide: Race, Power, and War in Rwanda* (Ithaca, NY: Cornell University Press, 2006).

24. BBC News, "Rwanda: How the Genocide Happened."

25. Johann Galtung, "Violence, Peace, and Peace Research," *Journal of Peace Research* 6, no. 3 (1969): 167–91.

26. See, for example, John Mearsheimer, *The Tragedy of Great Power Politics* (New York; Norton, 2001). In this volume, Mearsheimer, who is a quintessential realist thinker, puts U.S. foreign policy and the emergence of the United States as a great power in a broad historical context that takes into account the emergence of other major powers such as China.

27. Charles Tilly, *Coercion, Capital, and European States* (Cambridge, MA: Blackwell, 1992).

28. The quote is taken from Jack F. Matlock, *Reagan and Gorbachev: How the Cold War Ended* (New York: Random House, 2004), 302. This is an example of how an individual actor in a position of power can play an important role in affecting the direction of a particular nation-state.

29. Mikhail Gorbachev, *Perestroika: New Thinking for Our Country and the World* (New York: Random House, 2004).

30. Joyce P. Kaufman, *A Concise History of U.S. Foreign Policy*, 2nd ed. (Lanham, MD: Rowman & Littlefield, 2010), 118.

31. See Matlock, *Reagan and Gorbachev*, for a description of the role played by both women.

32. Cynthia Enloe, *Bananas, Beaches, and Bases: Making Feminist Sense of International Politics* (Berkeley: University of California Press, 2000), 1–2.

33. Paul R. Viotti and Mark V. Kauppi, *International Relations and World Politics: Security, Economy, Identity* (Upper Saddle River, NJ: Pearson Prentice Hall, 2009), 13–14.

34. Goldstein and Pevehouse, *Principles of International Relations*, 47.

35. Goldstein and Pevehouse, *Principles of International Relations*, 48.

36. See Robert Jervis, "Hypotheses on Misperception," *World Politics* 20, no. 3 (April 1968): 455–79.

37. Jervis, "Hypotheses on Misperception," 462.

38. Jervis, "Hypotheses on Misperception," 462.

39. The potential traps and possible safeguards are outlined by Jervis in "Hypotheses on Misperceptions," section 3, "Safeguards," 462–65.

40. Upon hearing that Soviet ships bearing missiles heading to Cuba had turned around at sea, then secretary of state Dean Rusk was quoted as saying, "We're eyeball to eyeball and I think the other fellow just blinked." This statement is quoted in any number of sources. The one used for this version of the quote was Max Frankel, "The President's 'Just-a-Minute Man,'" *New York Times Magazine*, September 12, 1965, at http://select.nytimes.com/gst/abstract.html?res = F10D13FC355F1A7B8EDDAB099 4D1405B858AF1D3&scp = 6&sq = Dean + Rusk%2C + %22eyeball + to + eyeball%2 C%22Cuban + Missile + Crisis&st = p.

41. Graham T. Allison, "Conceptual Models and the Cuban Missile Crisis," *American Political Science Review* 63, no. 3 (September 1969): 691. See also Graham T. Allison and Philip Zelikow, *The Essence of Decision: Explaining the Cuban Missile Crisis*, 2nd ed. (New York: Pearson, 1999).

42. Don Oberdorfer, "Cuban Missile Crisis More Volatile Than Thought," *Washington Post*, January 14, 1992.

43. Quoted in Martin Tolchin, "U.S. Underestimated Soviet Forces in Cuba during '62 Missile Crisis," *New York Times*, January 15, 1992.

44. Irving L. Janis, "Victims of Groupthink: A Psychological Study of Foreign-Policy Decisions and Fiascoes," *Abstracts of the American Psychological Association*, at http://psycnet.apa.org/index.cfm?fa = search.displayRecord&uid = 1975-29417-000 (accessed September 30, 2012).

45. "Kennedy Library Releases New Report on Cuban Missile Crisis—Study Documents Impact of Crisis on American Public Opinion," October 16, 2002, at http://www.jfklibrary.org/About-Us/News-and-Press/Press-Releases/Kennedy-Library-Releases-New-Report-on-Cuban-Missile-Crisis-Study-Documents-Impact-of-Crisis-on-Amer.aspx#.

46. "Kennedy Library Releases New Report on Cuban Missile Crisis."

47. One of the more interesting cases where this can be seen is regarding the taking of American hostages in Iran in 1979 during the Carter administration. In one poll taken in June 1979, before the event, Carter had a 20 percent approval rating. Immediately following that event, public opinion shifted dramatically to become strongly supportive of Carter and also hostile to Iran. For more details see Rose McDermott, *Risk-Taking in International Politics: Prospect Theory in American Foreign Policy* (Ann Arbor: University of Michigan Press, 1998), especially chapter 3, "The Iranian Hostage Rescue Mission," 45–74.

48. "Kennedy Library Releases New Report on Cuban Missile Crisis."

49. See, for example, Graham T. Allison, *Essence of Decision: Explaining the Cuban Missile Crisis* (Boston: Little, Brown, 1971). This is perhaps the classic book on the missile crisis. Also see Raymond L. Garthoff, *Reflections on the Cuban Missile Crisis* (Washington, DC: Brookings Institution, 1989); and Robert F. Kennedy, *Thirteen Days: A Memoir of the Cuban Missile Crisis* (New York: Norton, 1969), for a fascinating first-person account of the event by someone intimately involved. For a work that draws on previously secret documents from Russian and U.S. archives to offer further insights into the crisis, see Aleksandr Fursenko and Timothy Naftali, *"One Hell of a Gamble": Khrushchev, Castro, and Kennedy 1958–1964* (New York: Norton, 1997). Also see Michael Dobbs, *One Minute to Midnight: Kennedy, Khrushchev, and Castro on the Brink of Nuclear War* (New York: Knopf, 2008) for a detailed account of the crisis that draws on exhaustive and relatively new research.

Nonstate Actors and the International System

Thus far, we have moved through the basics of international relations and the primary actors who are involved with and are part of the international system. We started by looking at the international system as a whole; at the nation-state, which is traditionally the primary actor in the international system; and within the nation-state at the component parts that make up the nation-state. In this chapter, we are going to look at the range of nonstate actors that exist outside the traditional levels-of-analysis framework but have a marked impact on the international system and the actors within it. These nonstate actors range from international organizations, such as the United Nations and the European Union, which are made up of nation-states, to terrorist organizations, such as al-Qaeda, that are capable of mounting attacks against nation-states, as we saw on September 11, 2001. But we will look at other nonstate actors such as multinational corporations and nongovernmental organizations, which also play an important role in international political and economic systems today.

By the end of this chapter, you should have a more complete picture of the international system and the range of actors who make up that system and also a better understanding of the strengths and weaknesses of the traditional approaches to international relations.

THE CHANGING NATURE OF THE INTERNATIONAL SYSTEM

What are nonstate actors and why are these actors important? As we noted in chapter 2, the traditional levels-of-analysis approach to understanding international relations *assumes* the nation-state as the primary actor. It *assumes* that the international system is made up of nation-states that interact with one another and conform to certain norms and expectations that can be defined as international law. It also *assumes* that all nation-states have certain characteristics that determine and affect the ways in which they act. And the fact of the matter is, for much of the modern history of international relations, that was the case.

Furthermore, most of the traditional theories that were formulated to describe and explain international relations also assume that the nation-state is the primary actor, even though they vary widely in their understanding of the nation-state and its role. Although more recent theoretical approaches, such as the constructivists, look at the structures that influence international relations, they also assume that states have certain characteristics or patterns of behavior that are influenced by factors that were socially constructed. Thus, even though this is a different theoretical approach to and understanding of the nation-state, that actor is still prominently featured.

In thinking about international relations today, it is also true that the norms or patterns of interaction among the nation-states as the major actors has changed, especially since the end of World War II, and exponentially since the end of the Cold War. At the end of World War II, national priorities changed. The world settled into the Cold War, a period also known as "The Long Peace" for the relative stability that came with a bipolar world, but also kept in check with the knowledge of the devastation that might result if the balance of power were disturbed.[1] Countries that had been colonies sought their independence, resulting in a proliferation of new nations, especially in Africa and Asia. The countries of Latin and South America started to become more assertive at charting their own course of political and economic action, which often did not align with the direction desired by the developed countries of the North, their former colonial powers. Countries also tried to understand why cataclysmic events such as World War II happened, in the hope of preventing them from occurring again in the future.

We see even greater and more rapid changes since the end of the Cold War. The countries of the developing world have moved far beyond their secondary postcolonial status and are now emerging as international powerhouses that even the most developed countries, like the United States, have to deal with. China is no longer a third world country built on a peasant workforce tied to the land; rather, it is a military and economic force to be reckoned with. Brazil has joined China as one of the BRIC countries (Brazil,

Russia, India, China, and sometimes including South Africa), as an economic and political leader in South America. In fact, in the past decade since Luiz Lula da Silva (Lula) became president of Brazil in 2002, the percentage of the population living in poverty has dropped from 26.7 percent to 15.3 percent. (By way of contrast, the National Academy of Science estimates that the poverty rate in the United States *increased* from 12.1 percent in 2002 to 14.3 percent in 2009.[2]) Average real monthly income per person in Brazil has increased from 507.7 reais to 630.3 reais, and the average years of schooling have increased from 6.6 to 7.6.[3] Increased demands for Brazilian exports and a booming domestic market coupled with better social policies have helped countless Brazilians not only emerge from poverty but have a better life. And the pattern of rapid economic growth and social development that we see in Brazil is not unique but has been repeated in countless other formerly developing countries, such as South Africa, Nigeria, and India.

This change in the international order among nation-states has important implications for other aspects of international relations, such as international organizations. With the world no longer divided into developed and developing nations, power blocs have been realigned and more countries are asserting themselves in discussions on important global issues such as the environment. Within the established international organizations, such as the United Nations, these same countries are demanding more of a say, claiming that the Cold War order that provided the framework for the creation of these organizations and was tied to "major powers" no longer is appropriate. And, of course, globalization has made it not only possible but easier for more countries to play a role in and have an impact on the international economic system.

But we see the changing nature of the international system in other ways as well. For example, in an age in which countries are interdependent, the earthquake and tsunami that hit Japan in March 2011 disrupted life not only in that country, but in the countries that trade with Japan. Help came quickly not only from other countries, but from international organizations whose mission is humanitarian aid and assistance. It is easy to look at that case and to think that help from other countries was forthcoming because they needed Japan; a disruption in trade could easily have had global consequences. But that would hide a more important message. We can also look at the earthquake that struck Haiti in January 2010, resulting in the deaths of more than 300,000 people, injury to at least that number, and more than one million people left homeless. Haiti is not a major player in the international system, and yet supplies and aid were coming as quickly as twenty-four hours after the initial event. And the help came from other countries but also from nongovernmental organizations such as the Red Cross and Doctors Without Borders.

It becomes clear, then, that in addition to the realignment in the relative power of nation-states, one of the other major changes that we see in the operation of the international system as a whole is the emergence of nonstate actors who have come to play a role that is in some cases as large as or even larger than that of nation-states. These nonstate actors, also known as transnational actors because they operate across national borders, provide aid and help in the event of major catastrophes, both natural (such as earthquakes and tsunamis) and man-made (including the devastation caused by wars). They also help influence policy by raising issues to the front of the international agenda, as organizations such as the Sierra Club did for the environment or Amnesty International has done for issues of human rights. And they advocate for specific positions within countries and across countries on behalf of children, women, animals, the environment, and so on. Clearly, these nonstate actors influence important aspects of international relations and play a role that nation-states can't or won't play.

What Are Nonstate Actors?

Nonstate actors can fall into a broad range of categories, but on the whole, they fall outside the traditional category of nation-states; some have nation-states as their members and others are organizations or groups of individuals whose membership and goals cross the borders of nation-states. Some are organized to advocate for the common good, such as the environment, the rights of children, or health care, while others have expressly political motives, such as terrorist groups. What makes them so perplexing to deal with in IR terms, though, is that the major theories and levels-of-analysis framework have few ways to account for them or their behavior. These organizations don't fall within any of the major theoretical perspectives, yet they have a marked impact on the traditional actors in IR.

International organizations (IOs) are also known as intergovernmental organizations (IGOs), because their members are nation-states and, generally, their main role is to help bring order to the international system. This category encompasses a range of organizations, for example, the United Nations

(UN) or the European Union (EU), which bring sovereign nation-states together in pursuit of common goals. What becomes most interesting in these cases, however, is how states can join together to pursue common policies *without* infringing on their sovereignty as individual nations. This is a point we will come back to a little bit later in this chapter.

These international organizations also exist outside the traditional bounds of the levels of analysis, even though they are made up of nation-states. If you look carefully at the levels, you can see that there is no provision for such organizations, except as they exist within the international system.

Another group that has become more familiar to many are nongovernmental organizations (NGOs), whose members are individuals or groups rather than nation-states, and who generally have a specialized function. Often, they try to influence national or international policies and are created specifically to advocate for a specific policy that transcends national borders. Examples of these are Amnesty International, which fights for basic human rights worldwide; Doctors Without Borders (Médecins Sans Frontières), an international medical humanitarian group that provides medical assistance after a natural disaster, political violence, or in cases of extreme poverty; and Greenpeace International, which campaigns to protect the global environment, to name but a few of the better-known organizations. Such NGOs are another form of international organization that exists outside the formal levels of analysis but tries to bring pressure upon the actors in the international system, nation-states, and international organizations, in order to effect policy change.

Other entities, such as terrorist groups or even multinational corporations (MNCs), also can influence actors in the international system; they can even pose a threat of some kind to the international system and/or the actors within it, especially the nation-state. In the case of terrorist groups, the threat is pretty self-explanatory. However, MNCs are much more insidious in the role they play. While they exist outside the levels of analysis, they can exert a strong influence on the policies of nation-states and the international system as a whole. And for that reason, it is important to explore them.

In this chapter, we will consider each of these types of nonstate actors. Beginning with a general definition or description of each, we will explore their goals, their members, and the role they play in international relations. Since these groups of actors exist outside the bounds of the formal levels of analysis, we need to look at the impact that they do have and on what levels.

Thus, one of the major points to think about as we continue through this discussion is what level or levels of analysis they draw from or affect as actors in the international system.

In keeping with the themes of this brief overview of international relations, what we are going to turn our attention to first is at the more macro level, focusing on international organizations as a group of actors who have come to play a role in international relations. They are generally made up of nation-states as well as some NGOs, and they seek ways to bring nation-states together to discuss issues of common concern and to make policy that will affect all of them. In so doing, they help bring about a more stable and regulated order in the international system.

In chapter 3 we talked about the concept of collective security and how it was embodied in the charter of the United Nations. Our approach here will be to identify the purposes or functions that international organizations serve, the role(s) they can—or cannot—play in the international system today, and the type of influence they have. We will also try to see the ways in which different theoretical approaches view international organizations. We will then look quickly at examples of specific organizations in order to apply our understanding of them.

In this section, we will look at these various nonstate actors to see where they fit, whom they influence, and what impact they have on the international system and the actors that exist within it.

INTERNATIONAL ORGANIZATIONS

Within the subfield of international relations, there is a further subdivision that includes the study of international organizations (IOs). Generally, when we think of international organizations we think of those organizations whose members are national governments; therefore, these organizations are also known as intergovernmental organizations (IGOs). Within that broad category, organizations can be further subdivided; some have virtually universal membership, such as the UN, while others are regional organizations, such as the European Union.

Another way to look at these IGOs is by function. For example, there are organizations that were created to ensure the collective defense of their members. NATO is an example of that type, although on a larger scale, so is the UN. There are other organizations that were created to help stabilize the international economic system, such as the International Monetary Fund

(IMF), "an organization of 187 countries, working to foster global monetary cooperation, secure financial stability, facilitate international trade, promote high employment and sustainable economic growth, and reduce poverty around the world."[4] Then there are a plethora of regional organizations designed to facilitate free trade and openness among member nations. In addition to the EU, we can look at the North American Free Trade Agreement (NAFTA), which unites the United States, Canada, and Mexico into a big trading block. Asia-Pacific Economic Cooperation (APEC) is committed to increasing trade and opening markets in the Asia-Pacific region. APEC is an organization of twenty-one nation-states that border both sides of the Pacific Ocean. Hence, its membership includes the three NAFTA countries, but also Chile and Peru in South America and a range of other countries including China, Japan, Russia, and Vietnam. This illustrates the ways in which membership in organizations can often be overlapping rather than exclusive. And there is no limit to the number or types of organizations that a country can be part of.

Another important international organization is the Organization of the Petroleum Exporting Countries (OPEC), whose membership includes the oil-exporting countries Venezuela and Nigeria, as well as the major oil producers in the Middle East. Since it was founded in 1960 with five members, this organization has grown to a membership of twelve countries. In 2010, these twelve members produced almost three times the number of barrels of crude oil as did non-OPEC members.[5] Thus, although some oil-producing countries like Russia and Mexico are not OPEC members, this organization controls enough oil to manipulate the world markets. The "oil shocks" of the 1970s were a warning to the industrialized and industrializing nations that they needed to wean themselves from their dependence on imported oil and look to other energy sources. The disruptions in oil production and flows from the unrest in Middle Eastern countries such as Libya in the spring and summer of 2011, which further drove up prices, were another reminder of the power that a small group of countries can wield when they control an important international resource. That power can be manifested in other, less overt ways as well. For example, China's thirst for oil has contributed directly to its growing relationship with Nigeria, a major oil-producing nation. This partnership has given China an important stronghold in Africa.

And these are but a few examples of the types of international organizations that exist and the varied roles that they play internationally. What all of these have in common is that *their members are nation-states* that have joined the organization in the belief that doing so will further their national interest. Nation-states may be, and often are, members of more than one organization that reflects the different interests and priorities that nations have, e.g., security, economics, trade, regional, international, and so on.

We will now turn to a more detailed discussion of the different types of international organizations that, ultimately, will allow us to draw some important conclusions about the roles they play in the international system.

Intergovernmental Organizations (IGOs)

As noted above, IGOs are multilateral organizations whose members are nation-states. As we have suggested, this raises some interesting questions about the balance between the state's commitments to the organization while also ensuring its own sovereignty. In order to be able to answer that question of balance, we need to begin by determining why states join such organizations in the first place. Here the theoretical approaches can give us some insight, even if they appear to be conflicting.

There are certain general principles that are common to all IGOs and help describe the role(s) that they play in international relations. The assumption underlying the creation of IGOs is that each organization brings together independent states that adhere to the basic principles and goals of the organization and are willing to support its norms. Each organization also has its own set of rules of operation, ways to finance itself, a bureaucratic structure of some type, a voting or decision-making approach among its members, ways to punish member states that don't conform, and membership criteria. Since there is no single means of enforcing international law, IGOs often play an important role in ensuring that such laws, international agreements, and policies are enforced and violators punished. Beyond this set of generalities, however, international organizations vary widely.

The United Nations

The UN is a multilateral organization whose membership includes most nation-states. It is also a major and complex bureaucracy composed of many parts and agencies, with voting of the whole on broad policy issues coming through the General Assembly based on majority vote. So, in that forum, all states have an equal voice. In contrast, the Security Council of the UN has the primary responsibility for issues pertaining to international peace and security and can meet at any time. There are fifteen members, including five permanent members (China, France, Russia, the UK, and the United States), each of which has veto power, and ten additional members that are elected by the General Assembly to serve two-year terms. One of the major items of discussion lately has been whether the makeup of the Security Council is an artifact of the Cold War and needs to be broadened. That argument suggests that the number of permanent members should be expanded to more accurately represent the power distribution beyond the "major powers" of the Cold War period—for example, to include at least one of the BRIC states and/or a representative from different regions, including Latin/South America and Africa. Despite this apparent flaw in membership and the difficulty that the UN in general has had in adapting to changing international realities, it continues to play an important role in the international system as a forum for discussion, and also because of the specialized work it does through its various agencies.

One of the unique roles that the UN plays internationally has to do with peacekeeping. An extension of the collective security role that the UN was created for, the peacekeeping mission extends into regions in which there is violent political conflict. Because of its virtually universal membership and the fact that the deployment of UN peacekeeping forces is discussed, debated, and voted on in the Security Council, it is generally seen as playing an apolitical role, responding instead to the particular circumstances and to work for the greater good.

As noted initially in chapter 3, UN peacekeeping forces, also known as "blue helmets" because of their headgear, play an important and unique role in supporting missions designated by UN Security Council resolutions or other relevant organizations, such as NATO. In that regard they play a role that no single country can, injecting themselves into conflict situations not as combatants, but as representatives of an international organization deployed for a specific purpose and usually of limited duration. For example, UN peacekeeping forces patrol the green line between the North and South in Cyprus and the DMZ separating North and South Korea; supported the implementation of a peace agreement between the government and rebel factions in Sudan; helped maintain civil order in the Democratic Republic of Congo; were based in Kosovo to help administer that area and to support the reconstruction of a political process following the conflict; and have performed and still perform countless other missions in virtually every part of the world—all authorized by the international system through the United Nations. The forces are drawn from member countries, and their purpose is

> to capitalize on the moral authority drawn from their position as peacekeepers accepted in principle by all contending parties. As such, they were not to intervene in these conflicts, much less take sides. They were only to monitor the peace and to provide a necessary presence to dissuade the parties from resorting to force against each other.[6]

Ideally, of course, one of the goals of the UN's collective security function is to provide a forum for discussion and debate that allows for the peaceful resolution of conflicts before they escalate in armed violence. However, should the conflict escalate into armed violence, then the United Nations can help play the role of peacemaker and/or peacekeeper as needed.

But the United Nations plays a broader role than just dealing with conflict and peace. Through its various agencies, the UN performs other important tasks pertaining to human rights, children, women, social and economic programs, adjudicating international disputes, and other broad international issues as they arise. Each of these has its own structure and specialized mission, although there can be overlap. If you ever trick-or-treated for UNICEF, you were raising money on behalf of the UN organization specifically dedicated to helping children world-wide:

> UNICEF is the driving force that helps build a world where the rights of every child are realized. We have the global authority to influence decision-makers, and the variety of partners at grassroots level to turn the most innovative ideas into reality. That makes us unique among world organizations, and unique among those working with the young.[7]

In addition to agencies devoted specifically to children or refugees, for example, the UN has other agencies within it that address specific issues, such as population and the environment. In short, as a major international organization, the UN is designed to address and to find solutions to major global issues by bringing countries and NGOs together.

In addition to the accusation that the UN is tied too closely to Cold War values and political structure, it has also been criticized for its inability to confront some of the most difficult international issues. Because of the structure of the Security Council, a veto, or even the threat of a veto, from one of

BOX 5.1

MILLENNIUM DEVELOPMENT GOALS.

The UN Millennium Development Goals (MDGs) project was adopted by world leaders in 2000 to "provide a framework for the entire international community to work together towards a common end—making sure that human development reaches everyone, everywhere. These offer another example of how the United Nations can bring countries together to pursue goals for global benefit. If these goals are achieved, world poverty will be cut by half, tens of millions of lives will be saved, and billions more people will have the opportunity to benefit from the global economy." What makes these especially important is that they provide quantitative measures that can be used to assess progress on these goals at various points up to the projected end date of 2015.

The eight MDGs further break down into twenty-one quantifiable targets that are measured by sixty indicators.

Goal 1: Eradicate extreme poverty and hunger
Goal 2: Achieve universal primary education
Goal 3: Promote gender equality and empower women
Goal 4: Reduce child mortality
Goal 5: Improve maternal health
Goal 6: Combat HIV/AIDS, malaria, and other diseases
Goal 7: Ensure environmental sustainability
Goal 8: Develop a global partnership for development

Source: http://www.undp.org/mdg/basics.shtml.

the "big five" countries can limit the types of actions that the organization can take, often while conflict continues to rage. For example, in October 2011 as the civil war in Syria was escalating, China and Russia vetoed a measure proposed by Britain to impose "targeted measures" against the government of Bashar al-Assad. While this response provoked cries of outrage from other countries, the structure of the Security Council means that little could be done to move forward. One year later, with the conflict now a major civil war with no end apparently in sight, there has been virtually no formal action taken by the UN beyond issuing statements of "strong condemnation" and the creation of the position of a joint special representative for Syria who is supposed to explore a peaceful resolution to the ongoing conflict, thus far unsuccessfully.

Criticism aside, the UN has been able to endure and remain an important symbol of international cooperation and unity, as well as being an established forum for discussion of important issues. Many of the conventions and resolutions pertaining directly to women, for example, grew out of major UN-sponsored conferences that brought together political leaders and NGOs. Passage of conventions such as the Declaration on the Elimination of Violence Against Women, passed in 1993, and the 1979 Convention on the Elimination of All Forms of Discrimination against Women (CEDAW), described as the international bill of rights for women, brings the weight of the international system to bear on important issues, in this case pertaining specifically to women.

What this illustrates is the way in which the UN can be used to coalesce international opinion behind an issue and can contribute to international agreement.

North Atlantic Treaty Organization (NATO)

As noted above, there are any number of other IGOs that are either more limited in membership or that take on specific functions. Many of these were created after World War II by the then "great powers" as a way to stabilize and formalize some aspect of international relations. For example, the North Atlantic Treaty Organization (NATO) was created in 1949 by the then democratic countries of Western Europe, specifically to link them with the United States and also Canada to serve as a deterrent to Soviet expansion. The assumption was that this alliance would explicitly tie the U.S. nuclear deterrent to the European allies, and it would thereby balance the power of the Soviet Union. NATO enlargement to include the countries of the former Eastern bloc, beginning with Poland, Hungary, and the Czech Republic in 1997, was tangible proof that the Cold War had ended and that these formerly communist countries were now recognized democracies. But perhaps even more important, it served as an indicator that the old international order was changing, and along with that, so were assumptions about the need for a collective defense agreement directed against a single threat. Since then,

NATO has expanded its role greatly, most recently overseeing the conflict in Afghanistan and supporting the rebel forces in their fight against Gadhafi in Libya.

Especially since the end of the Cold War, the utility of NATO has been questioned. The decision to enlarge NATO in 1993 at the same time that the war in Bosnia was escalating raised serious issues about the role of the alliance after the Cold War. When NATO did agree to go into the Balkans, it was the first "out-of-area" mission, and it set a precedent for the expanded role for the alliance that we see today. In December 2001, two months after the decision to attack Afghanistan, NATO created the International Security Assistance Force (ISAF), and in August 2003, NATO assumed leadership of the ISAF operation. At that time, the alliance "became responsible for the command, coordination and planning of the force, including the provision of a force commander and headquarters on the ground in Afghanistan."[8] Hence, NATO has evolved from an organization designed specifically to protect the European allies by tying them to the U.S. nuclear deterrent, as envisioned when NATO was created in 1949, to one that is bringing together many countries to address major security issues in other parts of the world.

The International Monetary Fund (IMF) and the World Bank

There are many other examples of the creation of specialized IGOs created after World War II to serve specific purposes as envisioned by the major powers, given the political and economic realities of that time. As noted above, the International Monetary Fund (IMF) grew out of the Bretton Woods Conference in 1944, driven largely by the United States to promote international monetary cooperation and stability. The World Bank, which was also created at Bretton Woods, was originally designed to help facilitate the postwar reconstruction efforts in Europe, but it was subsequently expanded to provide loans to assist countries' development efforts. These organizations were designed to help foster financial stability, promote international trade and cooperation, and promote employment and economic growth worldwide through their policies. And much of the ideas underlying these organizations made sense at that time. But the situation has changed since then, leading to questions about their effectiveness today.

One of the major policies that both advocate are structural adjustment programs (SAPs) that "impose specific spending restrictions on governments, especially when it comes to social welfare, health and education programs, while encouraging expenditures on items such as infrastructure, more efficient revenue collection programs, tourist facilities, and tax rebates for foreign investors."[9] While these should lead to economic growth, they often ignore the costs to the people of the country.

The approach taken by these organizations to provide loans to the leaders or governments of countries has raised questions about who really benefits from those loans. In some cases the loans funded corrupt governments rather than the projects that were designed to reach the people. The structural adjustment programs that were supposed to help a country develop by offering lower interest rates on loans under certain conditions actually can have the opposite effect. And feminist theorists as well as some of the Marxist/radical theorists question "the harsh effects of structural adjustment policies imposed by the International Monetary Fund on Third World debtor nations [which] fall disproportionately on women as providers of basic needs, as social welfare programs in areas of health, nutrition, and housing are cut."[10]

The IMF and the World Bank have also been subjected to international criticism and questions about their role in a globalized world. At the most basic level, both of these organizations were created at a period of time that was quite different from the present, politically and economically. This can be seen in the leadership structure of each; traditionally, the World Bank has been headed by an American and the IMF by a European, representing the "old" order. When IMF Managing Director Dominique Strauss-Kahn stepped down because of a sex scandal in May 2011, there were questions about whether his replacement had to be a European. In fact, some countries argued that it was time to move beyond that assumption and to have a managing director from one of the emerging countries who could better understand those countries' needs. Although Christine Lagarde, then serving as France's finance minister, ultimately was elected to the post, the head of the Mexican Central Bank was also a contender for the position.

The five countries with the largest number of shares in World Bank capital (the United States, Germany, France, Japan, and the UK), have the greatest say. Again, this reinforces the charges that these institutions are artifacts of the Cold War and do not reflect current international reality. Furthermore, since their members are states, they cannot help but be subject to political rivalries that can call into question their decisions.

Regional Organizations: The European Union (EU)

The European Union now is a group of twenty-seven countries that have pledged to move toward a common economic, foreign, and defense policy, including the seventeen countries that make up the euro zone—those countries that have come to adopt the euro as their common currency although adopting the euro is not a requirement for being in the EU. By remaining outside the euro zone, which has given it a degree of independence, the UK has been able to emerge as a leader in establishing policy for the EU, and by virtue of its "special relationship" with the United States, it plays an important balancing role. On the other hand, because of its economic power, Germany has emerged as an important player in both the EU and the euro zone and has, in fact, dictated many of the economic policies that the countries in that group have followed. What cannot be overlooked is the fact that in a globalized world, the economic policies and issues surrounding the euro zone have a direct impact on the global economic system. The EU also stands as an example of the growing trend toward regional integration.

The EU has an interesting structure; each of the member nations has its own leader, typically a president, a prime minister, or both. But as an entity, the EU also has a president—actually two: a president of the European Council, and a president of the European Commission. The European Council is composed of the heads of state or government of each of the EU member nations, and it meets regularly to review common policies and initiatives. It is headed by a president who is appointed for a $2^1/_2$-year term, replacing the previous structure of a presidency that rotated among member nations. This body has been the driving force behind EU integration efforts. The European Commission is the executive body of the EU, and it is responsible for the implementation of policy and the day-to-day running of the EU. There are twenty-seven commissioners, one per member state, with the president proposed by the Council and then elected by the European Parliament.

Are you confused yet? How can an organization of twenty-seven sovereign states also be a member of another organization that also has its own parliament and president(s) and makes policy that each state is expected to support? That is one of the challenges of integration. The realists would say that states will remain in this organization as long as it is in their national interest to do so. The liberals would say that all countries benefit from this union of democratic countries because of increased trade and the advantages that come from a common security and foreign policy. The constructivists would note the ways in which these states and the people within them have been transformed because of the structural framework within which they are now interacting (the EU) and, in turn, that the structure itself has been transformed because of the member states. Regardless of your interpretation, the reality is that despite many challenges and disagreements, the EU has become stronger and more integrated over time.

Much of the EU's attention of late has been focused on how to deal with the financial crises that have affected the euro-zone countries of Greece, Spain, Portugal, and even Cyprus. According to one article on the topic, "For many countries in Europe, the debt problems of Greece or Portugal are little more than a distraction. Greece, which accounts for 2.5 percent of the gross national product in the euro zone, is not an important market for most large multinationals." However, it also raises a more important point: "One risk of the current crisis is that it will create a sharper divide between poorer Southern Europe and prosperous Northern Europe, adding to tensions about how to manage the euro-zone economy." And that is the crux of the issue. This is coming at a time when there are already some serious tensions and divisions within the EU and especially among euro-zone countries.[11] This point also highlights the dangers inherent in integrating the economies of independent sovereign states,

Addressing the economic crisis in the euro zone was the primary topic of discussion at a summit of EU leaders in June 2012. That summit reinforced the need for leaders to address the structural as well as financial issues sur-rounding the euro zone. Previously, a routine summit of EU leaders in March 2011 was followed by a euro-zone summit that included only the lead-ers of euro-zone countries. The plan that was adopted, known as "the pact for Europe," places the European Commission at the heart of the plan, spe-cifically by allowing it to supervise any new commitments while also provid-ing closer scrutiny of members' economic and budgetary policies. But this was not without controversy, as it raised questions about the good of the whole group versus the sovereignty of each of the states.

In many ways, it is clear that the EU nations have a common foreign and economic policy when they agree, but they generally resort to national poli-cies when they disagree. For example, the EU is the world's largest aid donor, which gives it clout in Africa and parts of Asia and the Middle East. Working as a group allowed it to take important (and unified) stands in Bosnia, Congo, Darfur, and Kosovo. Because the United States has no formal rela-tions with Iran, it has looked to the governments of the UK, France, and Germany—critical EU members—to facilitate discussion and to try to per-suade Iran not to build a nuclear weapon. All of these give the EU a great deal of power and influence internationally.

However, when the member nations disagree, it means that the EU working as a whole can do little or nothing at all. The primary example of this is the war over Iraq in 2003, where some of the member nations, such as the UK, Poland, and initially Spain, were strong supporters of the U.S. decision to go to war, as opposed to France, Germany, and Belgium, which were united in opposition. And the EU countries remain deeply divided over the issue of enlargement in general, and which countries to admit in particular. This is especially acute over the issue of membership for Turkey, a country that applied for full membership as far back as 1987 but has yet to meet the criteria for membership. The reality, though, is that issues of enlargement take a backseat to the economic crisis that the EU is experiencing, and finding ways to move forward as a bloc to address it.

The EU represents an interesting case study of a regional organization.

Other Regional Organizations

Increasingly, regional organizations in general have emerged to challenge—or complement—the place of global IGOs. Few of them have the international clout of the EU, but they do play an important role and are worth thinking about. Many of these reflect changing power relationships both regionally and internationally, and they have come to play important roles for their member countries. For example, the Organisation of African Unity (OAU), now called the African Union (AU), was created in 1963 to promote cooperation and solidarity among the states of Africa in order to ensure a better life for the peoples of the continent. As a continental organization,

> the OAU provided an effective forum that enabled all Member States to adopt coordinated positions on matters of common concern to the continent in international fora and defend the interests of Africa effectively. . . . Through the OAU Coordinating Committee for the Liberation of Africa, the Continent worked and spoke as one with undivided determination in forging an international consensus in support of the liberation struggle and the fight against apartheid.[12]

Clearly, one of the goals of this particular regional organization is to minimize dependence upon the developed countries of the North and West and to further the roles in which African countries can help one another. Even within the continent of Africa, there are many other regional and specialized organizations that exist to promote greater economic development and political cooperation.

Similar organizations exist in other regions, often with overlapping missions and members. Why is this important, and what does this brief review of IGOs tell us about the state of international relations today? First, the emergence of regional organizations that parallel the broader global ones suggests that states still believe in the importance of organizations that bring them together to pursue common goals. This also suggests that states do not see a conflict between the sovereignty of the state and the goals of an organization; rather, it suggests that countries see and support the idea that working together within the framework of a single organization can be in the national interest of the country.

Second, the emergence of regional organizations serves to reinforce the changing power structure within the international system. Countries no longer have to rely on the major powers for security or to ensure their economic well-being. While many organizations include some of the major powers—the United States is a member of many IGOs, including regional ones such as APEC, NAFTA, and the Organization of American States (OAS)—the organization does not depend on, nor even want, a major power like the United States to steer its course. Rather, the United States serves as another member of the group, albeit one with more resources than other members.

Third, many of the IGOs that exist today stress economic cooperation as a core value, rather than security. Admittedly, this is also an indicator of the changing and broadening understanding of security, which is also a function of the post–Cold War world. It is also vindication of one of the basic principles put forward by the feminist authors that the concept of security needs to be redefined so that it moves "beyond its association with military issues" to include economic and environmental threats, as well as ensuring basic values such as freedom.[13] It is instructive that the websites of so many regional organizations stress these values as fundamental to the organization.

Fourth, despite the criticisms of the global IGOs with their emphasis on the power of the developed countries and their outdated goals, these organizations remain important; they have not been supplanted by other organizations, either regional or functional, but rather they continue to exist and to play a prominent role internationally. One basic assumption of political life is that if an entity, such as an organization, stops being able to meet a need or perform a function, it will cease to exist or it will be supplanted by another entity/actor/organization that can better fill that gap. But that has not happened. Whereas the League of Nations disappeared when it became clear that it could not serve the function it was designed to, the UN continues to exist and to play an important role internationally. While that might not have been the role it was originally designed for, the organization has been able to adapt and evolve and, in doing so, has met other needs that were not necessarily envisioned when the UN was created.

These are important lessons if we really are to understand the role of IGOs today. Where you stand on this issue is, in part, a function of which of the philosophical traditions you support, which in turn will color your interpretation of the issues.

IGOs and IR Theory

If IGOs are an established part of the international system, how do they fit within the theoretical framework that we outlined earlier? As organizations whose members are nation-states, they clearly exist at a unique place in the levels-of-analysis framework and within the international system. They play a role as actors whose decisions and actions affect other actors, including nation-states, in the international system at various levels. And while they represent the interests of the states who make up their membership, they also enact policies that are separate from and influence the behaviors of other nation-states, both those that are their members and also nonmembers.

Realists start with the presumption that all states seek to maximize their own power and that they are rational actors. They would also be skeptical of the utility of IGOs and the role that they play in the international system, since such organizations do seem to go against the primacy of the nation-state. Logically, then, the next step would be to conclude that if states enter into such agreements or join IGOs they do so in the belief that membership will increase their power or leverage or that it would certainly not undermine their power and leverage in any way. That would certainly be the case with some of the examples above.

But there is also a healthy dose of liberal thought inherent in the creation of any IGO. Here the assumption is that countries choose to enter into them because they facilitate cooperation and collective action that all benefit from. All participating countries share basic values and work together to ensure that their values and norms are sustained. These IGOs reinforce the belief in the importance of interdependence and regional integration and see interdependence and regional integration as mutually beneficial. Furthermore, also underlying the liberal commitment to such organizations is the belief that the resulting cooperation and interdependence will make war and conflict less likely to occur, which is clearly another benefit.

Constructivists emphasize the structures that influence states, as well as the ways in which states and the individuals within them are altered by the structures with which they interact. So, as we saw above with the case of the EU, the various states in the organization are affected directly by its policies and the organization (in this case, the EU), in turn, is influenced and affected by the decisions of the states that are its members. In other words, the structure of the organization transforms and is in turn transformed by the actors within it—not only the states, but the individual leaders. Witness the critical role played by Angela Merkel in determining the fiscal policies of the euro zone. Thus, IGOs serve as a way in which the international system can be altered and the actions of that system changed—hopefully in a positive way.

The more radical theorists, such as Marxists, would probably discount the value of such organizations in the belief that even if they were not explicitly created by the more powerful countries, ultimately an unequal power balance will result, creating an outcome that will pit more powerful against less powerful states. In many ways, this is the charge often leveled against the UN, which is seen as perpetuating a structure based on pitting the developed versus the developing nations; even though that now appears to be an outdated political order.

It is also in understanding the role of IGOs that the feminist perspective again offers some important insights. On the one hand, the UN and some of the other IGOs have played an important role in identifying the inequities that exist among members of a population and in drawing attention to ways to address these inequities. The various world conferences on women hosted by the UN have drawn attention to the status of women worldwide and have led to the passage of resolutions specifically to ensure women's representation and that women's views are noted. However, feminists also note that since IGOs represent the views of the governments of the member states rather than the populations, women's views are underrepresented—as are women—in the discussions.

Regardless of which theoretical perspective you accept about the role or utility of IGOs, there can be little discussion or debate about the fact that they do exist as organizations with nation-states as their members, which play an important role in contemporary international relations.

IGOs and Sovereignty

One question we must come back to is: How do states reconcile the apparent contradiction between ensuring their own sovereignty and participating in such an organization? To respond to that, it is important to remember that any state can withdraw from the organization (or, for that matter, from any international agreement) at any time if it feels that participating will not be in its best interest or would undermine its sovereignty. An example of this can be seen with France and NATO.

In that case, France withdrew from the NATO unified military command structure in 1966 in the belief that remaining within the organization undermined its sovereignty and was not in its best interest. France did remain part of the political structure, however, which ensured that it had ongoing ties to the organization. In 2009, French president Nicolas Sarkozy announced that France would be returning to the military structure, claiming that "there was no sense in France—a founder member of NATO—having no say in the organization's decisions on military strategy." Sarkozy also said that "'this rapprochement with NATO ensures our national independence. . . . To distance ourselves would limit our independence and our room for maneuver.'"[14] Thus, Sarkozy was making the case that inclusion, rather than exclusion, offered more options for France and benefited its ability to make policy decisions internationally, rather than constraining it as previously believed.

But Sarkozy also noted, "'A solitary nation is a nation that has no influence whatsoever. We need strong diplomacy, a strong defense and a strong Europe.'"[15] This, in turn, suggests that the country's strength and power would be maximized from being part of NATO. Obviously, then French president Sarkozy saw that the advantages that accrue from being in the alliance outweigh the possible costs. This is an example of rational decision making. But it also stands as an example of how a country can choose when or whether to join or remain part of an IGO.

This particular case is especially illustrative for a number of reasons regarding the role that IGOs play internationally, but also applying the levels of analysis. From the perspective of an individual nation-state, it shows the ways in which a country's interpretation of sovereignty varied according to the individual leader of the country, in this case, then president Charles de

Gaulle in 1966 versus President Sarkozy in 2009. At the nation-state level it illustrates how the interpretation of national interests changed, and with those changes came a different relationship to NATO. From the perspective of the IGO, in this case NATO, it also shows that a unified organization is far greater than its individual parts.

In looking at the case of the UN, we can also see some of the apparent contradictions between sovereignty and the IGO. When it was envisioned in 1941, the United Nations was to be an organization that would unite sovereign states, all of which would be equal in terms of voting within the General Assembly. However, as sovereign states, none is bound by any determination made by the UN. Therefore, what binds them to the organization is commitment to international law and the obligations that come with that. However, because of the sanctity of state sovereignty and other central principles of international thinking, it has also proven to be powerless at times to address international crises, such as the genocide that has taken place in a number of countries and the proliferation of nuclear weapons. While it has been successful at bringing countries together to take a stand against such global issues—the imposition of sanctions against Iran is an example—it has not been able to put a stop to the actions of individual nations in all cases.

Nonetheless, it is also important to remember that the UN does hold moral suasion in that countries want UN approval for various actions. For example, the United States did look to the UN for support in its initial decision to go to war against Afghanistan following the attacks of 9/11. However, the decision to go to war against Iraq seriously divided the countries when it did not get UN approval.

> After reaching consensus to insist on Iraqi disarmament and send back UN weapon inspectors, the Security Council split on whether to authorize force against Iraq—the United States and Britain voted in favor; France, Russia, and China against. After France threatened to veto a UN resolution authorizing war, a U.S.-British coalition toppled the Iraqi government without explicit UN backing. UN Secretary-General Kofi Annan later called the war "illegal."[16]

This example illustrates some of the limits of IGOs, especially when there is a conflict between the goals of the nation-state and that of the organization. In this example, the United States took action in defiance of the will of the UN. Yet, the UN continues to exist with the United States as a member.

We will now turn to nongovernmental organizations, other nonstate actors that also play a role in the international system. What makes these especially unique, however, is that none of them is made up of nation-states, although what each does affects nation-states and, in fact, the entire international system.

NONGOVERNMENTAL ORGANIZATIONS (NGOs)

The prominence and role of nongovernmental organizations (NGOs) have grown as they have become recognized by other legitimate actors within the international system, such as nation-states, and other IGOs, such as the UN. Some transnational movements have grown up around very positive and progressive ideas, such as protecting the environment or human rights. Some coalesce around specific ideological causes, such as population control/family planning or immigration. What these social movements have in common is the desire to bring about change in international law or policy, or within an individual nation-state. And often they seek legal and legitimate ways to bring pressure to bear on numerous governments and the international system in order to achieve their goals without resorting to acts of violence.

Groups that are dedicated to cleaning up the environment (such as the Sierra Club) or human rights (such as Amnesty International) are examples of such NGOs that bring together people from different nation-states to work for or advocate for a larger global good. NGOs can also serve economic needs (such as chambers of commerce) or business-related functions (such as the International Air Transport Association [IATA], which coordinates airlines worldwide). Among the things that make NGOs especially difficult to define or characterize is that they vary quite a bit in terms of mission, size, membership, and resources.

Because they are not tied to any individual nation-state but cross state borders, NGOs are also in a unique position to effect change at the international level. Generally, they do not advocate for any single state's position but for issues pertaining to a group of people or an issue. And as the world has become smaller and more globalized, technology has enabled them to spread their message quite broadly and to appeal to a larger group of people.

What does all this tell us? If you google "NGO" you will get almost 20 million entries. And if you further subdivide these, you can get a good idea of the range and extent of these organizations. The point is that NGOs exist to advocate for almost any cause and purpose, and that these transcend polit-ical borders. Further, they can play an important role in influencing policy in the international system.

For example, when the UN organized the various conferences on women,[17] it included participation by NGOs representing women. In fact, the website for the UN Division for the Advancement of Women (DAW) states explicitly:

> The active participation of NGOs is a critical element. . . . NGOs have been influential in shaping the current global policy framework on women's em-powerment and gender equality—the Beijing Declaration and Platform for Ac-tion. They continue to play an important role in holding international and national leaders accountable for the commitments they made in the Platform for Action.[18]

In this case, NGOs based in various countries around the world came to-gether to contribute to an international agenda that promoted and recog-nized the role of women under the auspices of the UN. And there are many other such examples.

The United Nations has a website

> for our global NGO community (Non-governmental organizations associated with the United Nations). Its aim is to help promote collaborations between NGOs throughout the world, so that together we can more effectively partner with the United Nations and each other to create a more peaceful, just, equita-ble and sustainable world for this and future generations.[19]

In other words, there is a network linking UN-recognized NGOs to facilitate their collaboration.

One statistic notes that in 2009 there were approximately twenty-eight thousand documented NGOs worldwide. Furthermore, the "socially con-structed image of NGOs widely accepted throughout the world is highly positive—humanitarian movements dedicated to improving the human con-dition rather than seeking to benefit themselves at the expense of others."[20] This positive image has been reinforced by the public and also by the re-sponse of NGOs to natural disasters, such as the earthquake in Haiti in Janu-ary 2010 or the earthquake and tsunami in Japan in March 2011. Where countries were seen as lagging in their responses, it was international NGOs such as the International Red Cross and Doctors Without Borders that were the first to respond.

In many ways, NGOs play an important and otherwise unfilled role in international relations. But this also makes them vulnerable and makes them targets in situations of conflict. For example, one of the first buildings to be bombed in Sarajevo, Bosnia, in 1992 at the start of that war was the building housing the International Federation of the Red Cross (IFRC), which was identified by its flag.[21] Attacking that building was important symbolically because it was identified so strongly with the international community, and the bombing sent a message internationally about the gravity of the conflict. That destruction aside, the IFRC and its associated organizations continued their work in Bosnia during the war and after, including taking on the task of clearing land mines that had been planted during the war.

Here we can ask another important question, and that is: Who would take on these tasks if NGOs did not step up? For example, clearing land mines is tedious and expensive work that most militaries are reluctant or unable to do. And yet because land mines are so inexpensive to make and plant, they have become a weapon used in many civil conflicts. The International Campaign to Ban Landmines (ICBL), another NGO, was awarded a Nobel Peace Prize for its work in trying to enact an international treaty banning land mines. The Treaty to Ban Land Mines entered into force in March 1999, but thirty-six states, including the United States, have not yet signed. The ICBL also estimates that as of 2010, more than seventy states were still affected by land mines, primarily as a result of civil wars.[22] This NGO continues to work for the elimination of land mines and expanding the list of countries that are signatories. It serves as an example of an NGO that advocates for a cause that affects many countries and the people within them, which the countries are unwilling or unable to address themselves.

Those NGOs that advocate for a particular policy position, such as family planning, are seen as more controversial because of the stand that they take. While few would argue with the need to help a country or a people who have suffered because of an event not of their making, to advocate for the distribution of contraceptive devices flies in the face of some religious or cultural tenets or traditions. In those cases, the NGO often does not get the same level or type of support.

Here we get into the dangers of cultural imperialism as well: the imposition of one set of cultural norms on another country or group. While those in the developed West might advocate for the use of condoms for family planning purposes as a way to reduce the poverty rate of a country, ensure freedom for women from unwanted pregnancy, and reduce the rate of HIV/ AIDS, some in the target countries might see this as the West imposing its cultural norms on another group. Thus, what one NGO might advocate as a positive policy option for a host of reasons might elicit a negative response for cultural or social reasons.

Like the IGOs noted above, different theoretical traditions respond in different ways to NGOs and the roles that they play. Realists would question the validity of such organizations as playing any legitimate role internationally. Since they believe that power is tied to and derived from the nation-state, NGOs by definition do not and cannot play a role as independent actors. Any power that they might have internationally has to be granted to them by the nation-state.

Here we can also see the divergence among theoretical perspectives. Liberals, in contrast to realists, would see the growing role of NGOs as indicative of changes in the international system. They would argue that NGOs represent different perspectives and points of view, and that they actually help facilitate cooperation and collective action around policies that are designed to further the greater good. Thus, they would argue, NGOs play a unique role in coalescing support for policies such as improving the environment or protecting the rights of children worldwide. Constructivists too would see the emergence of NGOs as indicative of changes in the structure of international relations that can ultimately alter the policies of nation-states.

Feminists especially see the importance of NGOs, which emerged beyond the constraints of formal political channels and therefore can be far more receptive to the inclusion of women and to addressing the needs of women. In fact, "Women have a long history of nongovernmental political engagement at the international level. In the nineteenth century, women began to organize internationally over a broad range of issues such as antislavery, temperance, peace, and women's suffrage."[23] Clearly, women saw that they could play a role in influencing policy decisions, even if they could not yet vote. But it also is important to note that many of these women's movements were driven by generally elite women from the northern developed countries such as the UK and the United States. This, in turn, seemed to set a precedent "that international women's movements have tended to reflect the priorities of those in Western liberal states; this has given rise to legitimate claims from women in the South that their concerns have been ignored or misunderstood."[24]

Nonetheless, the international agenda for all women took an important step forward in the 1970s with the declaration of the UN Decade for Women and the subsequent women's conferences held under UN auspices. At these various conferences,

> there was an increasing recognition of the multiple experiences of women depending on their class, race and nationality; feminist concerns with difference and cautions about universalism were articulated by the activist community. A wide variety of issues was raised, including women's participation in informal labor markets, environmental issues, and violence against women.[25]

The point here is that the emergence and growing roles of NGOs internationally have made it possible to put policy issues on the international agenda that nation-states have had to address in a serious way. This is one example of the ways in which nonstate actors, in this case NGOs, can affect the behavior of nation-states and the international system.

TERRORISM: A CHALLENGE TO THE INTERNATIONAL SYSTEM

Thus far, we have looked at international organizations of various types that have been recognized as an ongoing and legitimate part of the international system. We are now going to turn our attention to a very different type of nonstate actor: terrorist groups. Terrorist groups, such as al-Qaeda, are among the nonstate actors that have gotten a lot of attention in the wake of 9/11 especially. But various other events, including two sets of bombings in the city of Mumbai, India, and bombings in London and Madrid and other European capitals, are examples of the types of events that have drawn attention to terrorist groups as nonstate actors that have had a significant impact on nation-states and the international system.

Terrorism: A Historical Perspective

In looking at terrorism, it is important to note that it is not a new phenomenon; examples of what could be called terrorist acts can be documented going back to ancient Rome. "Historically, the vast majority of terrorism of traditional societies has been religiously inspired; indeed, terrorists often claimed they were carrying out the will of God. These historical examples are a good reminder that religiously inspired terrorism—a major contemporary concern—is certainly not new."[26] However, what should also be remembered is that terrorism is not confined to religious extremism. In fact, it is often called the weapon of the weak, for its use by groups with political agendas that could not get access to the political system or groups that felt they had no other way of making their views known beyond resorting to acts of terrorism.

In fact, it was often the state that used tactics we have come to think of as terrorist in order to keep their citizens in check. For example, the "knock at the door" in Nazi Germany or Stalin's Russia was a way to remind people of the power of the state and of the fact that they needed to behave. The idea of purges, which Stalin engaged in as a way to control the population, can be seen as an act of state-sponsored terror. So the idea of the use of violence (either real or perceived) was often sufficient to get the citizens to comply with the desires of the government.

It was in the nineteenth century that individuals started to take advantage of many of the same types of arbitrary actions that the government used to keep citizens in line. The emergence of this type of *political terrorism* can be defined as

> the deliberate use or threat of violence against noncombatants, calculated to instill fear, alarm, and ultimately a feeling of helplessness in an audience beyond the immediate victims. Because perpetrators of terrorism often strike symbolic targets in a horrific manner, the psychological impact of an attack can exceed the physical damage. A mixture of drama and dread, terrorism is not senseless violence; it is a *premeditated political strategy* that threatens people with a coming danger that seems ubiquitous, unavoidable, and unpredictable. (emphasis added)[27]

That is, terrorism is a tactic that is specifically used to strike fear into innocent civilians and thereby threaten the stability of the state, which ultimately will pressure political decision makers to bring about the ends desired by the terrorists.

Terrorism can be used to support or change the status quo. And as noted above, it can be used by states as well as nonstate actors. But it is the latter that we have come to think of when we think of terrorism—usually groups that want to change the status quo, bring attention to their cause, change the political leader, and so on. It is also important to remember that terrorism can be and has been used by groups on both the left and right wings of the political spectrum, by secular as well as religious groups—but all resort to the same sorts of tactics in order to achieve their goals.

Terrorism can have an important impact on the policies of the nation by focusing primarily on the people *within* the nation. Thus, terrorist actions do not necessarily result in the desired outcome because the government gives in to the demands of the terrorists. Rather, what is more likely is that the terrorist actions have an impact on the people, who then bring pressure to bear on the government to change its policies.

Many of the tactics of political terrorism came into prominence in the nineteenth century in Europe and North America, at a time when the very nature of the state was changing. The Industrial Revolution and the growth of science and technology contributed to some important advances for the world at that time. But along with those came the growth of cities as the base for the new industries, and with that, laborers necessary to do the work in those industries. The UK is one of the classic examples of this movement from the rural areas to the industrial cities. But the United States, France, and to a lesser extent the other countries in Europe gradually went through similar transitions. While many people grew rich, especially those who owned the factories, many others became poor, and the urban areas gave rise to slums and poverty. It was out of that disconnect between those who owned the means of production and those who worked in them that Karl Marx and other communist theoreticians talked about the need for the workers to rise up, as noted in chapter 2.[28] In *The Communist Manifesto*, Marx, writing with Friedrich Engels, declared: "The proletarians have nothing to lose but their chains. They have a world to win. Working Men of All Countries, Unite!"[29] This became a rallying cry for rebellion against the state. This call gave rise to a group known as *anarchists*, who took it upon themselves to wage war against the emerging order. But it is also important to note that they waged their attacks primarily against the officials of the government, not innocent civilians.

The United States was a victim of this type of terrorist attack allegedly perpetrated by anarchists in the 1920 bombing of the J. P. Morgan Bank headquarters in New York. More than thirty people were killed and scores were injured in this bombing. While the bombers were never caught, a message was found in a mailbox of a building nearby signed "American Anarchist Fighters." This bombing coincided with a period in which the United

States was already focused inward, and this provided further reason to enact legislation that limited immigration, as well as repression against "undesirables" such as communists. In many ways, this presages what we see following the terrorist attacks of 9/11.[30]

After World War I and into the years preceding and following World War II, the nature of terrorism started to change. Often the goals of the new terrorist groups were tied to issues of self-determination and the desire to create a new and independent state using military force if necessary. During the Cold War, this often took on an ideological edge, contributing to the growth of "revolutionary movements," whose goal was to overthrow the existing dominant order. Often these terrorist groups had their roots in what they saw as their nationalist mission to bring to the country a different form of government most consistent with the goals of the peoples of that nation. And these groups also felt that the only way they could get their ideas across and make their point was to root it in acts of violence.

Terrorism also was tied to groups who were advocating a particular ideological path that they felt the government either had abandoned or was not following at all. By attacking innocent people within the country, these terrorist groups felt they could draw attention to their cause.

Terrorist acts were also committed in the name of nationalism, in which the groups felt they had to act in support of the peoples of their nation and against the state, even if that meant killing innocent civilians. In their viewpoint, no one could truly be innocent. For example, nationalism became part of the rallying cry for the Irish Republican Army (IRA) and its acts of violence directed against the British and the Union supporters in Northern Ireland. In this case, they were hoping that the campaign of violence would result in the British forces leaving Northern Ireland so that Northern Ireland could become an independent country free of Great Britain. Clearly, this did not happen, and the IRA's campaign of terror turned many people away from the cause that they were advocating. Eventually, the IRA leadership and the majority of people within the IRA concluded that they would be more successful negotiating for their goals, rather than continuing their campaign of violence. Gerry Adams, who was involved with the IRA, now serves as a member of the Irish Parliament for Sinn Fein, the political arm of the IRA.

Terrorism was part of the landscape from the time of the Balfour Declaration in 1917 and the Palestine mandate that would lead ultimately to the creation of the state of Israel in 1948, and perhaps surprisingly can be attributed to both sides. Prior to the formal creation of Israel in 1948, various Jewish organizations that were Zionist and nationalistic embarked on a series of terrorist acts directed against Palestinians but also against the British who were still in the region. One of the most notorious of those was the bombing of a wing of the King David Hotel in Jerusalem in 1946, resulting in ninety-one deaths and more than forty injured. But this act contributed to pressure on the British to leave, ultimately leading to the recognition of Israel as a Jewish state.[31]

On the Palestinian side, we see the growth of the Palestine Liberation Organization (PLO), which advocated for a Palestinian state and the concomitant destruction of Israel. The first of the PLO attacks came in the early 1960s; later attacks included the murder of Israeli athletes in the 1972 Munich Olympics and the massacre of civilians at the Rome and Vienna airports in 1985. Like the IRA, the PLO eventually moderated its tactics from acts of violence to pursuing its goals through political means, and the organization itself went from being a terrorist group to a governing political party that actually now negotiates with the government of Israel. However, in the case of both the PLO and the IRA, there are many who have not forgotten their acts of violence and continue to question their legitimacy.

Terrorism as a Political Tool

Why is terrorism effective? The fact that terrorism is so arbitrary means that everyone is potentially a target and a victim. Terrorism often does not target the military or the government, but innocent civilians, thereby disrupting the patterns of what might otherwise be termed "normal" life. It is able to amplify the impact it has because by targeting people in what otherwise would be normal settings—a market, a bus going to school or work, an airplane—it makes it clear that anyone is potentially vulnerable, which has a psychological effect on a far larger population than just those who were affected by the attack. Furthermore, increasingly terrorist acts are being committed by women as well as men, which changes the dynamics as well as the perception of terrorism and who is a terrorist.

If terrorism is a weapon of the weak, it has been used more effectively in a world that has gotten smaller and that has come to rely more heavily on technology. One of the dangers of a globalized world is that borders are harder to control, so people can move easily and quickly across them, enter another country, and settle there, potentially waiting years before mounting an attack. Along with the movement of people comes the ease with which arms and explosives of various types can cross borders, making it easier to arm terrorists or criminals and resulting in untold amounts of damage in lives and property. And as we saw with the events of 9/11, any terrorist who is intent on inflicting damage can find a means to do so, even to the extent of using commercial aircraft as a weapon of destruction designed to inflict terror.

Clearly, the United States has seen firsthand the impact of terrorism and why it poses such a challenge to the international system. Now that terrorist attacks are covered by the media and coverage is so instantaneous, as soon as the 9/11 attacks were reported we could all watch the second plane crash into the World Trade Center *in real time*. Virtually no one could be untouched by the scenes of death and destruction in Manhattan, but the imagery also brought home the important lesson that potentially everyone is vulnerable—no one is immune to terrorist attacks.

We started off by talking about new challenges to the international system. While terrorism has been around for a long time, for many of the reasons noted above it has become even more of a challenge to the international system. Furthermore, as a nonstate transnational actor, it can cross borders and affect many people in many states, thereby making it even more difficult for any single nation to arrive at a response.

Women as Terrorists

With the growth of terrorism as a political tool, the concept of what a terrorist looks like has changed. The proliferation of women as terrorists has made it even more difficult for states to identify a terrorist, respond to acts of terrorism, or even formulate policies about it. Women as terrorists—whether as suicide bombers, snipers, leaders of a rebellious guerilla group, and so on—runs counter to the commonly held perception of women as peacemakers and women as peaceful. Women have always been engaged as spies and even terrorists, since it is often easier for them to move through society without attracting the attention a man would. And with the increase in civil wars and wars of national liberation since the end of the Cold War, women have become more prominent. The "Black Tiger" Tamil women fighting for a state against the Sinhalese in Sri Lanka, the "Black Widows" who fought in Chechnya, and the women who made up the Palestinian "army of roses" are but a few of the cases in which women have been prominent as terrorists and even suicide bombers.

In many ways, the role of women as terrorists emerged prominently in the 1960s and 1970s, with the proliferation of terrorist groups in general. Although the "typical terrorist" was male, "several of the most active left-wing terrorist groups during this period had a strong female presence"[32]—for example, Ulrike Meinhof of the Baader-Meinhof group in Germany; Leila Khaled, who was actively involved with the Popular Front for the Liberation of Palestine (PFLP); and Fusako Shigenobu, founder and leader of the Japanese Red Army. But in giving these examples, it is also important to note that

> from modern terrorism's beginnings, women have tended to be more active as leaders and members of groups that have worked to *overturn* traditional values, rather than those seeking to restore old ones—stated another way, they have been less likely to play an active role in right-wing groups that idealize the past and incorporate sexism into the political ideologies. (emphasis added)[33]

It should also be noted that the emergence of these women as leaders of these left-leaning organizations coincided with the advance of the women's movement (second-wave feminism), a basic premise of which was to advocate the philosophy that women should not be bound to traditional "women's roles" and that both women and men would benefit from situations of equality. That means that both men and women could—and did—engage in acts of terrorism.

In looking at terrorism and terrorist groups and the role that they play in the international system, they "are more willing than states are to violate the norms of the international system because, unlike states, they do not have a stake in that system."[34] In fact, from a traditional levels-of-analysis perspective, it is questionable where they even fit within the system. Yet the impact that they have on that system cannot be debated.

MULTINATIONAL CORPORATIONS (MNCs)

We have been talking about various transnational actors that have had an impact on the international system. Some, such as terrorist groups, exist outside the law, and their goal is to make their point by inflicting fear and terror through the arbitrary act of violence, either threatened or real. We also talked about other groups like NGOs that have social or political issues in common and transcend traditional state boundaries, which work to influence the international policy agenda.

What we are going to look briefly at now are multinational corporations (MNCs), which are corporations or businesses based or headquartered in one country that produce goods or services and conduct operations in two or more other countries. It is important to remember that MNCs are not a new phenomenon but existed in earlier cycles of globalization, albeit on a different scale. For example, the Dutch East India Company was a critical force behind the exploration and colonization in the earlier era of globalization.[35] That company, based in the Netherlands, helped fund exploration to other parts of the world, looking for spices and other valuables. Those colonies then became the bases for their activities, which brought wealth back to the company, its investors, and the home country.

In many ways, that is analogous to the growth of MNCs that we see today, albeit on a larger scale. The growth of technology and globalization has made it easier for companies to be based in one country, have factories or the means of production in a number of others, and then sell their products in still other countries. Thus, MNCs have grown in size, scope, and power with the globalization of the international economy, especially since World War II.

Their size and the amount of money they command have given MNCs a great deal of power within the international system. According to data compiled in 2007 by the World Bank, if we look at gross national income (GNI), Wal-Mart Stores ranked twentieth, followed immediately by Exxon Mobil. The country of Turkey ranks next, followed by another oil company, Royal Dutch Shell. Fifty of the top one hundred countries and corporations by size of economy and revenue are countries, and the other fifty are MNCs. This wealth, as well as global reach, has made MNCs both hated and loved. Advocates for liberal free trade see such corporations as playing an active and important role in the international economic system. They can spur economic investment and improvement; often transmit ideas; move money to different places through their markets; and by ensuring competition, actually lower prices. This perspective moves beyond a world defined by states to one driven by economics and economic competition. Clearly, MNCs prosper in a stable international environment characterized by free and open trade and investment.

BOX 5.2

COUNTRIES AND CORPORATIONS: A RANKING
BY SIZE OF ECONOMY AND REVENUES

Rank	Country/Corporation	GNI/Revenues (billions of dollars)
1	United States	12,912.9
2	Japan	4,976.5
3	Germany	2,835.6
4	United Kingdom	2,272.7
5	China	2,269.7
6	France	2,169.2
7	Italy	1,772.9
8	Spain	1,095.9
9	Canada	1,052.6
10	India	804.1
11	South Korea	765.0
12	Mexico	753.4
13	Australia	673.2
14	Brazil	662.0
15	Netherlands	642.0
16	Russia	638.1
17	Switzerland	411.4
18	Belgium	378.7
19	Sweden	369.1
20	WAL-MART STORES	351.2
21	EXXON MOBIL	347.3
22	Turkey	342.0

Rank	Country/Corporation	GNI/Revenues (billions of dollars)
23	ROYAL DUTCH/SHELL	318.8
24	Austria	306.2
25	Saudi Arabia	289.2
26	Indonesia	282.2
27	Norway	281.5
28	BRITISH PETROLEUM	274.4
29	Poland	273.1
30	Denmark	261.8
31	South Africa	223.5
32	Philippines	223.1
33	Greece	220.3
34	GENERAL MOTORS	207.4
35	TOYOTA MOTOR	204.8
36	CHEVRON	200.6
37	Finland	196.9
38	Hong Kong, China	192.1
39	DAIMLER CHRYSLER	190.2
40	Portugal	181.3
41	Iran	177.3
42	Thailand	175.0
43	Argentina	173.1
44	CONOCOPHILLIPS	172.5
45	Ireland	171.1
46	TOTAL	168.4
47	GENERAL ELECTRIC	168.3

Rank	Country/Corporation	GNI/Revenues (billions of dollars)
48	FORD MOTOR	160.1
49	ING GROUP	158.3
50	CITIGROUP	146.8
51	AXA	139.7
52	VOLKSWAGEN	132.3
53	SINOPEC	131.6
54	Israel	128.7
55	CRÉDIT AGRICOLE	128.5
56	Venezuela	128.1
57	Malaysia	125.9
58	ALLIANZ	125.5
59	FORTIS	121.2
60	Singapore	119.8
61	BANK OF AMERICA	117.0
62	HSBC HOLDINGS	115.4
63	Czech Republic	114.8
64	AMERICAN INTERNATIONAL GROUP	113.2
65	CHINA NATIONAL PETROLEUM	110.5
66	BNP PARIBAS	109.2
67	ENI	109.0
68	UBS	107.8
69	Pakistan	107.3
70	SIEMENS	107.3
71	STATE GRID	107.2
72	New Zealand	106.3

Rank	Country/Corporation	GNI/Revenues (billions of dollars)
73	Colombia	104.5
74	United Arab Emirates	103.5
75	ASSICURAZIONI GENERALI	101.8
76	Hungary	101.6
77	J. P. MORGAN CHASE	100.0
78	CARREFOUR	99.0
79	BERKSHIRE HATHAWAY	98.6
80	PEMEX	97.5
81	DEUTSCHE BANK	96.2
82	DEXIA GROUP	95.8
83	Chile	95.7
84	HONDA MOTOR	94.8
85	MCKESSON	93.6
86	VERIZON COMMUNICATIONS	93.2
87	NIPPON TELEGRAPH & TELEPHONE	92.0
88	HEWLETT-PACKARD	91.7
89	INTERNATIONAL BUSINESS MACHINES	91.4
90	VALERO ENERGY	91.1
91	HOME DEPOT	90.8
92	Egypt	90.1
93	Algeria	89.6
94	NISSAN MOTOR	89.5
95	SAMSUNG ELECTRONICS	89.5
96	CREDIT SUISSE	89.4
97	HITACHI	87.6

Rank	Country/Corporation	GNI/Revenues (billions of dollars)
98	Romania	84.6
99	SOCIÉTÉ GÉNÉRALE	84.5
100	AVIVA83.5	83.5

Sources: Gross National Income (GNI), World Bank, 2007 World Development Indicators, 14–16; MNC revenues, Fortune, July 23, 2007, 133–40.

In contrast, however, MNCs are also the target of much hostility, as they are seen as taking jobs away from people at home, exploiting labor, and producing shoddy products. In the poorer, less developed countries, MNCs are perceived as subverting the sovereignty of the state, since the corporations have more money—and often more economic and political power—than the state appears to have. On the other hand, they create jobs in the poorer countries, often in areas where economic options are otherwise limited. This also means that the government is often dependent on the corporation.

In the first of a series of Pulitzer Prize–winning articles about Wal-Mart published in November 2003 in the Los Angeles Times, the authors wrote:

Wal-Mart's decisions influence wages and working conditions across a wide swath of the world economy, from the shopping centers of Las Vegas to the factories of Honduras and South Asia. Its business is so vital to developing countries that some send emissaries to the corporate headquarters in Bentonville, Ark., almost as if Wal-Mart were a sovereign nation. (emphasis added)[36]

The second article in the series, which focuses on the impact on the countries in which it has factories, also illustrates well this symbiotic relationship between corporation and government:

The company's size and obsession with shaving costs have made it a global economic force. Its decisions affect wages, working conditions and manufacturing practices—even the price of a yard of denim—around the world. . . . To cut costs, Honduran factories have reduced payrolls and become more efficient. The country produces the same amount of clothing as it did three years

ago, but with 20% fewer workers, said Henry Fransen, director of the Honduran Apparel Manufacturers Assn., which represents nearly 200 export factories.

"We're earning less and producing more," he said with a laugh, "following
the Wal-Mart philosophy."

That's harsh medicine for a developing country. The clothing industry is
one of the few sources of decent jobs for unskilled workers in this nation of 6
million. Many of those jobs depend on Wal-Mart.[37]

Another criticism leveled at MNCs—and the Wal-Mart example illustrates
this quite well—is that the MNCs not only control the wages of the labor
force but can also alter the wage structure, which has implications for the
social structure of the country. Women who might have previously partici-
pated in agriculture or creation of traditional arts and crafts turn to working
in the factories, often under deplorable conditions, because of the salaries
that they get. And in some countries, children are also hired to work in those
factories.

U.S. retailers began making their way to Bangladesh in the 1980s. They found
a large population of poor, young women willing to work from dawn to dusk
for a few pennies an hour. . . . Many factories lacked ventilation and fire es-
capes. Labor activists estimated in the mid-1990s that as many as 50,000 Ban-
gladeshi children were sewing apparel for companies such as Wal-Mart and
Kmart Corp.[38]

On the other hand, the wages are good in relative terms, and the work is
steady. For some, it's their only source of income.[39]

MNCs are often the target of much of what is seen as bad in the area of
globalization, but the reality is that the role of MNCs is complex as well as
controversial. It is clear that MNCs play a role in international relations, although what that role is and who benefits or is harmed can be unclear. To
some, MNCs are agents of their home national governments, which give
MNCs clear national identities. Or put another way, the image of the MNC
and the country become intertwined. The Wal-Mart example is a case in
point: Wal-Mart is equated with the United States. This, in turn, has contributed to the undermining of the "soft power" of the United States; when a
major U.S. corporation is seen as exploiting the people or infringing on the
rights of others or taking wealth out of the country, the United States is
blamed, rightly or not. Some actually make the argument the other way—

that is, that states exist as agents of corporations, and that state intervention is therefore specifically used to enhance the well-being of the corporation. This is the basis of some of the arguments that we saw underlying the invasion of Iraq, specifically that the United States invaded Iraq to protect oil interests and that the invasion benefited some U.S. corporations, such as Halliburton. As a subcontractor to the U.S. government, Halliburton was hired to perform a particular task at the lowest possible cost, and with a minimal amount of control by the United States.

When we look at the role of MNCs as actors in the international system, it is also important to remember that not only do they operate and work in other countries, but they own capital in them. These might include buildings, factories, and so on. This foreign direct investment in a country other than the home country of the corporation can be politically sensitive, as it gives them access to the political and economic system of that country and potentially some influence in what goes on in that country.

MNCs operate in the *host* country, while headquartered in the *home* country, and they can create both opportunities and problems for each. MNCs are chartered within one country and technically therefore function under the laws of the home country. However, when they operate in other countries, there are also a host of legal questions that come up. For example, when five Blackwater guards hired as subcontractors to work in Iraq were arrested and charged with the deaths of unarmed civilians in Baghdad in 2007, they turned themselves in to the authorities in Salt Lake City, Utah, and were not tried in Iraq. According to a news report about the incident in the *New York Times*:

> In an indication of the legal uncertainties surrounding the case in Iraq, where the law gives American contractors virtual immunity, Mr. Dabbagh [spokesman for the Iraqi Prime Minister] said decisions on specific legal steps would wait until the Americans completed their own investigation of the shooting and conferred with the Iraqis. It is not clear which provisions of American law would apply in this case.[40]

But incidents such as these, and the confusion surrounding jurisdiction and legalities, also complicate the situation for MNCs and the people who work for them.

One of the major changes regarding MNCs has been their origin or home countries, which in many ways is also representative of the changes in global power. Initially, most MNCs were housed in the United States, Japan, and parts of Europe. But more recently, we have seen that change with the emergence of companies based in China, for example, and other parts of Asia. Hence, MNCs are no longer the purview of the developed world of the North, nor can all blame for the behavior of MNCs be placed on just those countries.

Why are MNCs seen as controversial? As the role and wealth of MNCs have grown, so has their prominence in the international system, which has also made them a target for much of the hatred tied to globalization. For one thing, as wealth and power appear to be more concentrated, the larger MNCs seem to become even more powerful. Their global reach and power have enabled them to be involved in the internal affairs of nations—they are not only international nonstate actors, but they try to or actually do influence policies within nations. For example, MNCs actively lobby for the passage of legislation that will be to their advantage, such as on trade, tax policies, and so on. MNCs can actually serve as instruments of a nation's foreign policy— for example, Halliburton operating in Iraq as contractors, augmenting the U.S. military. More recently, we can see this in the flap that has erupted between the United States and its ally the UK over whether there was some connection between the release of Abdel Basset Ali al-Megrahi, the only person convicted in the bombing of Pan Am Flight 103 over Lockerbie, Scotland, and British Petroleum (BP), now a company of great interest to the United States because of the major oil spill from its drilling well in the Gulf of Mexico. That issue was the focus of much of the first meeting held in July 2010 between President Obama and new British prime minister David Cameron, overshadowing other major foreign policy issues, such as the war in Afghanistan. What this illustrates is the blurring of boundaries between corporations and nations' foreign policies.

Another thing that makes MNCs so difficult to deal with in the study of IR is the fact that, as nonstate actors, they really do not fall clearly within any theoretical perspective. But we do know that they have an influence on nation-states and even international relations. In looking at the roles that they play and who is affected by their actions, Marxist and feminist theorists can actually be of some help. The Marxists would look at the relationship between the corporation and the workers, especially those who are often exploited in order to ensure that the corporation makes as much profit as possible. Here we have an unequal relationship between those who have the power, the corporations, and those who work for the corporation, often at low wages and in poor conditions—i.e., the workers. There is clearly a tension that exists between these two groups, although in some ways, both benefit. The Marxists would also advise us to look at the relationships between the corporation and the various nation-states, as this also provides some important information in understanding their roles. What nations are the corporations based in, and where do they actually do their work (extracting oil, manufacturing clothing, and so on)? Are the nation-states equal, or do we see an unequal relationship between the countries? What does each country get from the relationship that enables the relationship to continue? This too should provide some insight into our understanding of the way international relations works, especially when there are asymmetrical relationships.

In order to truly understand the role of MNCs, the feminists would once again ask us to reflect with gender-sensitive lenses. When we do so, we can see that often corporations can only prosper because of the exploitation of women's labor. This is a point made in the articles about Wal-Mart, but it is also echoed in the feminist IR literature. But as Tickner also reminds us in her brief analysis of women and the global economy, there are some cases where women are being empowered through their ability to work, which comes at the expense of men.[41] So not only do we need to look at and understand the role of MNCs through gender-sensitive lenses, we also have to remove our cultural blinders and assumptions so that we can get a more balanced perspective on who is affected, who benefits (including the consumer), and the costs.

In this section, we wanted to raise a number of issues about MNCs and also to illustrate the complexity and ambiguities of the roles that they play in the international system today. MNCs will not go away. Rather, the challenge for the members of the international system is how best to deal with them.

SUMMARY

In this chapter, we looked at the actors that exist outside the traditional levels-of-analysis framework but have an important impact on the international system nonetheless. Because they do not fit neatly within the levels of analysis does not mean that we need to throw out that organizational framework or assume it is useless and out of date. It continues to serve as an important organizing principle in international relations. However, what we also need to be aware of is the fact that it is no longer as complete a model as it was when Kenneth Waltz put the idea forward in 1954, and then as it was developed further by J. David Singer in 1960. The world has changed a lot since then, while the levels-of-analysis approach really hasn't adapted. In fact, as we recognize the existence of other actors, we can modify the model a bit to take them into account, specifically by addressing the impact of each of these nonstate actors on the various levels, including the international system as a whole. Doing so will allow us to have a more complete picture of international relations in general and the actors within it specifically.

FURTHER READINGS

These additional readings are worth exploring and elaborate on some of the points raised in this chapter. This list is not meant to be exhaustive, but only illustrative.

Goldman, Abigail, Nancy Cleeland, et al., "The Wal-Mart Effect," *Los Angeles Times*, November 23, 24, and 25, 2003, at http://www.latimes.com/la-walmart-sg,0,7885 526.storygallery.

"NGO Global Network," at http://www.ngo.org/index3.htm.

UN Division for the Advancement of Women, "Non-Governmental Organizations (NGOs)," at http://www.un.org/womenwatch/daw/ngo/index.html.

NOTES

1. See John Lewis Gaddis, "The Long Peace: Elements of Stability in the Postwar International System," *International Security* 10, no. 4 (Spring 1986): 99–142.

2. See "Official and National Academy of Sciences (NAS) Based Poverty Rates: 1999 to 2009," accessed through the U.S. Census Bureau website, at http://www.census.gov/hhes/povmeas/data/nas/tables/2009/index.html.

3. "Lula's Legacy," *The Economist*, October 2, 2010, 30.

4. "About the IMF," http://www.imf.org/external/about.htm.

5. OPEC, "Annual Report, 2010," 11, at http://www.opec.org/opec_web/static_files_project/media/downloads/publications/Annual_Report_2010.pdf.

6. Paul Viotti and Mark V. Kauppi, *International Relations and World Politics: Security, Economy, Identity*, 4th ed. (Upper Saddle River, NJ: Pearson Prentice Hall, 2009), 215.

7. "About UNICEF: Who We Are," at http://www.unicef.org/about/who/index_introduction.html.

8. "About ISAF: History," at http://www.isaf.nato.int/history.html.

9. Mary Ann Tetrault and Ronnie D. Lipschutz, *Global Politics As If People Mattered* (Lanham, MD: Rowman & Littlefield, 2005), 172.

10. J. Ann Tickner, *Gender in International Relations: Feminist Perspectives on Achieving Global Security* (New York: Columbia University Press, 1992), 78.

11. Jack Ewing, "Some Winners Emerge from Europe's Debt Crisis," *New York Times*, June 20, 2010.

12. "AU in a Nutshell," at http://www.au.int/en/about/nutshell.

13. See, for example, J. Ann Tickner, *Gendering World Politics: Issues and Approaches in the Post–Cold War Era* (New York: Columbia University Press, 2001). Also see V. Spike Peterson and Anne Sisson Runyan, *Global Gender Issues*, 2nd ed. (Boulder, CO: Westview Press, 1999).

14. BBC News, "France Ends Four-Decade Nato Rift," March 12, 2009, at http://news.bbc.co.uk/2/hi/7937666.stm.

15. BBC News, "France Ends Four-Decade Nato Rift."

16. Joshua S. Goldstein and Jon C. Pevehouse, *Principles of International Relations* (New York: Pearson Longman, 2009), 59. There are a number of excellent books that detail the U.S. decision to go into Iraq despite UN and international reservations. See, for example, Thomas Ricks, *Fiasco: The American Military Adventure in Iraq* (New York: Penguin, 2006); Todd S. Purdum, *A Time of Our Choosing: America's War in Iraq* (New York: Henry Holt, 2003); and Richard N. Haass, *War of Necessity, War of Choice: A Memoir of Two Iraq Wars* (New York: Simon & Schuster, 2009).

17. The Commission on the Status of Women has been responsible for organizing and following up the world conferences on women in Mexico (1975), Copenhagen (1980), Nairobi (1985), and Beijing (1995). There was also a special session of the General Assembly on women held in June 2000 to follow up on Beijing. One of the things that marked the Beijing conference was the number of NGOs related to the status of women that attended.

18. UN Division for the Advancement of Women, "Non-Governmental Organizations (NGOs)," at http://www.un.org/womenwatch/daw/ngo/index.html.

19. "NGO Global Network," at http://www.ngo.org/index3.htm.

20. Charles W. Kegley with Shannon L. Blanton, *World Politics: Trend and Transformation*, 12th ed. (Belmont, CA: Wadsworth Cengage Learning, 2009), 190–91.

21. This was told to me at an interview with members of the IFRC delegation in Sarajevo in September 2000.

22. For more information, see International Campaign to Ban Landmines website, at http://www.icbl.org/index.php/icbl/content/view/full/2.

23. Tickner, *Gendering World Politics*, 117.

24. Tickner, *Gendering World Politics*, 117.

25. Tickner, *Gendering World Politics*, 117–18.

26. Viotti and Kauppi, *International Relations and World Politics*, 257.

27. Kegley, *World Politics*, 387.

28. See Karl Marx and Friedrich Engels, *The Communist Manifesto*. There are countless editions of this readily available. It is also available online at http://www.marx istsfr.org/archive/marx/works/download/manifest.pdf.

29. Marx and Engels, *The Communist Manifesto*.

30. See Beverly Gage, *The Day Wall Street Exploded: A Story of America in Its First Age of Terror* (New York: Oxford University Press, 2009).

31. For more context on this event, see "The Palestine Mandate and the Birth of the State of Israel," in William L. Cleveland, *A History of the Modern Middle East*, 2nd ed. (Boulder, CO: Westview Press, 2000), 233–66.

32. Cindy D. Ness, "In the Name of the Cause: Women's Work in Secular and Religious Terrorism," in *Female Terrorism and Militancy: Agency, Utility, and Organization*, ed. Cindy D. Ness (New York: Routledge, 2008), 13.

33. Ness, "In the Name of the Cause," 13.

34. Goldstein and Pevehouse, *Principles of International Relations*, 141.

35. For an excellent and straightforward explanation about the various stages of globalization, see Robert B. Marks, *The Origins of the Modern World*, 2nd ed. (Lanham, MD: Rowman & Littlefield, 2006).

36. Abigail Goldman and Nancy Cleeland, "The Wal-Mart Effect: An Empire Built on Bargains Remakes the Working World," *Los Angeles Times*, November 23, 2003. The series is available online at http://www.latimes.com/la-walmart-sg,0,7885526 .storygallery. It is important to note that I have used Wal-Mart as an example in part because of the insights offered in this series of articles. I take no position on Wal-Mart.

37. Nancy Cleeland, Evelyn Iritani, and Tyler Marshall, "The Wal-Mart Effect: Scouring the Globe to Give Shoppers an $8.63 Polo Shirt," *Los Angeles Times*, November 24, 2003.

38. Cleeland, Iritani, and Marshall, "Scouring the Globe."

39. For another perspective on this "feminization of labor," see V. Spike Peterson and Anne Sisson Runyan, "Gendered Divisions of Violence, Labor, and Resources," in *Global Gender Issues*, 2nd ed. (Boulder, CO: Westview Press, 1999), 113–62.

40. James Glanz and Alissa J. Rubin, "Blackwater Shootings 'Murder,' Iraq Says," *New York Times*, October 8, 2007, at http://www.nytimes.com/2007/10/08/world/ middleeast/08blackwater.html.

41. Tickner, *Gendering World Politics*, 83.

Pulling It All Together

INTRODUCTION TO THE CASES

In chapter 1, we introduced some basic concepts and ideas that are necessary for you to understand if you are going to master the study of international relations. Many of these concepts and theories were formulated to simplify a complex reality so that you can hold parts of it constant in order to focus on one piece at a time. Doing this is clearly an artificial construct, as we know that the various components of the international system—from the international system level to the nation-states within it, the cultures and societies of the nation-states, and the individuals who make decisions and respond to those decisions all exist and act together, not in discrete parts. But imposing these artificial boundaries also makes it possible to look at and answer a range of questions that would seem to be too big and difficult to address otherwise.

We also started the discussion by noting the impact of globalization on the international system and various components of it. Like it or not, globalization is here to stay. Therefore, what we need to do is to be able to understand the impact of globalization on the international system and what that means for anyone who studies international relations.

In chapters 2 through 5 we then went through the levels of analysis and focused on some of the big questions in IR: What do we mean by war and peace? Why do nations go to war? Why do some nation-states hold together and others fall apart, some peacefully and others violently? We even looked at the role that individuals play in influencing international relations. In doing all this, we also examined the various theories that were designed to help us describe what happened and explain why certain events occurred or why nation-states behave as they do.

As noted earlier, the nature of the nation-state system, which has defined international relations since the Treaty of Westphalia, is changing. For example, since the end of the Cold War nation-states have been characterized by patterns of both integration and disintegration in a way that we have not seen since the current international system came into being. Nation-states are further challenged by a scarcity of necessary resources, such as oil and water, which also has changed the pattern of international relations. We don't know yet whether this will lead to more conflict or cooperation. But no doubt it will require nation-states to rethink their relationships with other countries and nonstate actors.

The nature of power is changing as well. The major economic and military powers of Europe and the United States have become more integrated. The emergence of other democratic and capitalist countries made for even more integration. Yet these same countries are also vying for resources, such as fossil fuels. And countries have different understandings of how to meet that resource need in ways that will not destroy the environment. In short, the very nature of international relations and the international system is changing and no doubt will continue to change as priories shift and relationships are reordered.

In this chapter, we are going to try to pull all these ideas together in some way. The approach we are going to take is to look at some current international issues that affect virtually all members of the international system from the most micro (the individual) to the most macro (the system as a whole). We are not going to presume to provide answers. Rather, what we are going to do is outline a number of cases that the international system is grappling with at the present time. In order to reflect some of the changes in the current international political reality, we are going to stay away from the traditional "hard power" issues of military security and focus more on some of the other issues that are plaguing the international system. This is not meant to discount or minimize the impact or importance of these issues—quite the contrary. As illustrated by events in the Middle East, with a civil war in Syria and the threat from a possibly nuclear Iran, and what is going on in the South China Sea as China becomes more aggressive, these issues that we think of as "security" are an ongoing part of international relations. However, a lot of attention has been given to these issues. Far less attention is devoted to issues of human security or the assurance that all people have their basic human needs met.

For years the international community has struggled to agree upon standards for environmental protection and human rights. But it seems that all too often the concern to protect the environment seems to be in conflict with the goal of development and industrialization. While countries might support the importance of a clean environment, they don't want to enact any policy that will hurt their economic growth.

Immigration is another issue that we need to think about. Although it has been a factor for centuries—think of the pilgrims who left England to come to America in search of political and religious freedom—it has become a more prominent part of the international agenda relatively recently. A globalized world has made it easier for people to leave one country for another in search of economic opportunity. But it has also contributed to a growth of nationalism and nativist sentiments, which have contributed to race riots in France and the passage of anti-immigrant legislation in parts of the United States. At the same time, it has also increased pressure on the federal government of the United States to implement a new and more relevant immigration law.

Similarly, while countries might support the importance of basic human rights for all in theory, they also want to ensure that they—not the international system—determine what is best for their own people. And the case of women's rights not only puts forward issues pertaining to women, but it also raises questions about the difference between having the international community accept resolutions or treaties and the realities of implementing them.

As you go through these cases, your task will be to try to find ways to address these issues, given what you know about international relations and the actors who make up the international system. These cases represent only a brief starting point. There are many other cases you could explore, and I would encourage you to try to do that. What are some other prominent issues? How would you develop those into a case, and what would exploring that particular case tell you about international relations? And as you explore the three cases listed here plus any others that might interest you, how do the lessons of the cases contribute to your understanding of international relations today?

CASE 1: ENVIRONMENTAL PROTECTION AS A COMMON GOOD

Protecting the environment is one of the areas that falls under the heading of "common good" in that it is something that affects all countries and peoples;

environmental degradation knows no national boundaries. Countries can assume that it is not only in their national interest but in the interest of all nations to ensure that the quality of the environment is protected, and that it is incumbent upon them to work together to achieve this goal; this is a position that the liberal theorists would take. Or countries can take the "free rider" position and assume that other countries will take the lead, and that they do not have to spend the money or invest resources in this policy area since others will do it for them—and they will benefit anyway. In that regard, consistent with the more realist position, each nation-state would ask whether and how it is in their best interest to work on improving the environment and what will happen if they don't.

Countries are facing a number of severe environmental issues that have implications for each of them and for the world. Issues of deforestation, access to clean and safe water, and the contribution of pollution and greenhouse gas emissions to global warming are among the issues that transcend borders. The April 2010 oil spill in the Gulf of Mexico caused by an explosion at the British Petroleum (BP) Deepwater Horizon oil rig has shown that environmental issues can be caused by or attributed to corporate negligence, as well as national neglect or ignorance. However, the international system has few means available to make corporations take responsibility for any problems they cause. This illustrates clearly some of the problems caused by the reach of MNCs.

If environmental issues are to be addressed, countries will need to work together. But can they?

Background of the Issue

The Kyoto Protocol to the United Nations Framework Convention on Climate Change (known as the Kyoto Protocol) was adopted in 1997 and was set to expire in 2012. The Kyoto Protocol is linked to the UN Framework Convention on Climate Change (UNFCC) and

> sets binding targets for 37 industrialized countries and the European community for reducing greenhouse gas emissions (GHG). . . . The major distinction between the Protocol and the Convention is that while the convention *encouraged* industrialized countries to stabilize GHG emissions, the Protocol *commits* them to do so. (emphasis in original)[1]

To ensure that the goals associated with protecting the environment that grew from the Kyoto Protocol were met, subsequent meetings were scheduled annually to bring the international community together for further discussion and negotiation. In general, the goal of these various international meetings was to frame follow-up agreements to move forward issues surrounding climate change.

While 184 countries ratified the Protocol, many of its terms were controversial. For example, the agreement places a heavier burden on the developed versus the developing countries, a point that both sets of countries had problems with. The developed countries felt that this unfairly punished them, while the developing countries, which included India and China, wanted international assistance that would allow them to develop economically *and* provide assistance in helping them do so in an environmentally friendly way. At a time when India and China are among the fastest-growing economies in the world, labeling them "developing" countries underscores another of the problems that can be identified quickly when looking at this issue. Specifically, what really constitutes a developed or industrialized country versus a developing one?

Despite some of these flaws, the Kyoto Protocol was seen as an important first step toward achieving global emissions reduction. In addition, it provided a framework for the next steps that the international community needed to take in controlling greenhouse gas emissions.

Countries know that it would be virtually impossible to try to tackle all the environmental issues—greenhouse gas emissions, deforestation, ensuring biodiversity, promoting principles of sustainable development—at the same time. Therefore, one of the goals of the Copenhagen meeting of 2009 that was to build on Kyoto was to frame an agreement that would set priorities and guide countries' policies into the future.

In November 2009, prior to the start of meetings in Copenhagen, many were optimistic about the future when China announced its plan to reduce significantly its greenhouse gas emissions over the next decade. This was a departure from China's position to that point, and other countries saw it as a positive step. Despite the initial optimism, reaching an agreement proved to be difficult. An accord was finally reached on the last day, brokered in part by U.S. president Barack Obama, assisted by the BRIC countries China, India, Brazil, and South Africa. While the accord fell short of what some environmentalists hoped for, it accomplished the objective of getting countries to commit to keeping the maximum temperature rise to below 2 degrees Celsius. It also achieved a commitment "to list developed country emission reduction targets and mitigation action by developing countries for 2020; USD 30 billion short-term funding for immediate action till 2012 and USD 100 billion annually by 2020 in long-term financing, as well as mechanisms to support technology transfer and forestry." But, as UN official Yvo de Boer also noted, "The challenge now is to turn what is agreed into something that is legally binding in Mexico one year from now."[2]

That became the starting point for the conference in Cancun, Mexico, held late in 2010. Copenhagen "produced a lot of ill will and an 'accord' put together by only a small subset of nations. . . . In Cancun the ill-will faded and large chunks of that accord were at least translated into the official UN process."[3] Given the history of the meetings to that point, countries went into the Cancun summit in November 2010 with low expectations. Nonetheless, the Cancun Agreements provide emission mitigation targets and actions for approximately eighty countries, including Brazil, one of the world's largest greenhouse gas emitters. By agreeing to cut its greenhouse gas emissions, Brazil was aligning itself with the EU, South Korea, and other countries that had similarly adopted emissions targets. But it also reflects the views of many Brazilians who support a low-carbon economy and also the rise of the Green Party domestically. This is a clear case in which domestic politics, culture, and society have had a positive impact on environmental concerns.

One of the other reasons for success in Cancun was simply a change in process whereby under the rules set by the conference chair no country had the right to veto the will of others. Another thing that also made the agreement reached at the Cancun meeting unique is that it was able to identify and build upon areas of common concern between the developing and developed countries. Among these was a pledge to create a Green Climate Fund of $100 billion a year to go from the countries of the North (the developed countries) to those of the South (developing) to help pay for emissions cuts and climate adaptation by 2020. What pleased both sets of countries was the notion that the developing countries would be helped, along with the suggestion that not all the money has to come from the government, but that the private sector could contribute as well. A safeguard to protect the rights of indigenous people was also an addition that pleased a number of countries, while a new framework made dealing with climate change an integral part of the UN process. "All of these now need to be turned from paper agreements into practical ones."[4]

Another reason for the success at Cancun was that both the United States and China, two of the major players, got things that each wanted. China did not feel that it was "blamed" for failures, as it had been at previous conferences. And the United States wanted progress toward verification. But many attribute the level of buy-in to the fear that "failing to meet the very modest expectations of Cancun would have been fatal."[5]

Despite the successes, the agreement failed in other ways. The text did not address proposals on agriculture, a major greenhouse gas emitter equal to deforestation. The pledges made are not strong enough to really hold down climate change to an increase of 2 degrees Celsius, as some had hoped. Some claim that such specific targets will not be applied as long as some countries (notably the United States and China) object. And there is a danger that if that is treated as a make-or-break issue, then agreement will never be possible.

International experts were not optimistic going into the next set of talks in Durban, South Africa, in December 2011, as the developed countries (especially Japan, Russia, and Canada) had already indicated that they did not want to take on any additional legally binding responsibilities to cut their greenhouse gas emissions; the United States had never agreed to be part of the Kyoto treaty at all. Of the developed countries only the Europeans, who are responsible for about 13 percent of global emissions, agreed to consider being part of another round of cuts. And while the developing countries, including China and India, had already promised to cut the energy or carbon intensity of their economies, they refused to turn their pledges of commitment into legally binding pacts. "Their main concern is for their economies to grow rapidly, not least to help deal with the fallout of warming."[6] So part of the challenge that countries faced going into Durban and beyond is a very different set of needs and expectations.

The conference in Durban resulted in some agreement on the need to work toward a new global treaty and to make progress on the Green Climate Fund. Progress on the more contentious issue, a treaty, was made possible only after Brazil came up with wording all could agree upon, specifically that "the new deal is not to be 'legally binding.' It will, instead, be 'a protocol, another legal instrument or an agreed outcome with legal force.'"[7] The new protocol begins the process of replacing the Kyoto agreement "with something that treats all countries—including the economic powerhouses China, India and Brazil—equally." The expiration date and additional specifics are to be negotiated in the future. The Green Climate Fund "would help mobilize a promised $100 billion a year in public and private financing by 2020 to assist developing countries in adapting to climate change and converting to clean energy sources."[8] But questions about implementing the fund remain to be determined.

In November–December 2012, countries met in Doha, Qatar, for the annual UN climate change negotiations. Among the few accomplishments at this meeting was the agreement from the wealthier developed countries to provide funding in aid to those primarily developing countries that are most affected by climate change, thereby building on the idea of the Green Climate Fund. Looking forward to the 2013 meetings (to be held in Warsaw, Poland), it is important that countries begin to make progress toward finalizing a legally binding agreement that they hope will be concluded and signed by 2015 if the myriad issues pertaining to protecting the environment really are to be addressed.

It is apparent that if there really is to be progress made on these important environmental issues, countries need to move beyond generalities to the specifics of implementation. This makes clear one of the challenges of trying to address an international agreement: Reaching an agreement is only one part of the process. Implementing it is another part.

Issues of deforestation, access to clean and safe water, and pollution and emissions contributing to global warming are among the issues that transcend national borders. If these issues are to be addressed, countries will need to work together. The emission of greenhouse gases and other particulate matter generally has been attributed to the developed countries. However, as countries seek to develop rapidly in order to be able to compete in the global marketplace, they too have started to become major polluters. Countries that traditionally depended on their rain forests and other natural resources for their own survival are now depleting a natural resource, as they either cut down or burn the forests to make way for agricultural land or development. That policy decision has long-term implications, not only for that country but for others as well.

Clearly, countries are facing a number of severe environmental issues that have implications for the world. Many of these are issues that countries bring

upon themselves through the policy choices they make. For example, Indonesia, in order to support its growing population, has been deforesting its
land. As if that were not bad enough for the environment, burning that for-
ested land as a way to clear it contributes to air pollution—which in turn
contributes to health issues such as asthma. And Indonesia is not alone in
this. According to the United Nations, "From 1990 to 2005, the world lost 3
percent of its forests, an average decrease of 0.2 percent a year. Deforestation,
primarily due to the conversion of forests to agricultural land in developing
countries, continues at an alarming rate. . . . The rate of loss has been fastest
in some of the world's most biologically diverse regions."[9] Not only does this
then affect the loss of forest land, which in turn affects the air quality, but it
also affects the biological diversity of these regions. Hence, deforestation is a
significant environmental problem that affects the international community
as a whole.

Other environmental challenges, however, are the result of conflict or of
corporate irresponsibility. On April 20, 2010, an explosion "aboard the
Deepwater Horizon, a drilling rig working on a well for the oil company BP
one mile below the surface of the Gulf of Mexico, . . . led to the largest oil
spill in American history."[10] As of the end of June 2010, months after the
explosion, the oil was not yet contained; the well was not permanently sealed
until September 2010, which meant that oil continued to pour into the Gulf.
Government scientists estimated that before it was capped, nearly five million
barrels of oil flowed into the Gulf of Mexico. The full and lasting extent of the
damage to the environment, including sea and animal life, the marshlands of
Louisiana, and the coastline of the Gulf, has yet to be determined. That does
not even take into account the human toll on the people whose livelihood
depends on the Gulf of Mexico in some way.

A presidential panel convened to study the accident called it "a prevent-
able one, caused by a series of failures and blunders by the companies involved in drilling the well and the government regulators assigned to police
them."[11] As you can see, in this case corporate irresponsibility, interstate and
intrastate conflict, and poor policy decisions are among some of the many
man-made reasons for the ongoing depletion of the environment. All of these
have different causes and different environmental impacts, which makes it
even harder to determine how to solve the problems or even address them.

What this case illustrates is the fact that tied to the issue of sustainable
development is the need for countries to develop in an environmentally safe

way. This requires that countries do whatever they can to develop cleaner energy technology and fuels and simultaneously find ways to limit harmful CO_2 emissions that are associated with global climate change. But it will also require countries to work together and compromise, not only in reaching an agreement but in ensuring that the agreement reached will be implemented.

Analysis of the Case

The challenge posed by environmental issues gets to the heart of some of the issues we have discussed as they pertain to international relations. Environmental issues are difficult to address because they do not respect international borders. Thus, what happens in one country has a direct impact on other countries beyond its borders. Furthermore, countries and the people who live within them ideally would like to have a clean and safe environment. But how much is that worth if it comes at the expense of economic growth and development? Do all countries put the same value on ensuring a clean environment? If not, then the starting point alone is one of conflicting perspectives and priorities, which makes it even more difficult to come to a satisfactory outcome.

From a realist perspective, each country will only pursue those policies that are in its own best interest. From a liberal theoretical perspective, however, cooperating and moving toward achieving a climate change agreement will benefit all countries, those people who live in the countries, and the international system as a whole. Therefore it would make sense to cooperate in order to achieve a common good. To the radical or Marxist theoretical perspective, the dilemma is really about who controls the resources and, therefore, can make the decisions. The constructivists would look at this case as an example of changing international norms and the ways in which they affect the discourse of international relations. And each of these would assign a different priority to the environment as a policy issue.

But let's say we could move beyond the differences stemming from theoretical perspectives and countries could negotiate an international agreement. Even if such an international agreement on the environment were to be reached, we would then have a different set of issues that would have to be confronted stemming from differences in perspective. The developed countries would want to ensure that they are not burdened unfairly, either with the costs of implementing the agreement or in terms of the specifics of the agreement, which could impose more stringent requirements on them than on other countries. The developing countries, on the other hand, want to be able to industrialize and progress economically without feeling like they are impeded by an agreement. Thus, another way to look at the problem at the nation-state level is to look at what happens when what is in the best interest of the nation-state conflicts with the greater good or with the interests of the international system.

If we look within the nations, we see the issue still another way. For example, the people within a country want to know that they have access to potable water, that the air that they breathe is clean, and that the government will ensure that they have these basic necessities. These qualities are tied to their basic security and well-being. But in some countries, they also want to make sure that they have land to plant the crops necessary to feed their own families and perhaps provide a little extra to trade. If that means clearing part of the rain forest, can the government forbid them to do so?

This case also points out clearly the impact that MNCs can have as well as questions about who regulates and monitors them. In the case of the Deepwater Horizon oil spill, the drilling rig was actually owned by Transocean, Ltd., a Swiss company, and leased to BP, which owned the well. The rig and well were operating under a lease granted by the U.S. government. A settlement reached in January 2013 with the U.S. Justice Department resolved Transocean's role and required that company to pay "$1 billion in civil penalties and $400 million in criminal penalties and plead guilty to a misdemeanor charge of violating the Clean Water Act, according to a court filing." In November 2012, "BP agreed to plead guilty to 14 criminal acts in connection with the giant oil spill in the Gulf of Mexico in 2010 and to pay $4.5 billion in fines."[12]

And of course in this case, the NGOs play an important role. Not only can they bring pressure to bear on the government or even the international system by making sure that environmental issues are on the international agenda, but they can also lobby to bring about a specific outcome. They can serve as neutral monitors to ensure compliance with an agreement once it is reached, or they can even arbitrate in the event of disputes regarding interpretation or implementation. They can provide experts to work with the government to find ways to improve the quality of the environment, and they can work with the people to help them find the most efficient uses of their land.

Ultimately, it is up to the government to negotiate any international agreement and to determine whether to abide by it or abrogate it. International agreements are between countries. But as this case illustrates, what about corporations?

The greater good versus the good of the individual nation—who wins?

CASE 2: THE MOVEMENT OF PEOPLE IN A GLOBALIZED WORLD

Globalization has changed how countries interact in a number of ways. One of those is in the movement of people, where individuals travel to different countries either legally or illegally, in search of economic opportunity, to escape a conflict, to seek asylum from political persecution, and even to find food or water because of severe environmental crisis. At a time when many countries are struggling to find workers to fill the lowest-paid and unskilled jobs, often these same countries are finding a void at the upper ranks as well. Different countries have different labor needs; in a global economy that is increasingly interdependent, it seems only logical that countries look to one another to augment their own labor/workers.

The open borders that often come with the creation and growth of free trade zones have made the migration of workers from country to country, legally and illegally, even easier. But not all who flee one country for another do so for economic reasons, although ultimately they will need a way to ensure their livelihood in their new country. At a time of economic recession, many countries resent the influx of immigrants, who often make demands on the system (education, health care, etc.). This creates further divisions within the social structure of the country.

In the United States, the issue of illegal immigration has become a political "hot button," especially in the states of the Southwest that border Mexico. In the Middle East, the protracted civil war in Syria has contributed to a surge of émigrés fleeing the violence by crossing the borders into Jordan or Turkey. This has caused strains on both those countries. And sub-Saharan Africa has seen the movement of people who are fleeing current crises not only of war, but also of drought and famine. For example, the UN High Commissioner for Refugees (UNHCR) has estimated that hundreds of thousands have fled the violence and drought in the African country of Mali, and "with more than one million Somali refugees in the East and Horn of Africa and some 1.36 million internally displaced persons (IDPs) in Somalia, the country remains at the centre of one of the worst humanitarian crises UNHCR has faced."[13] In Europe, the arrest of immigrants accused of acts of terrorism has conflated the issue of immigration with terrorism. In short, the movement of people is a problem that affects virtually every part of the world, developed and developing, rural and urban.

In thinking about this issue, it is important to note that not all immigrants are terrorists, nor are all terrorists immigrants who seek to gain entry into a country for illegal and destructive reasons. Yet at a time when they already feel threatened, many immigrants (especially those from the Middle East, who look different and are often Muslim) resettling in places like Europe or the United States seem to be a symbol, as well as being easily identifiable.

Many countries want to do all they can to make sure that the needs of their own citizens are met at a time of budgetary constraints, which often means cracking down on immigration. Yet some countries, peoples, and NGOs also feel that all would benefit if an international agreement could be reached as to how best to monitor the movement of people and to guarantee protection to all migrants and immigrants, whether legal or illegal. Countries know that this will be a challenge but also that if they can come up with an agreement, it could be a classic "win-win" situation.

Given the range of issues involved as well as perspectives, this is a difficult task.

Background of the Issue

Globalization is a fact of twenty-first-century life. As we saw in chapter 1, in reality, the process of globalization began with the early years of exploration in the sixteenth century, when the original patterns of trade between and among countries were established. Along with that came the sale of human beings (slaves) who were bought and sold to provide the labor needed to ensure the economic benefit of the colonial power. What has made the globalization of the twentieth and twenty-first century different, however, is the growth of technology that can move people, goods, and ideas farther and faster than ever before.

Like so many things, globalization brings with it advantages and disadvantages. On the one hand, a globalized world in which trade is open means that all countries benefit, at least in theory. Each trades what it has or can produce with other countries based on what they don't have and need. On the other hand, the argument goes, rich countries get richer at the expense of poorer countries.

The same is true of the movement of people. In a world in which people can move freely and cross borders relatively easily, it is not unusual for people to leave one country and move to another in search of economic opportunity. The cases that seem to attract the most attention are those involving the movement of people for illegal or illicit reasons such as terrorism or human trafficking. Others, however, move between countries, often illegally but for legitimate reasons, such as the quest for better economic opportunity than they would have at home. These are often unskilled and uneducated people, who are willing to do whatever they have to do in order to leave one country and migrate to another in search of economic opportunities. Because they enter a country illegally, they can also be exploited and forced to work for very little, knowing that they have few legal options. Many of those cases are widely reported, as are the harrowing tales of what many of these émigrés have had to do in order to be able to leave one country and enter another.

Still other people leave one country to flee conflict or to escape persecution of some kind. Refugee camps have grown up in areas bordering wartorn states to shelter those people who hope to avoid war, but they often find that their new situation is almost as bleak. International organizations like the UN and NGOs often work with people in the camps to provide food, shelter, and basic health care, but that makes the refugees dependent on these organizations rather than offering them an alternative way of life.

It is important to note that not all of the immigrants who flee one country in search of opportunities in another do so illegally. In fact, some relatively wealthy households in the developing countries send family members out of the country for schooling, knowing that they will get better jobs and have more opportunities if they remain in their adopted country; they are not expected to return home. However, this contributes to a brain drain, which has made the plight of the developing countries even more dire, since it deprives the home country of individuals with much-needed education and talent. This is not a new issue; in 1999 the International Monetary Fund published a paper documenting brain drain trends from the 1960s to that time. As noted in that paper, "One important implication of the brain drain is that investment in education in a developing country may not lead to faster economic growth if a large number of its highly educated people leave the country."[14]

It is often the people who are the poorest and most desperate who become the victims of the trade in and sale of human beings, and they often take the greatest risk in trying to escape. Newspapers in the United States and Europe seem to have an increasing number of stories about migrants trying to flee their home country to enter another country illegally found dead or close to death. Some of these are illegal immigrants who are being sent from one country to another to enter into a life of servitude. Others, however, choose to leave voluntarily, often paying thousands of dollars to smugglers to bring them into another country safely. These immigrants are desperate to escape their plight at home and to find opportunity in another (and developed) country. Those who are able to escape safely can become success stories, sending hundreds or even thousands of dollars home to the families they left behind, which, in turn encourages others to try the same thing.

For example, the World Bank has found that remittances sent from migrants in one country to another hit a high of about $414 billion in 2008, with $316 billion of that sent to developing countries. Like many other things, the global economic crisis has had an impact on remittances, which dropped in 2009.[15] Thus, not only do these immigrants benefit economically, but their home countries do as well. The International Organization for Migration, an NGO, found that in 2010, "one out of every 33 persons is an international migrant," which translates into approximately 214 million migrants.[16]

At a meeting of the general assembly in September 2010, the director general of the International Organization for Migration noted, "Today more people are on the move than at any other time in recorded history: 214 million international migrants and 740 million internal migrants. In other words, one in every seven persons is a migrant—on the move."[17] In his remarks, he also noted the positive impact of some of this movement of people. For example, "migrant remittances—the money sent home by migrants—helps reduce poverty by providing families in countries of origin with additional, often vital, income." He also noted that the "increased feminization of migration—women migrating independently, or, as the 'breadwinner,'" can promote gender equality and empower women; nearly half of the world's migrants today are women. And through diaspora communities, migrants can develop ties that can aid their home country as well as their adopted country.[18]

Clearly, those remarks paint a more positive portrait of the impact of migration. But as noted above, there is a darker side to this movement of people as well. Migrants are especially vulnerable during economic crises, as they tend to be younger workers with less formal education who often get menial jobs—for example, doing manual labor or janitorial and cleaning work. This group is often among the first to lose their jobs, and they often do not have the protections that other workers have, such as unemployment or health benefits. Yet, many choose not to return home.

The UN secretary-general, in prepared remarks delivered to a global forum on migration and development, noted:

> Rising unemployment among natives and international migrants has spurred discrimination. The politics of xenophobia is on the rise. For millions of international migrants, life has become more treacherous. . . . Migration is more likely to benefit all stakeholders when it is safe, legal and orderly. Yet these opportunities for regular migration have diminished.[19]

The economic recession clearly has fostered the growth of anti-immigrant feeling in the United States and parts of Europe, which has made life more dangerous for migrants and immigrants. In April 2010, the governor of Arizona signed into law the toughest bill on immigration in the United States. According to one newspaper account, "its aim is to identify, prosecute and deport illegal immigrants." It was quickly condemned by President Obama and human rights advocates.

> The law, which proponents and critics alike said was the broadest and strictest immigration measure in generations, would make the failure to carry immigration documents a crime and give the police broad power to detain anyone suspected of being in the country illegally. Opponents have called it an open invitation for harassment and discrimination against Hispanics regardless of their citizenship status.[20]

It also illustrates clearly the depth of passion surrounding the immigration debate in the United States, as well as the anti-immigrant feeling at a time of economic recession.

In Europe, Greece has become the gateway for the vast majority of people trying to enter the EU illegally. "Of the 106,200 people detected trying to cross illegally into the European Union in 2009, almost three-quarters were stopped in Greece. Early data for 2010 suggest that, although absolute numbers are falling, Greece's burden has risen further, to about 80% of the EU total, up from 50% three years ago."[21] At a time when Greece is suffering financially, it cannot afford the estimated $103 million it spends each year to address the problem. And this amount is far from adequate, given the scope of the problem.[22] One of the reasons that Greece has been bearing the brunt of the wave of illegal immigration is that many of the other EU countries have signed bilateral deals with countries in Africa that have closed their borders. Examples are the bilateral agreement between Italy and Libya, and Spain's with Senegal and Mauritania.

"Recent data show an overall decline in illegal immigration into the EU. That might bring temporary respite. But as Europe's pummeled economies continue their recovery and labor demand picks up, the figures are likely to start rising again."[23] Thus, on the one hand, the economic decline has resulted in a drop in the number of illegal immigrants and has had a negative impact on those who are already in the country. On the other hand, however, as the economy starts to improve, one result is likely to be an increase in the number of illegal immigrants once again. Ironically, since "Greece's own economic problems make it a less attractive destination for would-be entrants, most of them plan to move on to the wealthier parts of the continent once inside the EU."[24]

Since 2007 the EU has been debating how to arrive at a sane and humane immigration policy. But the reason it has been so difficult to arrive at a policy is the lack of agreement on what immigration and migration mean. For example, on the one hand, "the union [EU] seems to view migration as a benign exchange: in one direction, labor to meet growing gaps in Europe's jobs market; in the other, a flow of remittances and knowledge to some of the world's poorest countries." On the other hand, some in the EU have been promoting new legislation that would allow for seasonal migrants (for example, to help with agriculture or construction when needed), but would require them to return home at the end of the contract period. These are being seen as "temporary work opportunities," which translates into a guest worker plan whereby workers are imported from the poorer countries, engage in manual labor, and never really integrate into society. While never adopted, this notion of "circular migration" tapped into the public's anti-immigration mood, which remains in place today.[25]

In addition to the passage of the anti-immigrant law in Arizona in the United States, the antipathy toward immigrants can be seen in the growth of right-wing, anti-immigrant political parties in Europe, which are becoming more popularly supported. Even in Sweden, long known for its liberal social policies, the right-wing and anti-immigrant Sweden Democrat party was able to gather enough votes to get a seat in Parliament in the election of 2010. Since that time, the party has continued its anti-immigrant, anti-"outsider" rhetoric.

The anti-immigrant fervor has been fueled even more in Europe with the conflation of immigration and terrorism, which has contributed to this anti-immigrant feeling. The suicide bomber identified as mounting an attack in Stockholm, Sweden, in December 2010 during the holiday shopping season was an émigré from Iraq. Swedish prime minister Fredrik Reinfeldt appealed to fellow citizens not to jump to "wrong conclusions" or "allow preliminary reports about the explosions to stir fresh tensions over Sweden's growing immigrant population, including about 450,000 Muslims."[26] Many of the suspects identified throughout Europe as terrorists plotting major attacks have been immigrants. For example, of five men arrested in Denmark and Sweden on December 29, 2010, following the bombing, three were Swedish nationals but one was a Tunisian citizen and the other an Iraqi asylum applicant living in Denmark.

Despite the passage of laws in the West, in Europe, and in the United States to try to stop the flood of illegal immigrants and to encourage sound migration policies, governments readily agree that it is extremely costly as well as very difficult to try to enforce them. As long as there is hope for a better life, people will continue to try to move from one country to another that promises them more. While in some cases, that might mask people who migrate specifically for illegal purposes, it appears that the majority do not have malevolent intentions.

It is apparent that no country acting alone can address all the aspects of the issues outlined here, which clearly cross borders and national boundaries. Not only do immigrants deal with the international system as a whole, because they cross borders, but they have an impact on the politics, cultures, and societies within countries—both the countries these émigrés flee from and the ones they go to. Thus, the issue crosses multiple levels of analysis, which makes it even more difficult to sort out and address.

Analysis of the Case

Like the environment, the movement of people is an issue that transcends national borders, affects many if not all countries in some way, and has been exacerbated by the globalization of the late twentieth and twenty-first century. It is also an issue that can be seen at all levels of analysis, which makes arriving at any solution especially difficult. The focus here, though, must start at the individual level, because it is individuals who make the decision to leave one country and to settle in another. Thus, in many ways, this becomes the starting point for understanding this issue. Who are these people and why do they choose to leave one country for another? What do they hope to find? Are they leaving legally or illegally, and conversely, what are their intentions regarding the host country in which they will be settling? These are all questions that must be asked at the individual level, which helps give this issue a very human dimension, more so than many other issues in international relations.

Continuing through the levels of analysis, we can then ask about the impact that these immigrants, migrants, or refugees have on the culture and society of their adopted state. Do they blend into an already dominant culture, or will they have an influence on it in some ways? Are they joining an already established national group within the larger nation-state (for example, the North Africans in Paris or Indians and Pakistanis in London), or will they be "outsiders" who will be expected to assimilate into the dominant culture? Will they become part of the educated workforce in their new country, even if that comes at the expense of their home country? What will they contribute in general, culturally, economically, socially, politically? And, of course, how does their departure affect what happens/happened at home? And these questions do not take into account those who resettle in another country specifically with the goal of causing harm in some way.

Implicit in the impact that the immigrants have on the society and culture, as noted above, is the impact on the political system. People who come to another country and see this move as a permanent one often want to become citizens and make a contribution politically, if just to vote so that their voices can be heard. But as we saw earlier in the example of the United States and the Cuban émigrés in Florida, an émigré population can have a marked impact on the political priorities of the adopted country. Different countries have different expectations and criteria for citizenship, and these too are political decisions sometimes specifically designed to limit that access. While some countries welcome immigrants, especially educated ones, that does not necessarily mean that they want them to have a say in how the country is run.

And of course, at the nation-state and international levels, the movement of peoples is a by-product of other decisions, whether benign or positive ones (such as accelerating free trade) or more insidious ones (such as conflicts). States will guard their own sovereignty and do not want to have the international system imposing regulations on them. They want to be able to determine who can and should enter their country. However, growing integration of countries makes that more challenging. For example, the Schengen Agreement signed in 1985 between five member countries of the then European Economic Community to gradually abolish checks at their common border has become part of EU law, establishing a borderless zone among all the EU countries.[27] And the issue of immigration has directly affected relations between the United States and neighboring Mexico.

Finally, nonstate actors come into play in this case in a number of ways. Clearly, terrorist groups can take advantage of a globalized world to move people from one country to another specifically for the purpose of inflicting death and destruction. But putting those aside, other nonstate actors also are factors here, as advocates for immigrants but also as interest groups advocating to limit immigration. The UN is a major player in this area, through its High Commissioner for Refugees and other specialized agencies. In this case, the UN is in a unique position to look at the international system as a whole and to make determinations about issues pertaining to the movement of peoples.

From the different theoretical perspectives, the movement of peoples gets to the heart of their understandings of the nation-state and its role in international politics. The very notion of the movement of people from one state to another raises issues about sovereignty, the sanctity of the state, and state security so central to the realist perspective. But it can be approached from other theoretical perspectives as well. Something like the Schengen Agreement can be understood by drawing on the liberal perspective and the idea that the movement of peoples across borders is really an issue of cooperation and not conflict or an infringement on sovereignty. Constructivists might ask what impact immigration has on the structure and policies of the new country, as well as on the country that they left. They could easily explore the issues of understanding national identity and what changing national identities then might mean for the state as well as the people within it. Even the Marxists could contribute to this discussion by asking in what ways economic development has contributed to immigration as the trend toward capitalism has changed the working relationships within a country, thereby contributing to movement from one country to another. And of course, the feminists would ask us to look at the people themselves to see who has been affected, in what ways, and why.

In many ways, the issue and approaches to it fit more comfortably into the theoretical perspectives that focus on the individual, such as the liberal, Marxist, and feminist perspectives. But as noted above, depending on the way in which you frame the question you are asking about the issue, any of the theoretical perspectives could provide some insight into our understanding of it. What we are really asking in this case is this: If the movement of peoples has become a fact of globalization, how can we best account for it and understand where it fits within traditional international relations—or does it?

CASE 3: WOMEN'S RIGHTS AS HUMAN RIGHTS

In 1975, the UN held the First World Conference on Women in Mexico. This became a catalyst for drafting any number of resolutions that pertained specifically to the rights and roles of women, both within countries and also internationally. Part of the impetus for the conference and the subsequent passage of a number of resolutions was the growing international attention to violations against women. Some of those were the result of cultural practices, but some were due to conflict and to the fact that women were being used as weapons of war. With little international law behind them and with little desire to implement the laws that were in place, the UN took the lead in starting to recognize the role that women can and do play, and also to ensure that there are international guarantees in place to protect women.

The Convention on the Elimination of All Forms of Discrimination Against Women (CEDAW) was passed in 1979, and it is seen by many as the international bill of rights for women. Since then UN Security Council Resolution 1325 on Women, Peace, and Security[28] was passed in October 2000, followed by Resolution 1820, Eliminating Violence Against Women and Girls[29] in June 2008. Resolution 1325 was passed following the Fourth World Conference on Women, held in Beijing in 1995, which stressed the importance of the full participation of women if peace and security in any country is to be assured, as well as the need to increase women's role in decision making pertaining to conflict prevention and resolution, and the need for postwar reconstruction. Resolution 1820 was passed by the Security Council to demand the "immediate and complete cessation by all parties to armed conflict of all acts of sexual violence against civilians," [and] expressing its deep concern that, despite repeated condemnation, violence and sexual abuse of women and children trapped in war zones was not only continuing, but, in some cases, had become so widespread and systematic as to "reach appalling levels of brutality."[30]

Capping a day-long ministerial-level meeting on women, peace, and security, the fifteen-member council unanimously adopted Resolution 1820 (2008), which noted that "rape and other forms of sexual violence can constitute war crimes, crimes against humanity or a constitutive act with respect to genocide." It also affirmed the council's intention, when establishing and renewing state-specific sanction regimes, to consider imposing "targeted and graduated" measures against warring factions who committed rape and other forms of violence against women and girls. While most nations applaud and support the goals of these resolutions, there are virtually no mechanisms in place to enforce them.

Once the resolutions are passed and become part of the canon of international law, one of the challenges facing the international system is to determine how to implement those resolutions that are in place to protect civilians, especially women and girls.

Background of the Issue

When the United Nations was created, of the original 51 member states, "only 30 allowed women equal voting rights with men or permitted them to hold public office." However, the Charter of the UN refers to the "equal rights of men and women" and declared the UN's "faith in fundamental human rights" and "the dignity and worth of the human person."[31] These phrases suggested that working for the rights of women would be a critical part of the mission of this IGO and that the weight of the UN would ensure compliance by all countries.

During the first three decades, the work of the United Nations on behalf of women focused primarily on the codification of women's legal and civil rights, and the gathering of data on the status of women around the world. With time, however, it became increasingly apparent that laws, in and of themselves, were not enough to ensure the equal rights of women.[32]

Rather, the UN realized that there would have to be significant specific efforts made if there was to be true equality for women worldwide.

To begin to address this issue, the UN convened conferences specifically to develop strategies and action plans for the advancement of women. The First World Conference on Women was held in Mexico City in 1975 to coincide with International Women's Year. This was observed "to remind the international community that discrimination against women continued to be a persistent problem in much of the world."[33] The General Assembly also launched the United Nations Decade for Women (1976–1985) to open a broader dialogue on equality for women. At the first conference and each of the three subsequent ones, key objectives and a plan of action were set that would define the work of the UN on behalf of women.

Three critical objectives were set for the 1975 Mexico City conference: "1) full gender equality and the elimination of gender discrimination; 2) the integration and full participation of women in development; and 3) an increased contribution by women in the strengthening of world peace."[34] The conference adopted a World Action Plan that set guidelines for governments and the international community to follow in order to pursue the key objectives. It also set minimum targets to be met by 1980 "that focused on securing equal access for women to resources such as education, employment opportunities, political participation, health services, nutrition and family planning."[35]

One of the things that made the Mexico City conference unique was that women played a key role in shaping the discussions. Including the official delegations and a parallel NGO forum, approximately four thousand participants attended. Many of the official delegations were headed by women.

From the beginning, though, women were far from unified in their perspective on what should happen. For example, women from the Eastern bloc "were most interested in issues of peace, while women from the West emphasized equality and those from the developing world placed a priority on development."[36] In other words, the division among the women attending reflected their own national, political, economic, and social perspectives and experiences. Nonetheless, the conference was deemed a success because of its ability to set in motion a process that would unite women and the international system, behind set goals that would benefit all women.

Within the UN framework, in addition to the Division for the Advancement of Women, the International Research and Training Institute for

Women and the United Nations Development Fund for Women (UNIFEM) were also created. Then in 1979, the General Assembly adopted the Convention on the Elimination of All Forms of Discrimination Against Women (CEDAW), which became known as the international bill of rights for women. This convention, which requires states to report regularly on steps that they have taken to remove obstacles they face in implementing the terms of the convention, has been ratified by 165 states. "By 2006, 182 states—over 90 percent of UN's membership—had ratified it. Many countries, including Uganda, South Africa, Brazil and Australia, have incorporated CEDAW provisions into their constitutions and national legislation."[37]

The second conference on women met in 1980 in Copenhagen specifically to review progress that had been made on the action plan. Despite the strides made since 1975, the Copenhagen conference "recognized that signs of disparity were beginning to emerge between rights secured and women's ability to exercise these rights." To address these, this conference identified three broad areas that would require focused action if the goals identified in Mexico City were ever to be achieved. These three areas were "equal access to education, employment opportunities and adequate health care services."[38]

Deliberations at the Copenhagen conference identified various factors that have kept women from achieving full rights. These included lack of involvement of men (decision makers) in improving women's roles and a shortage of women decision makers; lack of political will; lack of recognition of women's contributions and attention to women's needs; insufficient services, such as child care, that would help and support women; lack of financial resources; and lack of awareness on the part of women about opportunities. The Copenhagen Program of Action called for a set of measures that would address these factors in order to promote the status of women.

"The movement for gender equality had gained true global recognition as the third world conference on women, The World Conference to Review and Appraise the Achievements of the United Nations Decade for Women: Equality, Development and Peace, was convened in Nairobi in 1985."[39] The conference itself, combined with the parallel NGO forum, was seen as "the birth of global feminism" for the way it united women under the goals of equality, development, and peace. While this was seen as a positive development, the conference also brought to light how little had actually changed regarding improvements in the status of women. In general, women in the developing world had seen only marginal improvement at best. This suggested that most of the objectives identified earlier had not been met.

The conference developed and adopted the "Nairobi Forward-Looking Strategies to the Year 2000" as a blueprint for the future of women to the end of the century. "The Forward-looking Strategies for the Advancement of Women during the Period from 1986 to the Year 2000 set forth in the present document present concrete measures to overcome the obstacles to the Decade's goals and objectives for the advancement of women." The document explicitly recognizes the failures to that point, attributed in part to the economic crises affecting the developing nations that have impeded their ability to implement programs in support of women. And it was explicit in recognizing that full participation for women was essential to the development of all states:

> The role of women in development is directly related to the goal of comprehensive social and economic development and is fundamental to the development of all societies. Development means total development, including development in the political, economic, social, cultural and other dimensions of human life, as well as the development of the economic and other material resources and the physical, moral, intellectual and cultural growth of human beings.[40]

After identifying the obstacles to achieving the goals, the document then identified basic categories for achieving equality at the national level, although it was left up to individual governments to set their own priorities. First, "political commitment to establish, modify, expand or enforce a comprehensive legal base for the equality of women and men and on the basis of human dignity must be strengthened." This, in turn, would require legislation. Other categories were: (2) social and cultural changes that would lead to equal access to education and training for all people; (3) along with legislation to improve the status of women, the need for educating the public and, if necessary, altering some of the social and cultural norms that worked against the advancement of women; (4) ongoing research about and collecting data to track the changing status of women within each country; and (5) fostering the equality of women in political participation and decision making at all levels of government by identifying and implementing strategies to enhance access for women. The document lists countless others, as well as identifying the obstacles to achieving these goals.[41] In effect, the document that grew from the conference asserted that all issues are women's issues, and that society in general would benefit from an expanded role for women that could be achieved with true equality. From a levels-of-analysis perspective, the document provided a blueprint for what could and should be done at each level in order to achieve the stated goals.

By 1995, when the Fourth World Conference on Women was convened in Beijing, there was a renewed commitment to the empowerment of women globally. The conference adopted the Beijing Declaration and Platform for Action, which was an agenda for women's empowerment. It outlined twelve critical areas concerning women's lives: poverty; education and training; health care; violence against women; armed conflict; unequal access to resources (the economy); power and decision-making structures; need for mechanisms to promote women effectively; guarantee for human rights for women; access to means of communication and media; environmental concerns; and discrimination against female children.[42]

The Beijing Conference, therefore, allowed women to come together to raise a range of issues that affected them, and it gave governments the opportunity to commit to including a gender dimension to their institutions, policies, planning, and decision making. In endorsing this program for action, the UN General Assembly called upon all states, international organizations, and NGOs to begin to implement the recommendations in order to further the goals pertaining to equality for women.

UN Resolution 1325 grew in part out of the attention that the Beijing Platform for Action gave to armed conflict. In 1995 when the Beijing Conference was held, there was growing international attention given to the ethnic and civil conflicts that had emerged in the wake of the Cold War; the war in the Balkans, with its ethnic cleansing and the public attention given to women as refugees and as weapons of war, made apparent the concerns regarding the impact of conflict on women and children. Hence, the UN Security Council in passing Resolution 1325 recognized both the impact of war on women and also the contributions that women could play in conflict resolution and in building sustainable peace. As a result, the Security Council affirmed

the important role of women in the prevention and resolution of conflicts and in peace-building and stressing the importance of their equal participation and full involvement in all efforts for the maintenance and promotion of peace and security, and the need to increase their role in decision making with regard to conflict prevention and resolution.[43]

However, even though it was unanimously adopted by the Security Council, Resolution 1325 is virtually impossible to implement.

In further recognition of the impact of conflict on women, in 2008 the Security Council also passed Resolution 1820, against sexual violence in conflict. Resolution 1820 builds on Resolution 1325 in that it reaffirms

the important role of women in the prevention and resolution of conflicts and in peacebuilding, and stressing the importance of their equal participation and full involvement in all efforts for the maintenance and promotion of peace and security, and the need to increase their role in decision-making with regard to conflict prevention and resolution.[44]

This resolution makes it clear that violence against women during conflict is a war crime and that ultimately states are responsible for the behavior of their citizens and for ensuring that such behavior does not occur. However, as was the case with Resolution 1325, there really is no implementation or enforcement mechanism.

Despite the many conferences on women and the recognition of the roles that women can and should play in resolving conflicts and ensuring the creation of a postconflict society that is safe for all people, the reality is that women have not made progress in many of the areas identified. Furthermore, the proliferation of ethnic conflicts has shown that women still suffer greatly from the impact of conflicts, and that they remain excluded from the decision making that is central to the rebuilding of a conflict-torn society.

The resolutions that were passed made important political statements about the treatment and role of women. However, they also made it clear that ultimately it is the nation-state that is responsible for the behavior of its citizens—to ensure that women and children are protected during wartime, but even in peace to ensure that women have a say in the political processes of the state and to set their own priorities. But they also note that ultimately there will need to be social and cultural changes within the nation-state if the role and responsibilities of women are ever to change significantly.

Analysis of the Case

As we begin the analysis of this case, it is important to remember that it is not just a "women's issue," but the broader issue really is about basic human rights, which is a value that many states espouse and which pertains to human security writ large. In this case, though, we see the important role played by the UN (an IGO) and various NGOs in moving forward the issues pertaining to women. We also see the problems/challenges inherent in such an approach. Clearly, despite the support of the international system in passing these various resolutions, ultimately the impact will be limited unless or until nation-states take up the cause and make changes consistent with the implementation of the points made in these resolutions.

This points to a very important failing in the international system, especially pertaining to international law: the absence of any enforcement mechanism. It also reinforces the realist position that ultimately it will be up to individual nation-states to make policy determinations in their own best interest, and that they will conform to the dictates of international law when it suits them to do so. Clearly, this flies in the face of both the liberal and constructivist perspectives, both of which would advocate for cooperation in this issue, which reinforces an important value or norm. Liberals would see women's rights as an issue of human security that *should* be on the international agenda. Similarly, constructivists would draw attention to this norm as a way to influence and/or change both individual and state behavior. And the feminist theorists would support the importance of recognizing women and the role that they can and do play as actors in the international system.

This case also points out the relationships that exist among the various levels of analysis. Here we have an issue that was agreed upon by nation-states acting within an IGO and facilitated by NGOs, which ultimately would have an impact on groups of people within the state and would result in changes to the political, social, and cultural components of the state.

In this case, what we need to ask ourselves is what impact have Resolutions 1325 and 1820 actually had? The short answer is: not much beyond raising awareness of the issue. Since the passage of Resolution 1325, conflicts have continued to be resolved with little or no involvement by women. Similarly, since the passage of Resolution 1820, there have been numerous examples of civil conflict in which women and children were violated despite the protections that 1820 was supposed to offer. And in a globalized world with the media ubiquitous, the international community cannot say that they were unaware of the problems.

The feminist theorists would ask us to think about who makes the decisions and who has been affected by the decisions. These questions are especially relevant at a time when there seems to be a proliferation of civil conflicts, many of which have resulted in the displacement of civilians, especially women and children. And many of these conflicts have also changed the nature of warfare, where what might have previously been the protected domain of the home, which is generally seen as women's space, has become part of the battlefield. Suicide attacks do not distinguish between civilians and combatants as their victims, nor do pilotless drones. What had been private space has become public, as the battle lines have become blurred.

Perhaps an even more important question to think about at this point is: What happens after war ends? How is it possible for a society to rebuild and knit itself back together, unless all people, including women, are part of the peacemaking and peace-building processes? In many ways, it is questions like these that Resolutions 1325 and 1820 were designed to address. But implementing them requires decision makers to comply with the terms.

LESSONS OF THE CASES: UNDERSTANDING INTERNATIONAL RELATIONS IN A GLOBALIZED WORLD

The purpose of these cases was not only to introduce you to some important global issues, but to show you clearly how difficult it is to deal with them. When you started reading each of these issues, I am sure you already had your own point of view. After all, who could not be in favor of ensuring a clean environment? Issues pertaining to the movement of people can be more complicated, but you probably still had your own bias and perspective as you started. And who could not be for expanding the role of women internationally, especially if it would help stabilize a worn-torn country and therefore minimize the risk of future violence? But as you could see from studying these cases, different theoretical perspectives make different assumptions about the role of the nation-state and the desired outcomes. And examining the case from different levels of analysis will also lead you to draw very different conclusions.

As noted at the start of this chapter, the same type of analysis could be done for virtually any current international issue, whether it pertains to the traditional view of security or human security. Pick up any major newspaper any day, and you will see examples of these issues. The drug war in Mexico: Who is affected and what does it mean for relations between the United States and Mexico? The civil war in Syria: Who is fighting, who is suffering, and what impact has it had on neighboring Turkey, not to mention the dangers should the war spread and envelop the region? The United States and South Korea modified their bilateral agreement to extend the range of South Korea's ballistic missiles as a way to offset concerns about North Korea's intentions. But while that might help ensure South Korea's security, it raises other fears of a regional arms race, threatening other countries in Asia. Those examples are drawn from the news of just a few days in October 2012, and any of them could be developed further into a case or issue to study that could help illustrate the reality of contemporary international relations.

So what do the cases we included here tell us about international relations in a globalized world? First, they remind us that there are many actors to consider, both within and outside the nation-state, which in turn makes it more difficult to arrive at easy or set answers about how to address current global issues. All of these actors can play a role in any policy decision or in implementing policy. Often they work at cross-purposes, which means that what might appear to be a sound policy decision does not get implemented. And as we have also seen, in the international system without any form of global governance, implementing any decision is virtually impossible unless states want to do so.

Second, these cases show us how the borders between nation-states have broken down as they have become more interdependent. It is not only the easy movement of people that is a result of these transparent borders. We also see increased trade patterns leading to economic interdependence, which in turn has broken down some of the old distinctions between the developed and developing countries and, along with that, has brought a changing understanding of which countries truly are powerful. But another aspect of this interdependence is the rapid flow of information. Media coverage is virtually instantaneous now, not only through the established media outlets like CNN, but through cell phones and Twitter. As we saw in the revolutions that swept the Arab world in spring 2011, even repressive states have a difficult time controlling the flow of information.

Third, we learned that these global issues are raising important questions about the role of the nation-state as the central actor in international relations. Clearly, these cases illustrate the role of IGOs and NGOs in influencing policy, even in those cases where the policy requires or presumes a change in the political, cultural, and/or social levels within the nation-state. We can argue that the third case, the changing role of women, stresses the continued sovereignty of the nation-state, as the policy changes advocated by the UN resolutions would not/could not be implemented without state compliance. On the other hand, there are far more actors, both within and outside the state, who can bring pressure to ensure compliance. This is a relatively new concept and one that suggests rethinking the nature of the traditional approach to understanding the role of the nation-state as the primary actor.

Fourth, we learned that although there are flaws in the traditional levels-of-analysis approach to understanding international relations as envisioned when the approach was articulated decades ago, it still provides a framework that allows us to answer some important questions. By understanding the flaws or weaknesses in the approach, which should have become relatively apparent here, we can be better prepared to address them, thereby ensuring that we can arrive at a more complete picture of or answer to the questions or issues discussed. Furthermore, we have yet to arrive at a comprehensive theoretical framework to replace it as a starting point for analysis.

Fifth, we saw clearly how the different theoretical perspectives diverge in their understanding of issues, perspectives, and approaches to the international system and the actors within it. And as is the case with the levels-of-analysis approach (above), we can also identify more readily the weaknesses or failings in these approaches.

We concluded chapter 1 by noting that "understanding IR in a globalized world also means going beyond the traditional state-centered approach that the field has often had. We need to be able to see the limits of that approach, and to expand our understanding and definitions in order to incorporate the roles of nonstate actors."

As you have learned the fundamentals of IR and how to understand some of the questions inherent in this approach to political science, we hope that you will now be better able to pick up a newspaper and to understand why a state did what it did, and the ways in which others responded. You should now be able to understand more about the ongoing discussions of trade pacts and why they are important. You should be better able to analyze why war broke out within a country, and how that conflict can be resolved in a way that can help ensure peace rather than future conflict.

Is this easy to do? No. But you should now have the tools to be able to do all this and more. And as you are doing this and arriving at your own answers to some of these fundamental questions, you should also be able to determine whether you are a realist in your thinking or a liberal, or whether you can formulate your own approach that will help you describe, explain, and perhaps even predict international relations in a globalized world.

FURTHER READINGS

Much of the information for these cases was drawn from UN documents, which present the best starting point for specific international agreements. The specific references are listed in the notes. The UN home page is http:// www.un.org/en/.

It is also possible and often wise to get the perspectives of a particular country or organization. For example, the European Union website (http:// europa.eu/index_en.htm) provides an excellent starting point in understanding EU policies and the evolution of those policies.

For U.S. policies on many of these issues, a good starting point is the State Department website, at http://www.state.gov/. This includes U.S. policy regarding other countries and also U.S. policy on a range of international issues. Virtually every country has a similar resource that is easily accessed.

NOTES

1. "Kyoto Protocol," at http://unfcc.int/kyoto_protocol/items/2830.php.

2. United Nations Framework Convention on Climate Change, at http://unfccc .int/2860.php.

3. "The Cancun Climate-Change Conference: A Sort of Progress," *The Economist*, December 18, 2010, 16.

4. "Climate-Change Diplomacy: Back from the Brink," *The Economist*, December 18, 2010, 121.

5. "Climate-Change Diplomacy: Back from the Brink."

6. "Climate-Change Talks: Wilted Greenery," *The Economist*, December 3, 2011, 74.

7. "A Deal in Durban," *The Economist*, December 17, 2011, at http://www.econ omist.com/node/21541806.

8. John M. Broder, "Climate Talks in Durban Yield Limited Agreement," *New York Times*, December 11, 2011, at http://www.nytimes.com/2011/12/12/science/ earth/countries-at-un-conference-agree-to-draft-new-emissions-treaty.html?scp = 2&sq = Durban%20climate%20change%20conference&st = cse.

9. United Nations, *The Millennium Development Goals Report, 2007*, 23.

10. "Gulf of Mexico Oil Spill," *New York Times*, at http://topics.nytimes.com/top/reference/timestopics/subjects/o/oil_spills/gulf_of_mexico_2010/index.html?scp=10&sq=Oil%20spill%20in%20the%20Gulf%20of%20mexico&st=cse.

11. "Gulf of Mexico Oil Spill," *New York Times*, updated January 3, 2013, at http://topics.nytimes.com/top/reference/timestopics/subjects/o/oil_spills/gulf_of_mexico_2010/index.html.

12. "Gulf of Mexico Oil Spill."

13. UN High Commissioner for Refugees (UNHCR), "2013 Country Operations Profile: Africa," at http://www.unhcr.org/pages/4a02d7fd6.html.

14. William J. Carrington and Enrica Detragaiche, "How Extensive Is the Brain Drain?" *Finance and Development* 36, no. 2 (June 1999), at http://www.imf.org/external/pubs/ft/fandd/1999/06/carringt.htm.

15. International Organization for Migration, "Remittances and the Movement of Workers," at http://www.ilo.org/wcmsp5/groups/public/—ed_emp/documents/presentations/wcms_142202.pdf.

16. International Organization for Migration, "Remittances and the Movement of Workers."

17. Remarks by William Lacy Swing, director general, International Organization for Migration, September 22, 2010, General Assembly Hall, United Nations Headquarters, New York, at http://www.migration4development.org/sites/m4d.emakina-eu.net/files/IOM/pdf.

18. Remarks by Swing.

19. The UN Secretary-General, "Message to Global Forum on Migration and Development," November 8, 2010, Puerto Vallarta, Mexico, at http://www.un.org/esa/population/migration/openingremarks-sg-puertovallarta.pdf.

20. Randal C. Archibold, "Arizona Enacts Stringent Law on Immigration," *New York Times*, April 23, 2010, at http://www.nytimes.com/2010/04/24/us/politics/24immig.html.

21. "Border Burden," *The Economist*, August 21, 2010, 43.

22. "Border Burden."

23. "Border Burden."

24. "Border Burden."

25. "In Search of an Immigration Policy," *The Economist*, June 2, 2007, 54.

26. Burns and Somaiya, "After Attack Hits Sweden, Focus Turns to Suspect," at http://www.nytimes.com/2010/12/13/world/europe/13sweden.html?sq=Bombing%20in%20Stockholm&st=cse&scp=1&pagewanted=print.

27. For more background on this, see the EU summary sheet, "The Schengen Area and Cooperation," at http://europa.eu/legislation_summaries/justice_freedom_security/free_movement_of_persons_asylum_immigration/l33020_en.htm.

28. UN Security Council Resolution 1325 on women, peace and security, October 31, 2000, at http://www.un.org/events/res_1325e.pdf.

29. UN Security Council Resolution 1820 on eliminating violence against women and girls, June 2008, at http://www.unfpa.org/webdav/site/global/shared/swp/2010/SC1820_eng.pdf.

30. UN Department of Public Information, "Security Council Demands Immediate and Complete Halt to Acts of Sexual Violence against Civilians in Conflict Zones," at http://www.un.org/News/Press/docs/2008/sc9364.doc.htm.

31. United Nations, Division for the Advancement of Women, "The Four Global Women's Conferences 1975–1995: Historical Perspective," at http://www.un.org/womenwatch/daw/followup/session/presskit/hist.htm.

32. United Nations, Division for the Advancement of Women, "The Four Global Women's Conferences."

33. United Nations, Division for the Advancement of Women, "The Four Global Women's Conferences."

34. United Nations, Division for the Advancement of Women, "The Four Global Women's Conferences."

35. United Nations, Division for the Advancement of Women, "The Four Global Women's Conferences."

36. United Nations, Division for the Advancement of Women, "The Four Global Women's Conferences."

37. Sanam Naraghi Anderlini, *Women Building Peace: What They Do, Why It Matters* (Boulder, CO: Lynne Rienner, 2007), 14.

38. United Nations, Division for the Advancement of Women, "The Four Global Women's Conferences."

39. United Nations, Division for the Advancement of Women, "The Four Global Women's Conferences."

40. "Report of the World Conference to Review and Appraise the Achievements of the United Nations Decade for Women: Equality, Development and Peace," Nairobi, 15–26 July 1985, at http://www.un.org/womenwatch/confer/nfls/Nairobi1985report.txt.

41. See "Report of the World Conference to Review and Appraise the Achievements of the United Nations Decade for Women."

42. See Anderlini, *Women Building Peace*, 15; and United Nations, Division for the Advancement of Women, "The Four Global Women's Conferences."

43. UN Security Council Resolution 1325.

44. UN Security Council Resolution 1820.

Glossary of Key Terms

affective biases. The impact of emotions as they affect policy decisions that are made.

alliances. A union of two or more countries that agree to coordinate policy in order to achieve common goals, generally to ensure greater security.

anarchy. A situation in which the major actors in the international system are not subject to any rules or regulations and therefore behave solely in their own interests.

balance of power. The assumption that conflict will be minimized and therefore peace maintained when military power is distributed roughly equally, thereby preventing any country from dominating.

bipolarity. The assumption that there are two major centers of power and that the power between them is roughly balanced. Most of the period of the Cold War was bipolar.

BRIC. An acronym for the countries of Brazil, Russia, India, and China, all of which have emerged as major players. When they act together, as they have in a number of areas (along with South Africa, BRICS, and sometimes Nigeria), they can be a powerful bloc in the international system.

capabilities. Materials and resources that a country has relative to other countries and is willing to use in order to achieve its desired goals or ends.

civil war. Any armed conflict that takes place *within* the state. This might be due to ethnic, religious, nationalist, tribal, or other conflicts between and among different groups of people within the nation-state.

coalition of the willing. As opposed to the more formal *alliance*, a group of countries that come together for a specific purpose. The term was widely used to describe the group of countries that joined together to fight Saddam Hussein in 1991 after Iraq's invasion of Kuwait.

cognitive biases. Biases or distortions in thinking that affect policy decisions.

Cold War. The period that extended roughly from the end of World War II (1945) until the breakup of the Soviet Union in 1991, which was characterized by tension between the United States and its democratic allies in Western Europe and the Soviet Union and its client states in Eastern Europe. The Cold War was a period of political, economic, and military rivalry and competition between the two sides, each of which sought to balance the power of the other.

collective defense. Variant of the concept of collective security, but with the assumption that there will be alliances made up of nations that pool their power or capabilities in order to balance the power of other states or alliances.

collective security. A formal relationship of nation-states that hopes to keep peace by deterring any act of aggression with the knowledge of a collective military response.

common good. Something that affects all countries and peoples and does not know or respect borders. For example, ensuring a clean environment is a common good that requires countries to work together.

conflict. Disagreement over interests or desired outcomes that may be settled peacefully or lead to war.

conflict spiral. A situation often found during a crisis when decision makers overestimate the hostile intentions of the adversary while underestimating their own hostile intentions. The crisis situation exacerbates this interaction, which then contributes to an ongoing sense of crisis.

constructivist theory (also known as "social constructivists"). A major theoretical approach in international relations that assumes that states are critical players, but that their actions and behaviors are socially constructed or affected by the system(s) in which they operate. It assumes that states will act upon their own constructions of reality.

core interests. The values that tie directly to a country's security and are central to its national interest.

credibility. The perception of a country's willingness to use its resources to achieve its desired goals or ends.

cultural imperialism. The imposition of one set of global norms or values on another country or group.

democratic peace. The notion that democratic countries are more peaceful because they do not go to war against other democratic countries.

dependency theory. The idea that the poorer countries of the developing world (also known as "third world") would remain tied to and dependent upon, as well as exploited by, the major developed countries.

developing countries. A category that is used by the World Bank to identify low-income countries, specifically those who, in 2011, had a Gross National Income (GNI) per capita of $1,025 or less.

diplomacy. The formal process of interaction among the members of the international system, carried out by diplomats who are asked to implement a country's policy.

disintegration. The competing forces that result in the breakup of a country into other smaller entities that then seek statehood, either relatively peacefully (e.g., Czechoslovakia and the Soviet Union) or because of major armed conflict, as seen with the former Yugoslavia.

empire. An entity composed of many separate units, all of which are under the domination of one single power that asserts political and economic supremacy over the units, all of which accept that relationship. One of the goals of an empire is to perpetuate itself and to continue to expand its domain and therefore its wealth. All wealth and allegiance flow from the separate units to the central power, usually the emperor.

engagement. A foreign policy orientation that allows the country to be actively involved with a range of countries and with the members of the international system.

ethnic cleansing. The systematic extermination of one group by another (i.e., genocide), often with the approval and support of the state.

Eurocentric. Putting Europe at the center of the discussion or analysis.

European Union. A regional bloc of twenty-seven sovereign states that united first economically and then more broadly, to create a common foreign and security policy.

euro zone. An economic and monetary union of seventeen of the EU countries that have agreed to adopt the euro as their common currency.

feminist theoretical perspectives. A relatively recent approach that suggests that it is impossible to understand international relations without addressing the role that gender plays in making decisions. It asks who is affected by the decisions that are made, and more broadly, "Where are the women?"

foreign policy orientation. The particular type of foreign policy decision made by a country that should, theoretically, further its national interest.

These include isolationism, unilateralism, neutrality and nonalignment, and active engagement.

free rider. The idea that since others will act to create a common good, it is not necessary for any individual actor to join in, since they will benefit from the work of the others at no cost to themselves or expenditure of resources.

gender-sensitive lenses. If we are to get a more complete picture of international relations, we need to refocus our questions and approaches specifically to include women in our analysis.

globalization. The assumption that all states and international actors interact and are interdependent in some way.

government. The entity within the nation-state that is responsible for ensuring the collective well-being and security of the state and the people within it.

groupthink. The tendency for members of a group to suppress dissent in order to arrive at a single decision.

"guns versus butter." The descriptor that suggests that a state can fund the military (guns) *or* the society (butter), but that often it is not possible to do both and that, therefore, there is a trade-off.

hard power. The use of a country's military power to influence events or the outcome of decisions.

hegemon. A state with the predominance of power, thereby enabling it to dominate political, economic, and/or political relations.

human security. A broad set of issues necessary to human survival such as protecting the environment, freedom from hunger, access to potable water, and so on.

integration. The merging of ideas and policies so that individual sovereign states start to blend into a unified whole. This can result in larger regional blocs, such as the European Union.

intergovernmental organizations (IGOs) (also known as "international organizations" [IOs]). Organizations that have nation-states as their members and represent regional organizations, such as the EU, or the international system, such as the UN. Some have been created for a specific purpose, such as the collective security of their members (NATO), while others are broader in scope. Within these organizations nation-states work together to pursue common policies on behalf of the whole that are not seen as infringing upon the sovereignty of the individual nations.

International Monetary Fund (IMF). An organization of 188 countries that work together to help stabilize the international economic system. It was established in 1945 and grew from the Bretton Woods meetings, which brought representatives of forty-five countries together to arrive at a framework for international economic policies that would minimize the possibility of another Great Depression.

international relations. A field of study within political science that addresses the relationships between and among actors in the international system and the impact of decisions made by any one actor on another actor or other actors.

international system. The framework for international relations in which the system itself is composed of nation-states and nonstate actors that interact in some way and, in so doing, affect the behavior of one another.

isolationism. The foreign policy orientation that has a country turn inward and minimize political or military involvement with other countries.

just war doctrine. The moral criteria that states should use when going to war, in fighting a war, and in ending a war.

Kyoto Protocol. An international agreement negotiated in Kyoto, Japan, in 1997 that extended the UN Framework Convention on Climate Change and set targets for reducing greenhouse gas emissions.

legitimacy. The notion that political power ultimately rests with the people, who then accept the leader or government. Thus, political power is derived from "the consent of the governed."

levels of analysis. An approach to understanding international relations by breaking down the various actors who are involved with the making of international relations decisions and the impact of those decisions on the various actors.

liberal theory. A major theoretical approach to understanding international relations that grows from the confluence of economics and politics and believes that all states will benefit from the flourishing of free trade and the open exchange of ideas. It also assumes that countries will benefit from cooperating with one another and advocates pursuing policies that are in the "common good." This is also known as the pluralist approach.

"Long Peace." One of the ways in which the Cold War has been referred to, in part because of the relative stability that came with a bipolar balance-of-power system that ensured peace between the superpowers.

Marxism. Theory derived from Karl Marx and the assumption that there is an inherent conflict that exists within and across societies and even nations that pits the "have-nots" against the "haves." Marxist theory suggests that economic factors shape a country's relationships, with the richer oppressing the poorer. Inherent in this is the idea that those who are oppressed by the dominant (capitalist) economic system will rise up against it.

monolithic actors. The assumption that states will behave as if they were one single entity, rather than as many individuals and groups.

multinational corporations (MNCs). Major corporations or companies that are based in one country and do business of some kind in at least one other country.

multipolar system. A system in which there are a number of power centers with alliances shifting among them. This is perceived as the least stable type of system.

nation. A group of people with similar background, culture, ethnicity, and language, who share common values.

national interest. A defined goal that furthers what is best for the country and guides that country's foreign policy decisions. States must be able to define what is in their national interest before they can act.

nationalism. Commitment to a central (national) identity or consciousness rather than loyalty to the ruler or the state. Hence, a situation where the primary loyalty of the group rests with the nation (the peoples and the group) at the expense of the state.

nation-state (also known as a "country"). A two-pronged concept that embodies the concepts of the *nation* and the *state*. A nation-state is made up of a group of individuals who live within a defined territory and under a single government. Together, they form a society that has certain values and beliefs in common. Generally referred to as a country. See **nation** and **state**.

negotiation. A dialogue or process of give-and-take on a particular issue that will result in an agreement that both or all sides can accept. This is an important tool of foreign policy used by allies as well as adversaries, in the hope of reaching an agreement or arriving at common ground.

neutrality. The decision not to commit a country's military forces or engage in a military or security alliance with other countries. This orientation recognizes that the country has special status within the international system and that other countries should respect, and not infringe on, that neutrality.

nonaligned. A status designated during the Cold War, when some countries declared that they would not politically or militarily support either the Soviet Union or the United States.

nongovernmental organizations (NGOs). Organizations that operate across international borders whose members are individuals, rather than countries or nation-states. Often they try to influence policy or to advocate for an issue that transcends international borders, such as the environment or human rights. Some NGOs also provide humanitarian and/or medical aid and assistance in the event of natural disaster or catastrophic events, such as earthquakes or tsunamis.

nonstate actor. An actor, entity, or group of any kind (e.g., terrorist group, MNC, or international organization) that is not a unique nation-state but plays a role in the international system and in international relations.

North American Free Trade Agreement (NAFTA). An agreement signed by the United States, Mexico, and Canada to create a trilateral trade bloc among the countries of North America. It went into effect in 1994.

North Atlantic Treaty Organization (NATO). A formal alliance created in 1949 to unite the United States with the democratic countries of Western Europe and Canada in order to deter a Soviet attack. The heart of the NATO treaty is Article 5, which states that an armed attack on any one would be considered an armed attack against all, which embodies the notion of collective defense.

peace. A situation characterized by an absence of hostility and also characterized by feelings of trust, a sense of security, and cooperation among peoples.

peace building. The actions that take place following the end of a conflict that contribute to strengthening and rebuilding the government structure and institutions in order to prevent conflict in the future.

peacekeeping. The efforts of third parties, such as the United Nations, to keep warring parties apart so that they do not continue to resort to hostilities. Peacekeeping forces may be inserted during the process of negotiating an end to a conflict. UN peacekeeping forces are often known as "blue helmets" because of their headgear.

peacemaking. The process of ending an armed conflict and resolving the issues that contributed to the conflict in the first place.

polycentric. An international system in which there are many national or regional centers of power.

power. The ability of one actor to influence another or to influence the outcome of events in order to achieve desired ends. Power is one of the central concepts in international relations.

proxy wars. During the Cold War, battles between the United States and the Soviet Union that were fought indirectly, through allies, rather than directly, thereby minimizing the risk of major nuclear confrontation.

"rally round the flag." A recognized phenomenon where a crisis galvanizes public support for the political leader.

rapprochement. Diplomatic term meaning a policy to reestablish a positive relationship.

rational actor. The assumption that an actor makes decisions based on a rational decision-making process.

rational decision making. The assumption that decisions will be made based on a logical process that allows for the assessment of choices, weighing of costs and benefits, and review of alternatives before arriving at a final decision that will further the actor's self-interest.

realist theory. One of the major approaches to understanding international relations, which assumes that states are the center of the international system and that all states will make decisions based on their national interest, which is defined by power.

Realpolitik. A German term that refers to foreign policy tied primarily to power and to maximizing power.

revolutionary movements. Seen primarily during the Cold War, the emergence of military movements whose goal was to overthrow the existing political order and replace it with a different one that was often more radical.

security. Ensuring the safety and protection of the people and the continuation of the state.

security dilemma. A situation in which one state improves its military capabilities in order to ensure its own security, but in so doing becomes a direct threat to another country, which responds with its own military buildup. The result is military buildup and feelings of insecurity and threat, rather than protection.

self-determination. The desire for a people to be recognized as a nation that is able to govern itself. The belief that each group of people should be allowed to determine who is responsible for leading or governing them.

smart power. The ability to combine hard and soft power in order to influence policy.

soft power. Influencing others through cooperation or co-option by drawing on common values, ideals, and shared cultural norms.

sovereignty. Within any given territory, recognition of the government as the single legitimate authority. No external power has the right to intervene in actions that take place within national borders. The authority is derived from a monopoly over the legitimate use of force. The concept originates with the Treaty of Westphalia (Peace of Westphalia).

state. An entity with a defined border under the rule of a governmental structure that is accepted by the people within the border.

state-centric. The assumption that the nation-state or country is the primary or critical actor, thereby dismissing the roles of other (nonstate) actors.

stateless people. A group of people who seek to create their own state with defined borders and a government that is sovereign. They often have the trappings of statehood, including a governmental structure and a single dominant nation, but they do not see themselves as part of any existing state. The Palestinian peoples are one example of this group, as are the Kurds, who straddle a number of different countries.

structural adjustment programs (SAPs). Economic programs that impose specific spending restrictions on governments, especially pertaining to social welfare, health care, and education programs, while encouraging expenditures in other areas, such as for infrastructure, which should lead to economic growth.

structural violence. A situation in which violence and inequality is built into and is a part of the structure of a particular political system, which results in the unequal distribution of resources, opportunity, and power.

theory. A linked set of propositions or ideas that simplify reality in order to describe events that have occurred, explain why they happened, and predict what might happen in the future.

threat. The perception that a country, people, or way of life is under attack either by an external actor or by a group or even an idea within a country. A threat can be military, economic, political, or even cultural, such as when there is a perceived attack on values.

transnational actors. Another name for the broad group of nonstate actors that operate across national borders.

Treaty of Westphalia (Peace of Westphalia). Treaty of 1648 that ended the Thirty Years' War in Europe. The concepts of the modern nation-state and sovereignty have their origins in this document.

unilateralism. A foreign policy orientation that advocates a policy of political and military detachment but acknowledges the need to interact with other countries in a range of areas, such as economics and trade.

war. Acts of armed violence either within or across states involving two or more parties, designed to achieve a specific objective or outcome.

World Bank. Created as part of the Bretton Woods system (like the International Monetary Fund) and originally designed to help facilitate the rebuilding of Europe after World War II. It subsequently expanded to provide loans to developing countries and to promote foreign direct investment in those countries.

world systems theory. A theoretical perspective that claims that the world is divided not just into rich and poor and developed and less developed states, but into a core of strong and well-integrated states and a periphery of states that depend on a largely unskilled labor pool. The assumption is that the core group of nations exploits those at the periphery.

Index

Page locators in italics refer to boxes, figures, and maps.

Balfour Declaration (1917), 190–91
Balkans, 173
Bananas, Beaches, and Bases (Enloe), 146
Bay of Pigs (Cuba), 152
Beijing Declaration (UN Resolution
    1325), 184, 205n17, 227–28, 232
Belfast (Good Friday) Agreement, *106*
bilateral arrangements, 92
bin Laden, Osama, 1, 3–5
bipolarity, 50, 81
"Black Tiger" Tamil women, 192
"Black Widows" (Chechnya), 192
Blackwater guards incident, 201
blocs, 78–79
Bosnia, 108, 173, 185
Bosnia-Herzegovina, 108, 140
Bosnian Muslims, 140
bourgeoisie, 64
brain drain, 220
Brazil, 162–63, 212, 213
BRIC countries (Brazil, Russia, India,
    China, South Africa), 162–63, 169,
    211
Britain, 87
British Petroleum (Deepwater Horizon)
    oil spill, 202, 210, 215, 217
Bush, George H. W., 12–13, 101–2, 109
Bush, George W., 2–3, 4, 55, 93, 102,
    109–10, 149; democratization in Iraq,
    122–23

Camp David Accords, 133–34
capabilities, 39–40, 42, 90
capitalist system, 31, 53, 63–65
Carter, Jimmy, 133, 135, 159n47
Chávez, Hugo, 144
Chechnya, 16, 78
Cheney, Dick, *122*
Chiang Kai-shek, 117
child labor, 200

China, 3, 42, 51, 162; class struggle, 65;
    development, 23; diplomatic
    opening, 49; empire, 82; environment
    and, 211, 213; Korea, investment in,
    117; oil requirements, 167; rise of, 51;
    U.S. nonrecognition of, 117–18
church, role of, 82–83
citizenship, 121; gendered, 113n30, 119,
    129
civilians, targeting of, 100, *101*, 102,
    113n25, 228, 235
class struggle, 63–65, *64*
Clausewitz, Carl von, 99, 100
Clean Water Act, 217
Clinton, Hillary, 43
coalition of the willing, 12–13
Coercion, Capital, and European States
    (Tilly), 102, 112n5
cognitive biases, 150
Cold War, 117; alliances, 16–18, 88–90;
    bilateral arms control negotiations,
    94–95; class struggle rhetoric, 65;
    collective defense, 88–90, *89*;
    containment policy, 49; Cuban
    missile crisis, 35–36, 151–55, 158n40;
    end of, 15–16, 24; NATO and, 92,
    172–73; realist view of, 50; United
    Nations and, 169, 170–71
collective defense, 88–90, *89*
collective security, 29, 86–88; Congress
    of Vienna, 86–87; Delian League,
    81–82; international organizations
    and, 166, 168–70. *See also* security
colonialism, 21, 23, 83, 162, 194
Commission on the Status of Women,
    205n17
The Communist Manifesto (Marx), 189
comparative politics, 5
conflict, 16, 24, 98, 128; intractable,
    135–40; Marxist view, 63–65, *64*;

nationalism and, 132–35; within nation state, 116; neorealist view, 51; power relations, 39–41, *40*, 49; structural violence, 107. *See also* war

conflict spiral, 154

Congress, 4, 36

constitution, republican, *124–25*

constructivism, 8, 11, 29, 42, 59–62, 80, 111, 162; alliances, view of, 85–86; democratization, view of, 120; environment, view of, 216; ethnic conflict, view of, 143; European Union, view of, 175–76; individuals, focus on, 13; international organizations, views of, 179–80; limitations and critique of, 62; peace, view of, 104; relationship-based, 60–61; women's rights, view of, 234

consumers, 1–2, 5, 6–7

continuity/discontinuity, 31

continuum of actions, *41*, 95

cooperation, 13, 15, 29, 32, 42, 52, 87–88, 104; arms control negotiations, 90; Cold War, 90; liberalist view of, 54–57, *56*

core and periphery, 65

core identities, 79–80

core interests/values, 33–34, 59, 94, 178

corporations, 1–2, 5

country. *See* nation-state

credibility, 40, 90

crisis decision-making, 151–55

Croatia, 140

Croats, 140

Cuba, 131

Cuban missile crisis, 35–36, 151–55, 158n40

cultural imperialism, 129

cultural level, 34–35, *35*, 96

cultures and societies, 129–43, 154–55; ethnic enclaves, 130–31

Cyprus, 96, 104, 109, 169

Czech Republic, 15, 78

Czechoslovakia, 15, 18, 78

Dayton Agreement, 108, 110

decision making, 1, 2, 30; biases, 149–50; changing international environment and, 144–45; Cuban missile crisis, 151–55; foreign policy orientations, 91–93; gender and, 43, 129; individual level, 35–36, 115; by individuals, 31–32; levels-of-analysis approach, 4–5; range of explanations, 152; by rational actors, 148–51; safeguards, 150–51; war, 2–3. *See also* levels of response

Delian League, 81–82, 85

demilitarized zone (DMZ), North/South Korea, 109, 169

democracy: as "best," 120–21; democratic peace, 120–26, *124–25*; elections not equal to, 118–19; feminist perspectives, 119, 128–29; liberal view, 53, 55, *56*, 57; patriarchal/hierarchal assumptions, 24–25, 129; responsibilities and requirements, 121

democratic peace, 120–26, *124–25*

democratization, 120–29, *122–23*, *124–25*; economics and, 120, 126; liberalist view, 120–21, 123, *127*

dependency theory, 23–24, 63–64, 65; developing countries, 162–63, *171*; environment and, 211–12; structural adjustment programs (SAPs) and, 173–74

development, 23–24

dialectic, 63

About the Author

Joyce P. Kaufman is professor of political science and director of the Center for Engagement with Communities at Whittier College. She is the author of *A Concise History of U.S. Foreign Policy*, 2nd ed. (2010) and *NATO and the Former Yugoslavia: Crisis, Conflict, and the Atlantic Alliance* (2002) and coeditor with Andrew M. Dorman of *The Future of Transatlantic Relations: Perceptions, Policy, and Practice* (2011). She is also the author of numerous articles and papers on U.S. foreign and security policy. With Kristen Williams, she is coauthor of *Challenging Gender Norms: Women and Political Activism in Times of Crisis* (2013), *Women and War: Gender Identity and Activism in Times of Conflict* (2010), and *Women, the State, and War: A Comparative Perspective on Citizenship and Nationalism* (2007). She holds a BA and MA in political science from New York University and a PhD from the University of Maryland.